Critical Essays on
GALWAY KINNELL

CRITICAL ESSAYS
ON
AMERICAN LITERATURE

James Nagel, General Editor
University of Georgia, Athens

Critical Essays on
GALWAY KINNELL

edited by

NANCY LEWIS TUTEN

G. K. Hall & Co.
An Imprint of Simon & Schuster Macmillan
New York

Prentice Hall International
London • Mexico City • New Delhi • Singapore • Sydney • Toronto

G. K. Hall & Co.
An Imprint of Simon & Schuster Macmillan
1633 Broadway
New York, New York   10019

Library of Congress Cataloging-in-Publication Data

Critical essays on Galway Kinnell / edited by Nancy L. Tuten.
    p.   cm. — (Critical essays on American literature)
   Includes bibliographical references and index.
   ISBN 0-7838-0030-4 (cloth)
   1. Kinnell, Galway, 1927–   —Criticism and interpretation.
I. Tuten, Nancy L. II. Series.
PS3521.I582Z64 1996
811'.54—dc20   96-43050
                                    CIP

10 9 8 7 6 5 4 3 2 1

Printed in the United States of America

For Sandra Saulisbury Lewis and William Joseph Lewis

Contents

General Editor's Note

◆

This series seeks to anthologize the most important criticism on a wide variety of topics and writers in American literature. Our readers will find in various volumes not only a generous selection of reprinted articles and reviews but original essays, bibliographies, manuscript sections, and other materials brought to public attention for the first time. This volume, *Critical Essays on Galway Kinnell,* is the most comprehensive collection of essays ever published on one of the most important modern poets in the United States. It contains both a sizable gathering of early reviews and a broad selection of more modern scholarship as well. Among the authors of reprinted articles and reviews are Donald Hall, Harold Bloom, Jay Parini, Sarah Cahill, Jane Taylor, Susan B. Weston, and Morris Dickstein. In addition to a substantial introduction by Nancy Lewis Tuten, there are also two original essays commissioned specifically for publication in this volume: an extended review by Fred Moramarco of *Imperfect Thirst* and a new study of Kinnell's "Domestication of the Transcendental" by Lorrie Goldensohn. We are confident that this book will make a permanent and significant contribution to the study of American literature.

JAMES NAGEL
University of Georgia, Athens

Publisher's Note

◆

Producing a volume that contains both newly commissioned and reprinted material presents the publisher with the challenge of balancing the desire to achieve stylistic consistency with the need to preserve the integrity of works first published elsewhere. In the *Critical Essays* series, essays commissioned especially for a particular volume are edited to be consistent with G. K. Hall's house style; reprinted essays appear in the style in which they were first published, with only typographical errors corrected. Consequently, shifts in style from one essay to another are the result of our efforts to be faithful to each text as it was originally published.

Acknowledgments

The success of any project depends upon the support of many people. I am grateful to Professor James Nagel and the editors at G. K. Hall for giving me the opportunity to be a part of the Critical Essays series. For permission to quote liberally from Galway Kinnell's poems, I thank Teresa Buswell at the Houghton Mifflin Company and Michael Greaves at Knopf. Thanks also to Bobbie Bristol and Galway Kinnell for working with the editors at both presses to secure these permissions.

The English Department at Columbia College generously covered administrative costs and provided the services of our administrative assistant, June Mullinax, who consistently renders valuable support to all of us in the department. I owe a debt of gratitude to Bryan Sinclair and Jane Tuttle, reference librarians at Columbia College who skillfully assisted me in the research process. Two Columbia College undergraduate students provided help as well. Amanda Holling tracked down a number of reviews and essays in libraries around the state, bringing to bear her well-honed research skills. Wendy Floyd took charge of the tedious task of cutting and pasting reprinted pieces.

On a more personal note, I wish to thank my colleagues in the English Department at Columbia College for listening to me fret about the deadline for this book. I owe a debt of gratitude to my husband, Tom, for his constant encouragement and patience. My parents, Sandra and Bill Lewis, selflessly gave of their time to help care for our young daughter when I needed blocks of time to write. I have dedicated this book to them with heartfelt gratitude for a lifetime of unwavering support.

Introduction

♦

NANCY LEWIS TUTEN

As early as 1953—seven years before the publication of his first book of poetry—Galway Kinnell wrote an essay in which he outlined his philosophy of the nature and purpose of poetry. The eleven volumes of poetry he has published in the forty years since that time stand as evidence that even at the age of twenty-six, he could clearly articulate the vision that has consistently defined his poetic career. Placing himself firmly within the romantic tradition, Kinnell explains what he finds problematic about modernist poetry: The "problems of structure and meaning," he writes, "appear to be less successfully handled by modern poets than the problems of achieving specific effects in individual lines and images." When poets find themselves in "slavish obedience" to the formal concerns of stanza, rhyme, and meter, says Kinnell, "meaning is . . . thought of as a peg on which to hang the poetry" and "odd language and startling imagery tend to become ends in themselves." What the poet must remember, Kinnell asserts, is that "only meaning is truly interesting." The danger he finds "illustrated by all but the best of modern poems, . . . is that the poems, by occupying themselves with their discrete effects, lose real connection with nature itself. The reader's interest is fixed at the verbal level, on how a thing is said, and seldom seriously on the thing itself."[1] Nearly twenty years after that denunciation of modernist tendencies in poetry and in the same year that *The Book of Nightmares* was published, Kinnell explained that as poetry moves away from "formal beauty," it is better able to "discover the glory of the ordinary." His is a "poetics of the physical world," devoted to "the most ordinary thing, the most despised" that, like Emily Dickinson's fly, "may be the one chosen to bear the strange brightening, this last moment of increased life."[2]

Nonetheless, despite the fact that Kinnell overtly asserted his intention to move poetry in a direction different from that of his immediate predecessors, reviewers with a modernist bent found much to applaud in Kinnell's ear-

1

liest work. Clearly Kinnell had articulated his intention to create, in effect, a neoromantic approach to both form and content that addresses twentieth-century concerns, but his verse had not yet been weaned from the influences of William Butler Yeats and Robert Frost. Although containing the Whitmanesque poem "The Avenue Bearing the Initial of Christ into the New World"—a work that critics still regard as one of Kinnell's finest—the poet's first published collection provided modernist scholars with poems that held their own when scrutinized for their handling of irony, imagery, and symbol and for their melding of form and content. Melvin Walker La Follette was one such scholar. His commentary on Kinnell's "First Song" applauds the "subtle handling of rhyme, half-rhyme, and internal rhyme, as well as the pleasing imagery" in the poem. While he points out that the symbols "spring directly from the substance of the material," he nevertheless finds the poem successful largely because it "functions ably on all its levels of meaning." He concludes by praising the poet's "skillful musical effects in the handling of language" and "a choice of symbolic material which is the organic outgrowth of a specific narrative context."[3] In the following year, in response to La Follette's comments, Gene H. Koretz directed his attention to the content of "First Song," taking issue with La Follette's "excessive Freudian" interpretation that the poem is about a young boy's sexual awakening. He reveals a basic misunderstanding of Kinnell's poetics, however, when he states in the final lines of his commentary that "the poem's subject is not sexual growth, but spiritual growth."[4] For Kinnell, as for Whitman, the sexual is inextricably linked to the spiritual; to suggest, as do both of these early critics, that Kinnell's poetry could be about one and not the other is to overlook the poet's romantic insistence that the spiritual realm can be found solely in and through the physical, sensual world. The scholarly world still had much to learn about the nature of postmodern romanticism in general and about Kinnell's poetry in particular.

Between 1957 and 1959, Kinnell lived on the Lower East Side of New York City and gleaned subject matter for the most critically acclaimed poem in his first volume, *What a Kingdom It Was* (1960). "The Avenue Bearing the Initial of Christ into the New World" is a fourteen-part, 450-line poem re-creating what John Logan describes as "the sounds, textures, odors, melodrama and pathos of Manhattan's Avenue C." Logan calls Kinnell's first published collection "one of the finest books of the past decade" because it represents for him a middle ground of poetry "between the bland and the horrendous in our diet of verse," falling somewhere between tedious ("better magazine") verse and "something with the blood and hair still bristling on it, untamed, uncooked, having to be washed down with much wine ('beat' poetry)." Although Logan senses the presence of what he calls "Father Whitman," he points out that in addition to "Avenue C," the poems in *What A Kingdom It Was* include also the "charming, naive, almost Elizabethan 'First Song' " and several poems "which conjure up the spirit of an intense and rather romanticized Robert Frost."[5] Indeed, in retrospect it is clear that in this earliest volume Kinnell had only begun to test the limits of free verse and was still, despite conscious efforts to the contrary, writing poetry that at least nodded in the direction of formal concerns.

Critics were by and large impressed with *What a Kingdom It Was* and hailed "Avenue C" as the most ambitious poem therein. Selden Rodman, who had predicted as early as 1948 that "the future of American poetry . . . lay in the footsteps of Walt Whitman," finds "Avenue C" "the freshest, most exciting, and by far the most readable poem of a bleak decade" and praises Kinnell's "capacity to identify rather than intellectualize."[6] Louise Bogan notes the volume's gift for being "remarkably unburdened by this or that current influence" and devotes most of her review to the final poem, in which Kinnell "feels the vitality" of the people who inhabit Avenue C.[7] Stanley J. Rowland Jr. describes Kinnell's voice as "lyrical and exuberant, if sometimes uneven" and laments the lack of "subtlety and structural tightness" found in "very good contemporary" poets. "Avenue C," however, he describes as a "long, loosely knit and beautifully lyrical poem," and he applauds Kinnell's "ability to make us glimpse the wonder of being" as he "transforms the rubble and slums" in New York City.[8]

At least one reviewer was more guardedly optimistic about Kinnell's poetic future. Poet and novelist James Dickey, although claiming to admire Kinnell's poems for "their wholehearted commitment to themselves," found them nevertheless "dishearteningly prolix" and went so far as to call some of the poems "almost too trivial to be believed." He, too, however, admired in "Avenue C" a "genuine presence, an integrated personal reality, powerful and *projected*." While he said of the volume that "poetry [could] do better than this," he found Kinnell promising because of the interplay between his poetry and the "actual events of his life," a "necessary involvement" that Dickey believed could be "in the end magnificent."[9]

What Dickey regarded as prolixity other critics recognized as Kinnell's earliest attempts to stretch the poem further than it had ever gone into the realm of prose. Glauco Cambon noted as early as 1962 that Kinnell's "current experiments with open form in free verse authorize bold expectations about this poet's future achievement." In his pamphlet *Recent American Poetry,* Cambon labels Kinnell "an American Expressionist," citing his "readiness to risk the prosy and the informal." Cambon recognized early in Kinnell's career several features that have been central to every subsequent volume: his tendency "to build his poems by accumulation and expansion," his "joyous attention to nature," and his "pictorial and tactile sensuousness." Like Dickey, though, Cambon complains that while the "Whitmanic spirit" empowers the poet "to dare to write richly," this influence reveals itself in less positive ways as well: in "the incidental failures of thickness, loose diction, and commentary."[10] Similarly, while Joseph Bennett praises Kinnell's "surface realism that is effective and spare, never gaudy," he later notes that Kinnell will have to "slough off the excesses" as he aims, in future work, for a "poetry of essences."[11]

A year later, in his essay "Galway Kinnell: Moments of Transcendence," Sherman Hawkins called Kinnell's work "bold in its continuing development towards a more radical insight and a freer style." Hawkins traces through Kinnell's verse the influences of Frost, Yeats, and Whitman, asserting that while Frost held sway in the earlier poems and Whitman in the later ones, Yeats had been a constant. Hawkins discerns in Kinnell's work a clear commitment to writing about the "holy . . . incarnate in the real" and explores Kinnell's "notions of transcendence," which, according to the poet himself, "derive from Plato and the Transcendentalists, especially Thoreau" (a timely observation since in this same year Kinnell's participation in a voter registration campaign for the Congress of Racial Equality in Louisiana cost him a week in jail). Once again "Avenue C" is held up as evidence that Kinnell was moving deliberately toward Whitman as a model not only for form but for content and meaning as well. Hawkins writes, "here at last the real and ideal are not juxtaposed in contrast or set in transcendent sequence: they blend and mingle; they become one."[12]

The turbulent decade of the sixties was important for Kinnell both professionally and personally. During that time he published not only his first collection of poetry, but also two subsequent volumes of verse, *Flower Herding on Mount Monadnock* in 1964 and *Body Rags* in 1968; a novel, *Black Light,* in 1966; and two translations, *Poems of François Villon* in 1965 and Yves Bonnefoy's *On the Motion and Immobility of Douve* in 1968. He received a grant from the American Academy and Institute of Arts and Letters in 1962, a Guggenheim Fellowship in 1963, and the Brandeis Creative Arts Award in 1969. One year after the publication of *Flower Herding,* Kinnell married Inez Delgado de Torres, a union that lasted twenty years before their divorce in 1985. His daughter, Maud, was born in 1966, and his son, Finn Fergus, in 1968. These two births greatly influenced the creation of the work that is still considered Kinnell's most powerful, *The Book of Nightmares,* which appeared in 1971.

Critics reviewing Kinnell's second volume of poetry, *Flower Herding on Mount Monadnock,* were generally positive. In her brief remarks about the book in *Poetry,* Mona Van Duyn claims that "the poems in Galway Kinnell's second book work their way along the surfaces of things, creating as they go glimmerings and intimations of a view of the world, the mark of major poetry."[13] Herbert C. Burke describes this "second, disciplined offering" as possessing the "pellucid imagery we expect" when reading Kinnell.[14] De Witt Bell asserts that *Flower Herding* has "the virtues of his first [collection]—strength and surprising innovations of technique" while offering "a new subtlety, depth and simplicity."[15] Writing in the *Virginia Quarterly Review,* Fred Bornhauser describes Kinnell as "a rhapsodic poet with restraint, a Whitmanesque bard with a more rarefied sensibility" who "only occasionally flirts with banality" in these most recent poems.[16] While S. J. Rowland Jr. finds *Flower Herding* "less daring and more uncertain" than *What a Kingdom It*

Was, he nonetheless praises it for being "more various and exploratory."[17] John Malcolm Brinnin, in his 1967 commentary in the *Partisan Review,* observes that the "quotient of 'nature' poems in this volume is . . . perhaps too high." He writes, "While many poems in this vein are as economical as line drawings, a certain sameness of attitude dominates a run of them and threatens to fix the poet in the dead stance of man-against-the-sky. In the city, on the other hand, this man has things to say."[18] Once again, as they did for Kinnell's first volume, critics of *Flower Herding* were more attracted to the Whitmanesque poems of the city than to the Frost-like depictions of the individual facing an indifferent nature.

So impressed was Robert Pack with Kinnell's now-famous city poem "Avenue C," in fact, that half his 1964 review of *Flower Herding* is devoted to it despite the fact that it appeared in the 1960 volume. Ironically, although Kinnell seemed clearly to most reviewers (and had himself by this time overtly declared on several occasions) to be consciously breaking with the modernist tradition, Pack compares "Avenue C" with T. S. Eliot's "coherence, verbal richness, controlled evocation through images and mythic reference" in "The Waste Land." He goes on to say that "Avenue C" resembles Eliot's work "in every way, in fact, but one: it is not an attempt to break from a particular tradition." His conclusion is that Kinnell's poem thus "lacks the fascination of innovation."[19]

One other analysis of *Flower Herding* bears particular attention: in his review subtitled "Three American Poets," R. W. Flint makes an observation that perhaps explains the reservations James Dickey expressed in his review of *What a Kingdom It Was.* Flint asserts, "Galway Kinnell and James Dickey belong together like yin and yang, like a parable of North and South, Catholic and Protestant. It's encouraging to think the continent still has room for two 'nature poets' as different and as good." He explains that "where Dickey's poetry seems a condensation of light and space, a Wordsworthian openness to wonder and terror, Kinnell's is as cool as a proposition in Aquinas." In *Flower Herding,* Flint finds that Kinnell "develops this gift for a kind of luminous, feeling sobriety."[20]

Although it was published in 1969, Jane Taylor's study of Kinnell's poetry focuses on the first two collections, ignoring the 1964 publication of *Body Rags.* In greater depth than anyone before her she discusses Kinnell's "sense of place," which "almost always provides the occasion for and defines the nature of Kinnell's perceptions." She goes so far as to argue that "in many poems the dominant myth is that of the land itself," pointing to specific passages as examples of how the landscape provides an analogy "to the discovered meaning in the poet's own inner voyage." She further explores Kinnell's "attempts to establish the possibility of the holy in an unholy world" and explains how the "secular wonder which informs so many of his poems sometimes takes the form of a religious inquiry—in which religious images can only be used ironically." In her concluding lines, Taylor notes that "the dis-

tinctive features of Kinnell's poetry . . . can sometimes become a poem's liabilities rather than its virtues." She lists those features as "the easy expansiveness of the poet's speaking voice, the slow accumulation of meaning, and the
laxness of metrical and verse patterns"[21]—three qualities Kinnell was consciously honing in his movement away from modernism.

Black Light, Kinnell's only attempt so far at novel writing, was published
in 1966 and turned for its inspiration to the poet's stay in Iran as a Fulbright
lecturer and journalist in 1959 and 1960. The publisher's note characterizes
Black Light as "a voyage of discovery and transformation" in which the Iranian
"Jamshid, a quiet simple carpet mender, . . . suddenly commits a murder and
is forced to flee."[22] As one might expect in a novel written by a poet, metaphors
abound, and the result is a kind of Middle Eastern *Pilgrim's Progress*—or perhaps *Pilgrim's Regress,* for, as Phoebe Adams points out, "the real story is in the
stripping away of all Jamshid's fragile, self-righteous little virtues."[23] Despite
her assertion that the novel is ambiguous, Adams applauds the book's "con-
densed, austere, and effective writing," but a writer for the *Virginia Quarterly
Review* describes it as "quite without substance."[24] Mona Van Duyn finds the
"existential 'idea' of this novel a tired one, unassisted by the easy paradox of
the title," but she regards the style as "flawless, neither too rich nor too
spare."[25] Kenith Trodd calls *Black Light* a "melancholy *conte*" and praises
Kinnell's ability to write "with a spare and archaic lucidity, convincingly near-
Eastern and beneath the skin of his poor Moslem."[26] In general, reviewers con-
cur that Kinnell's efforts were best spent writing poetry, but most, like
Gwendolyn Brooks, value Kinnell's effort to assert through this brief departure
from poetry that fiction "should aim at something more than reportage."[27]

Over three times as many reviews appeared for Kinnell's next volume of
poetry, *Body Rags,* as had appeared for either of his first two collections.
Included in this volume are two of Kinnell's more highly acclaimed poems,
"The Last River" and "The Bear," the latter his most often anthologized.
These two, along with "The Porcupine," were frequently cited by reviewers as
the most powerful poems in *Body Rags.* In John Logan's words, the two animal poems contain "some of the best poetry to be found any place today," and
"The Last River," he continues, "is one of the most pertinent and ambitious
poems of the time."[28] Michael Benedikt hails Kinnell's third volume as "one
of the most radical transformations of both matter and manner we have." He
points out that while Kinnell's "first two collections, with their perturbed pictures of the junk-ridden modern city, and their relatively straightforward pre-
sentations of the landscape, seemed to recommend withdrawal from the
urban syndrome in favor of nature," in *Body Rags* "we feel the breadth of his
interpretation of the natural ideal."[29] Michele Murray calls it "a satisfying,
mature book, . . . honest, solid, beautifully written,"[30] and Richard Dillard
praises Kinnell's "sense of line and word that can crackle like a dry, cold morning" as well as his "poet's sense of the truth in things and the truths beyond
things."[31]

Repeatedly reviewers note the many strengths of this volume but include in their comments some reservations as well. Dillard was troubled by the "sad tries for shock and communion with the poor and out by means of the quick vulgarity."[32] While Laurence Lieberman finds "individual lines, images, and whole passages in nearly every poem . . . unforgettably poignant," he nevertheless feels that Kinnell "operates on just two cylinders in disproportionately many of his new poems." He considers "The Porcupine" and "The Bear" to be "major performances, . . . fiercely self-transcending invasions into the incredible otherness of mysterious animal being," but he argues that other poems in this collection are "conspicuously marred in structure." What Kinnell would no doubt have considered Whitmanesque catalogues in these poems, Lieberman calls "random collecting," regretting that "whatever connects these fragments in Kinnell's inner life is not available to the reader."[33] Writing for the *London Observer,* Ian Hamilton deems Kinnell "very much the public bard, speaking in passionate diction of the sufferings of others," but he goes on to add that "too often his eloquence runs away with him and seems flashy."[34] Another British reviewer, Alan Brownjohn, admires most the "shorter, less ambitious poems" in which he finds "an achieved clarity of image and statement that doesn't get mawkish or pretentious."[35] Jerome Judson begins his review by wishing Kinnell "would restrain his steaming imagination and concupiscent vocabulary," but he points to "The Bear" as an example of "how powerful Kinnell is when his strengths all work together."[36] Like nearly every other reviewer, Hayden Carruth calls attention to "The Porcupine" and "The Bear," asserting that "these two poems . . . are the sort that are born to be famous." Finding "The Last River" only "a shade less successful" than the animal poems, he nonetheless calls it the "strongest single piece of writing the [Civil Rights] Movement has produced so far." Largely because of these three powerful poems, *Body Rags* is, Carruth concludes, "a very fine book indeed."[37]

In 1969, Richard Howard published an impressive study entitled *Alone with America: Essays on the Art of Poetry in the United States since 1950.* His chapter on Kinnell traces the fire imagery that recurs throughout the three books of poetry, one translation, and one novel published by that time. Kinnell's poetry, Howard argues, "is an Ordeal by Fire. It is fire which he invokes to set forth his plight, to enact his ordeal, and to restore himself to reality. It is fire—in its constant transformation, its endless resurrection—which *is* reality, for Kinnell." In *What a Kingdom It Was* and *Flower Herding,* Howard argues, Kinnell describes "the apocalypse": everything "has gone through the refining fire, has been *made clean.*" In *Body Rags* Howard senses a "still small voice" wherein "life for Galway Kinnell becomes a matter of sacred vestiges, remnants, husks" that the individual confronts "after the fire."[38]

By 1970, critics were able to look back at *What a Kingdom It Was* and note, as does Ralph J. Mills Jr., that it was "one of those volumes signalling decisive changes in the mood and character of American poetry as it departed from the witty, pseudomythic verse, apparently written to critical prescription, of the 1950s to arrive at the more authentic, liberated work of the 1960s." In a lengthy, two-part article in the *Iowa Review,* Mills traces "how Kinnell, using the considerable imaginative and linguistic powers at his command from the beginning, explores relentlessly the actualities of his existence to wrest from them what significance for life he can."[39] Mills concludes with close readings of both "The Porcupine" and "The Bear," calling the latter a "powerful dream-poem of the poet's initiation, which seems . . . in spite of its harshness to be ultimately quite strong in its affirmation of existence."[40]

In that year, also, Kinnell published two books: a translation of Yvan Goll's *Lackawanna Elegy* and a limited edition of his earliest poems—works which predated by as many as fourteen years the publication of *What a Kingdom It Was.* In the "Author's Note" to *First Poems: 1946–1954,* Kinnell comments, "It might have turned out better for me if, during that period of my life, I had written less and given myself more to silence and waiting. At least those arduous searches for the right iambic beat and the rhyme word seem now like time which could have been better spent." He explains that in most cases he found he preferred earlier, unrevised versions of his poems to those which had been polished to meet those poetic standards he held in his late teens and early twenties.[41] While it is difficult to imagine the author of these highly structured poems writing something so dramatically different as "Avenue C," Kinnell's readers will nonetheless recognize in the early work themes and images that are central to his work nearly fifty years later.

Kinnell's mentor and friend Charles Bell published in 1970 an entry on Galway Kinnell in *Contemporary Poets of the English Language.* It is important not only for the biographical background it provides but also for the perspective from which Bell was writing. After tracing Kinnell's movement from highly formal poetry to free verse, and after applauding the younger poet's adherence to the romantic "titanism of the last century," Bell notes that he has before him "various sketches of a new long poem, *The Book of Nightmares.*" Even in an unpolished state, these lines struck Bell as unique not only when compared to Kinnell's earlier work but when held up against other contemporary poetry. After quoting from "Maud Moon," a poem about the birth of Kinnell's daughter, Bell writes, "What distinguishes this from the work of any other poet . . . is the intuitive immediacy of its entrance into prebirth and subhuman organic nature." Bell draws parallels to Theodore Roethke, Rainer Maria Rilke, and Whitman, concluding that "of all the poets born in the twenties and thirties, Galway Kinnell is the only one who has taken up the passionate symbolic search of the great American tradition."[42]

One year later, with the publication of *The Book of Nightmares,* critics recognized immediately that this long poem in ten sections represented what Robert Langbaum called "an unforeseeable leap forward for Kinnell." While Kinnell's earlier work hinted at what was to be achieved in *Nightmares,* Langbaum asserts, "there is nothing on this scale, nothing that extends man's spiritual dimensions so high and so low, nothing that extends the range of man's connections so far into the biological and cosmic process." In the romantic tradition, Kinnell "tries to pull an immortality out of our mortality" even as he teaches us to "give ourselves up to death and thus to the perpetuation of life." Langbaum traces the development of this theme through the sections of this poem, concluding that "even with its weak spots, its few lapses in intensity, *The Book of Nightmares* is major poetry."[43]

Nearly every other review is equally laudatory. Donald Hall maintains that "Kinnell's transformations compel us, and the hypnosis of his rhythm possesses us. . . . We do not enter *The Book of Nightmares;* it fills us up. The loss of ego is the greatest gain; it is *poetry.*"[44] Thomas Lask finds *Nightmares* to be Kinnell's "most integrated book, a work of one mood, one subject really, a tormented cry of what the poet is and feels at this moment." Noting that Kinnell's nightmares "are not nocturnal happenings or hallucinatory experiences of the mind but those constrictions of the heart that are a function of living," Lask identifies the "one thought" that dominates this entire book: "the realization of our mortality." He writes, "The violence of the jailer, the rough companionship of the imprisoned, a chance meeting with a woman on a plane, a musician's playing Bach all reinforce his consciousness of the worm in the bud, of the skull beneath the flesh." "After reading it," he concludes, "one turns without plan or forethought to the beginning and starts anew."[45] In his review for *Poetry,* Michael Benedikt praises the work's "technical, philosophical, and metaphorical strengths," noting that structurally "Kinnell's is a decidedly baroque approach."[46] Arthur Oberg observes that *Nightmares* "extends this poet's ventures, in previous books and in talking and writing about poetry, in the creation of a shared *persona,* an inclusive 'I' which will be selfless." In this long poem, Kinnell moves, according to Oberg, "toward the achievement of voice and voicelessness." Calling the work "major poetry," Oberg describes it as "full of sustained, achieved writing that matches anything in the earlier books of Kinnell" that had impressed him most.[47]

William Virgil Davis traces the thematic structure of *The Book of Nightmares* in what is more an explication than a review. He notes, for example, that "Little Sleep's-Head Sprouting Hair in the Moonlight" is the "seventh poem of ten poems each in seven parts" and is "the thematic and structural center of this 'bridge which arcs' across a landscape of nightmare; it points both forward and back" with lines that recall both the first and last sections of the book.[48] Writing for *Commonweal,* Rosemary F. Deen contends that "the long, seven-part form in which all the poems are cast stretches a few poems beyond their substance or unity . . . and some beyond their possibility of variety." She is "also uneasy with the affirmations of some of the poems," but she concludes that "at least the first five of these big poems are stunning and beautifully unified."[49] Even one critic who had, up to that time, been otherwise unimpressed with Kinnell's work found much to be excited about in *The Book of Nightmares;* James Whitehead, writing for the *Saturday Review,* claims that while he had regarded Kinnell's second and third collections as "superpoetic" ("Robert Bly with very few *deep* images"), *Nightmares* seems "in most ways a wonder."[50]

M. L. Rosenthal, writing for the *New York Times Book Review,* acknowledges that while "some readers might well consider Kinnell's description of the birth process as grimly realistic, . . . the net effect of the reconstructed experience is rather glorious and buoyant." After quoting lines from "Under the Maud Moon," he asserts that "the real triumph, which is considerable, lies in just such moments of concrete realization, when the language exults at and transforms literal reality." He finds "more dubious" Kinnell's "projection of some unclarified personal complex of sufferings" onto his subject matter: "Naturally, the unresolved sexual guilts and the broodings over war and death that saturate the poems are irrefutable sources of depression. But they are, if in varying proportions, our common lot, and there is nothing in the way Kinnell handles these themes that makes them particularly his." Arguing that the work "needs stripping down," he asserts that "although some exciting effects of cosmic imperviousness to human affairs, heartbreaking and beautiful, are achieved, the structure is overloaded." Rosenthal finds the ending particularly anticlimactic, but holds that "the real power of [Kinnell's] book comes from its pressure of feeling, its remarkable empathy and keenness of observation, and its qualities of phrasing—far more than from its structural thoroughness or philosophical implications." He concludes, "Whatever its weaknesses, *The Book of Nightmares* grapples mightily with its depressive view of reality and with essential issues of love, and it leaves us with something splendid: a true voice, a true song, memorably human."[51]

Kinnell is a meticulous reviser of his verse, rearranging lines and changing words in draft after draft until his work reflects as closely as possible the poetry inherent in human speech. As he shifted away from formal verse, some critics naturally mistook Kinnell's conscious movement toward prose as inattention to the criteria that define traditional poetry. Reviewers of *Nightmares* were no exception. In the *Partisan Review* Richard Howard argues that while *Nightmares* is "wonderfully ordered" and coherent, "it is not memorable enough." He writes, "it is not written in verse, it is written, merely, in poetry, and there are findings of loss in the performance which founder in a waste of invention." He concludes, though, that this "translator of Villon and Bonnefoy has a justified confidence in his own compositional energies . . . the power to make up a poetry out of a hope, a wonder, a question."[52] In a similar vein, Richmond Lattimore complains that in Kinnell's *Nightmares* "[t]he series strings on and on in non-metre; Kinnell's ear is good, but the lengths after a while cry out for more shape."[53] Robert Peters charges that Kinnell has "become repetitious and flawed; his self-critical sense . . . diminished." Although claiming to have admired the poet for some years past, Peters theorizes that perhaps since Kinnell had "become a star, no editor dares give him the criticism he needs." He argues that Kinnell "overstates here, is sentimental there, overuses certain words until they become tags—Kinnell-words setting off easy Existentialisms." Throughout this scathing review Peters accuses Kinnell of having "reached the bottom of his bag of tricks," of being predictable, pretentious and portentous, and of crossing the line into sentimentality, particularly in the poems about his children. Early on in his commentary he concedes that "there is still the energy, originality, and power in Kinnell to nurture several lesser poets," but his conclusion laments a poetic career that he finds "mired midway." Peters writes, "I sincerely hope that his new work will indicate fresh turnings free of self-pity, stale romantic writing, and a stifling Existentialism."[54]

Lattimore is disturbed not only by what he calls the "non-metre" of Kinnell's verse but also by the "sufficiently revolting effects" which become for him "a weariness."[55] Jane Taylor McDonnell, on the other hand, recognizes Kinnell's "wilderness and slum settings" and "preoccupation with violence" as "a deliberate descent into the underworld, a deliberate psychological risk-taking—the entertaining of visions for the sake of exorcizing them." She admits that the book "is not without sensationalism" and that the "deliberate excesses of some of the imagery . . . account for the overstated and embattled tone of some of the poems." She also points out, though, that two poems in which Kinnell is most guilty of such excess are the two central poems, which the poet consciously "planned as the ultimate nightmare images of the sequence, the central images of death, hatred, destruction, and war, before the poet . . . comes to terms with his fears." Other poems in the book are "more effective," she argues, "partly because they are Kinnell's personal assumption of the common nightmare . . . and partly because of their remarkable combination of affection and tenderness with anguish, of wonder and forgiveness with horror." Quoting passages from "Little Sleep's-Head Sprouting Hair in the Moonlight"—a poem that she deems "typical of the best poems in the volume"—McDonnell insists that "Kinnell has achieved a new sort of success in this poem and in others in *Book of Nightmares*." She admits that this book is different from his others but sees those differences as strengths: This collection, she contends, surpasses Kinnell's earlier work "not only in its greater density and continuity of imagery, in its emphasis on horror rather than wonder, but also in its convincing personal assumption of our common nightmare."[56]

In the years between 1971 and 1973, Kinnell published three essays, all of which, for the most part, discuss poetry other than his own but which nonetheless provide valuable insights into his own philosophy of poetry. In "The Poetics of the Physical World," he begins by explaining why form was important to the earliest English poets and why it has become necessary to abandon it in the twentieth century. When poets could sustain a belief in a supernatural harmony, poetic form was a way of exercising order over the chaos of nature. However, Kinnell asserts, "For modern poets—everyone after Yeats—rhyme and meter, having lost their sacred and natural basis, amount to little more than mechanical aids for writing." He turns to a discussion of

Whitman—"the first poet in English wholly to discard outward form," the first to understand that "the chaos of the world, which he *loved,* couldn't be turned into neat stanzas without suffering betrayal"—and eventually asks, "Why does it seem, in the modern poem, that the less formal beauty there is, the more possible it is to discover the glory of the ordinary?" The best modern poetry will be about pain and death, he explains; it will represent "the poetics of the physical world."[57]

The second essay, titled "Poetry, Personality, and Death," although written before the publication of *The Book of Nightmares,* seems to anticipate the few negative remarks it generated. In response to those who would regard as pretentious his internalization of universal suffering, he asserts, "We move toward a poetry in which the poet seeks an inner liberation by going so deeply into himself—into the worst of himself as well as the best—that he suddenly finds he is everyone." And to those critics who would be leery of the affirmative ending of *Nightmares,* he explains that he seeks in poetry a "death of the self," but not a "drying up or withering." Instead, he explains, "it is a death . . . out of which one might hope to be reborn more giving, more alive, more open, more related to the natural life."[58]

Adrienne Rich, in an essay titled "Poetry, Personality and Wholeness: A Response to Galway Kinnell," challenges male poets in general and Kinnell in particular to "confront the closed ego of man in its most private and political mode: his confused relationship to his own femininity, and his fear and guilt toward women." Although Kinnell asserts, in Rich's words, "that we desire a poetry in which the 'I' has become all of us," Rich points out the problem with Kinnell's alignment of women with nature:

> Women are less alienated from nature, according to Kinnell (and this may be true, if only as a result of their historic lack of participation in man's world of struggle and conquest); certainly they are so "in the imaginations of men." But then, in man's imagination, is woman "human" in the generic sense, or is she "nature"—part of that same nature from which man has severed himself through objectification and domination? . . . Masculine ambivalence toward nature consists, on the one hand, in reducing it to the object of his desires, seeking to possess and dominate it at the cost of real relationship to it; and on the other hand, mythifying and frequently sentimentalizing it, e.g. in terms of the mystery of womanhood, the purity and innocence of childhood. Neither of these attitudes—domination and idealization—leads to that state of being which is named in *The Book of Nightmares,* "Tenderness toward Existence." This contradiction between these attitudes lies not only beneath the white American's oppression of blacks, as Kinnell has pointed out, but more universally beneath man's historic ill-faith toward woman.[59]

Rich asserts that she has singled Kinnell out "not because . . . his blindness is greater but his potential for vision more" than that of other masculine writers who must face the same difficult questions if they are "[t]o become truly universal." Although Richard Howard, in his review of *Nightmares*, mentions that "any competent Women's Liberatrix" could see in Kinnell's exaltation of fatherhood an opposition to motherhood,[60] no other critic before Rich had approached Kinnell's work from a feminist perspective—and only Lorrie Goldensohn, in her 1984 essay that has been updated for this collection, has elaborated on the place of women in Kinnell's poetics. The subject deserves a great deal more attention, particularly given the centrality of sexuality as a means through which Kinnell achieves transcendence. Critics wishing to break new ground in Kinnell studies would do well to continue the discussion of women and the feminine in his poetry.

Two years after "Poetry, Personality, and Death" Kinnell published "Whitman's Indicative Words." Here he blames the "intense anglophilia" of the nineteenth century and the "very theoretical approach to poetry" of the twentieth century for Whitman's failure to be recognized as little more than a "queer cultist or a blethering yokel" until very lately. Just as easily, though, Kinnell could be talking about reactions to his own poetry when he criticizes those who, "from their cerebral heights, . . . could only patronize this poet who lived on instinct." The essay is Kinnell's attempt to explain his attraction to Whitman and, indirectly, to elucidate his own poetic goals. First he focuses on what he calls the "mystic music" of Whitman's verse, the natural "iambic flow [that] is never regular, never counted out, and connects seamlessly to surrounding passages that don't use iambs at all." He goes on to discuss Whitman's "love of words . . . as physical entities . . . which could only become physical through absolute attachment to reality." Kinnell's own fascination with moving poetry in the direction of prose can in part be explained by his respect for Whitman's ability to choose words that are "photographically descriptive" and "belong, it's true, to the realm of prose." In defense of Whitman and, less directly, of his own poetry, Kinnell writes, "At his best Whitman goes far beyond photographic description. His adjectives do not merely try to categorize, give colors, shapes, likenesses. They try to bring into language the luminous, nearly unspeakable presence." Whitman "indicated to poets to come," Kinnell concludes, "that one's poetry, and also one's life, is not to be a timid, well-made, presentable, outward construction. It is to be the consuming enterprise, leading if possible to intensified life, even to self-transfiguration."[61]

By 1973, when Charles Molesworth wrote "The Rank Flavor of Blood: Galway Kinnell and American Poetry in the 1960's," critics had begun to define more clearly the neoromantic movement, what Molesworth calls "a new post-modern aesthetic in contemporary American poetry." Poets of the 1960s endeavored to move out of the "modernist cul-de-sac of irony," and for Kinnell such a shift meant "a virtual rediscovery of how to view objects intensely, while continuing to avoid any prescribed system." The danger for postmodernist poetry, Molesworth argues, is that "as it rejects or moves beyond irony, [it] runs the risk of sentimentality on the one hand or the 'loosely oracular' [Theodore Roethke's term] on the other." He concludes, however, that in *The Book of Nightmares* Kinnell has "discovered for his own voice . . . a tough, but complexly responsive, sense of form." What some critics had rejected as flabby non-poetry Molesworth recognizes as Kinnell's "own way to look at things," a way which he believes has strengthened American poetry.[62]

In 1974 Kinnell's next book-length publication appeared. *The Avenue Bearing the Initial of Christ into the New World: Poems 1946–1964* brought together in one volume *First Poems, What a Kingdom It Was,* and *Flower Herding on Mount Monadnock.* In a prefatory note, Kinnell writes, "Reading these poems over, I find I have not become at all detached or objective about them, as I had imagined I would. . . . for as I read through them I remember my life, and even more, the persons, events, and places surrounding their composition." He points out that poems from *Kingdom* and *Flower Herding* "appear in versions slightly different from those in the original editions" because of changes he had made during the course of numerous readings of the poems to audiences. He explains, "Standing at the podium, just about to say a line, I would feel come over me a definite reluctance to say it as written. Gradually I learned to trust this reluctance. I would either drop the line altogether . . . or else invent on the spot a revision of it."

As Patrick Keane points out, one of the reasons the one-volume *Avenue C* is valuable is that for the first time readers have in print those "on-the-spot excisions and alterations" that Kinnell had been making orally since the poems were first published. Keane adds that while many readers will turn to *Avenue C* expecting it to be a kind of invention exercise for *The Book of Nightmares,* these earliest of Kinnell's poems stand on their own merit. "Galway Kinnell has emerged," Keane concludes, "as one of the most powerful and moving poets of his generation."[63] Although he finds the title a "wounded snake," Vernon Young remarks that "Kinnell is a poet of astonishing incarnations," one who "never seems to be where you last met him and [who's] always secure in his new adaptations."[64] Christopher Ricks discusses the effect of humor in this collection, noting, "The American artist who cuts himself off from humor, or is not good at it, may be cut off, not just from some valuable ways of looking at life but from a national source of energy, the hiding places of the best American power." While he argues that in some poems Kinnell's "humor curdles to sarcasm," Ricks commends the poet for "the intelligent *exclusion* of humor," a tone which is "dramatically right" for some poems.[65] Finding it remarkable "that these earlier poems should constitute in themselves such a major work," James Atlas contends that "Kinnell is in possession of a gift that so few poets have now, with their emphasis on subdued, laconic diction." One of the few critics to recognize what Kinnell was trying to achieve in the form of his verse, Atlas argues, "He is so close to his subject, the natural world in all its tyranny and splendor, that his sympathies are readily translated into the richness of cadence and language that poetry should always have.[66] Terry Comito's review in *Modern Poetry Studies* is useful for its close attention to the images and themes in the collection and for its brief discussion of Kinnell's debt to Yvan Goll and Yves Bonnefoy, two poets whom he had earlier translated.[67] While the first part of Jerome McGann's review adds little in the way of analysis that had not been said before, he attacks Kinnell's poetry midway through the essay, alleging that the poet is a "great poetic extremist" in whose work "the sensible world is forever strangled in imagination." In this work McGann sees "a world of city and country landscapes in which lonely and scattered individuals are encountered, but never met."[68]

Donald Davie's review rails against Kinnell's poetry in particular and contemporary poetry in general, the effect of which he believes has been "to disperse and dissipate the artistic and intellectual riches accumulated by the great decades of American poetry earlier in this century" and "to take American poetry back out of the 20th century into the 19th." According to Davie, from "astringent and sophisticated" modernism, contemporary poets like Kinnell have moved "back into the world of Emerson and Whitman," back to a "spiritual hunger which refuses to take the steps necessary to appease itself." His thirteen-page harangue concludes with Davie supposing that *Avenue C* was published by Kinnell as a way to ask "in effect, whether there was any way back for him into the twentieth century from the blowsy nineteenth-century titanism in which he has snared himself." Davie's remarks about "The Bear" characterize—both in tone and thesis—the rest of this review. He maintains that in this poem,

> the poet, determined to reach the absolute one way if not another, and unable to leap above his humanity into the divine, chooses to sink beneath it into the bestial. It is a sort of transcendence, certainly. But what a fearsome responsibility for a poet to lead his readers into bestiality. . . . A challenge worthy of a titan. So Charles Manson may have thought. Will Galway Kinnell choose to be a titan or a human being?[69]

So hostile, in fact, are Davie's comments that Ralph J. Mills Jr., whose essay on Kinnell is singled out by Davie, felt compelled to respond, pointing out what he calls distortions and misrepresentations used by Davie in order to make clear his distaste for contemporary romantic poetry. This critical debate deteriorated even further when *Parnassus* published in the same issue as Mills's letter a rebuttal by Davie in which he defends his right to be "hostile to the ways of thinking and reading about poetry which [Mills's] essay represents."[70] While we would hope for better from scholars, the argument between Davie and Mills nonetheless represents the tension underpinning many studies of Kinnell's work: Critics and reviewers vacillate between praise for the poet's daring movement away from modernism and unease about his movement closer to the realm of prose.

In 1973 Kinnell was awarded the Shelley Prize from the Poetry Society of America, and in that same year three studies of his poetry appeared in addition to the reviews of *Avenue C*. William E. Thompson, writing for the *Gypsy Scholar*, insists that "only since the publication of *The Book of Nightmares* in 1971 has it been possible to assess the overall thematic development of Galway Kinnell." The work prior to *Body Rags*, he maintains, is overwhelmed with questions and "doubts overshadow hopes." Divided into two parts, the first devoted to *Body Rags* and the second to *Nightmares*, his study concludes that *Body Rags*, culminating in "The Bear," represents a quest, while *Nightmares* "is a meditation on the results of a search," in effect "a story of mistakes made, searches undertaken, doubts and questions which have no absolute concrete answer, and a message from the present to the future— from father to daughter—from the past to future generations."[71] In another study, a book-length work titled *Out of the Vietnam Vortex: A Study of Poets and Poetry Against the War*, James F. Mersmann places Kinnell in a school of contemporary poets who believe "that all poetry is rightly political just as all poetry is religious because it attempts to break through, rend, or transcend the barriers and veils that separate men from one another and from the divine." Mersmann briefly explores how the backdrop of the Vietnam war colors even those of Kinnell's poems that reject overt reference to it.[72] John Hobbs's essay in *Modern Poetry Studies* explicates the often anthologized poem "The Bear," explores possible origins for its images, and places the poem within the larger framework of Kinnell's poetics.[73]

As further evidence of the momentum his career gained during the seventies and after the publication of *The Book of Nightmares*, Kinnell received the Medal of Merit from the National Institute of Arts and Letters in 1975 and was the subject of three published explications in that year. Focusing on form and imagery in the poem "Spindrift," Linda Wagner asserts that Kinnell has moved beyond modernism to fulfill "poetry's traditional purpose, to depict ways of living and thinking which would move readers because of the aptness and beauty of the language used."[74] Writing for the *Explicator*, J. T. Ledbetter suggests the now widely accepted reading of "The Bear": that it is an allegory for the act of writing poetry.[75] The longest of these three studies is Conrad Hilberry's discussion of the structure of *The Book of Nightmares* with emphasis on the symmetrical pattern of the first poem, "Under the Maud Moon," and the image of that pattern reflected in the book as a whole. Hilberry maintains that the opening poem "moves from fragmentation to wholeness and back to fragmentation; the whole book moves from Maud's birth . . . to the relentless meditation on death in Poem V and the hellish picture of human depravity in Poem VI, and then back to the birth of Kinnell's son . . . and the qualified celebration in the last poem."[76]

The publication of *Nightmares* prompted critic William Virgil Davis to explore the nightmare paradigm in poems preceding that collection. He asserts that in "The Bear" the hunter/poet "sets the scene for the nightmare visions which are to follow" as he becomes increasingly aware of the significance of having become the bear, the hunted—the poet who must spend the rest of his life "blessed with the curse of poetry."[77] Glauco Cambon also turns to *Body Rags* in his 1977 study of Kinnell's "Last River," arguing that this poem is not merely modeled after Dante's *Inferno* but represents "a recognition of affinity between [Kinnell's] own mode of perception and the medieval Florentine's mode," one wherein poetry serves as a "criticism of life."[78] In the same year, Andrew Taylor traced the evolution of Kinnell's mythic vision, claiming that "all the best of Kinnell's poetry" consists of "three essential components." First, the poet suffers and undergoes a "death of the self, . . . a withdrawal to a pre-human or pre-conscious state." Not a death in the usual sense, "it is a withdrawal to . . . an animal state," as seen in the second component, Kinnell's pervasive animal imagery. Finally, the poet is reborn back "into life" with a sense of "rejoicing, wonder, or awe." Through this transformational process, Taylor concludes, Kinnell successfully "approaches the condition of myth," a fact establishing him as "a major mythic poet."[79]

Two other studies written in the late seventies include discussion of Kinnell's work in the context of a broader thesis. In chapter 12 of his book *The American Moment: American Poetry in the Mid-Century*, Geoffrey Thurley delineates what he regards as the weaknesses of Kinnell, Robert Bly, and Charles Simic in an attempt to portray them as inferior to the Beat poets before them. Thurley faults Kinnell for lacking "fundamental . . . engagement in the subject." The poet, according to Thurley, had yet to develop a "real voice or creative personality"—qualities that even his most harsh critics generally give him credit for exhibiting.[80] Takako U. Lento explores the prevalence of death wishes in contemporary American poetry, using "The Bear" as a prime example of Kinnell's "death of self" theme that in many poems transforms the poet/speaker from an individual into a Whitmanesque "all inclusive identity."[81]

As part of the University of Michigan Press *Poets on Poetry* series, Kinnell published in 1978 a collection of revised interviews titled *Walking Down the Stairs*. J. Boening, writing for *World Literature Today*, is bothered by the fact that the original transcripts were greatly changed in the process of removing what Kinnell regarded as "notably dull, rambling, self-involved, self-serving, falsely modest, or otherwise unpleasant." As a result, Boening argues, "we no longer have real interviews" but instead "eleven short dramatic pieces."[82] Susan Weston chooses to focus on the content of the collection, highlighting those elements of Kinnell's poetics that the interviews elucidate. Addressing the issue of the conversations having been edited, Weston offers this defense:

> [T]he difference between these and the original interviews is not as great as the title would suggest . . . and is worth noting only because the unedited versions confirm what one suspects from *Walking:* the public man—good-natured, eager to help the interviewer, optimistic—has few of the acerbic, ironic, or horror-stricken moments that possess the hugely floundering, hugely loving,

hugely possessed speakers of Kinnell's poetry. If there is a fiction here, it is less that the poet has revised his conversations than that he himself has been revised by the occasion, the circumstance of being interviewed.[83]

In his preface to *Walking,* Kinnell explains why he revised the interviews:

> While a single interview should keep fairly close to the original conversation . . . an entire book of interviews is another matter. Unless you can be spontaneous *and* articulate—which I can't—a little spontaneity goes a long way. I do think it's necessary that the answers be fairly thoughtful and coherent if a book of this kind is to be at all readable.[84]

Although Kinnell claims in the preface that a poet is, perhaps, the last to know what a particular poem is "about," scholars and critics have found much in this collection to assist them in explicating his poems and in formulating an understanding of his poetics.

Between 1980 and 1990, Kinnell published four volumes of poetry and a children's book (*How the Alligator Missed Breakfast,* 1982), received the American Book Award (cowinner with Charles Wright) and the Pulitzer Prize in 1983, and was the subject of no fewer than twenty-three studies—not counting reviews—including two book-length discussions of his poetry and a collection of critical essays on his work. In 1982 he participated in "An Evening to Support Humanitarian Relief for the Children of Lebanon," and that same year he spearheaded "Poetry against the End of the World," a nuclear arms protest. When *Mortal Acts, Mortal Words* appeared in 1980, nine years had elapsed since *The Book of Nightmares.*

Publisher's Weekly praises Kinnell in *Mortal Acts* for having "an eye for catching the wonder in simple things,"[85] but several reviewers struggled to reconcile the subdued tone of this volume with the intensity they had come to expect from Kinnell after *Nightmares.* Katha Pollitt is one such critic, noting in the *Nation* that while *Nightmares* is a "book of great scope and verve, saturated with rage and terror and tenderness," *Mortal Acts* presents "a more relaxed, conversational voice and a new concern for daily domestic life and [Kinnell's] own immediate circumstances." She poses the question that every reviewer—and perhaps every reader of Kinnell's oeuvre—grappled with when the book first appeared: "Is this a roundabout step forward, or a straightforward step back?" And, also like other reviewers, she hedges her bets. Admitting that "there are fine poems drawn from the natural world, as precise as any he has written," she nonetheless finds "more numerous . . . moments in which spontaneity bogs down in garrulity" and where the poet is guilty of "preachiness" and "overblown profundities."[86]

Other reviewers reacted with similarly guarded praise. Also writing for the *Nation,* Robert B. Shaw calls *Mortal Acts* a "puzzlingly mixed performance." He admires most the shorter poems and those whose subjects are Kinnell's close friends and family, but he argues that the "longer pieces are by contrast disappointing—flaccid and sprawling."[87] Commenting in the *New York Times Book Review*, Harold Bloom criticizes Kinnell for what he calls "a certain over-ambition that makes of each separate poem too crucial an event." He admits, however, that "it is difficult not to be grateful for a poem as generous, honest, and open as 'There Are Things I Tell to No One,' or for a lyrical closure as precise as that in 'The Gray Heron.'" While he concludes that "this does seem . . . the weakest volume so far by a poet who cannot be dismissed," he nonetheless praises "Mr. Kinnell's descriptive powers, which are increasing to a Whitmanian amplitude."[88] Peter Serchuk deems the poems in *Mortal Acts* "intensely moving" but "loaded with technical problems" that he attributes to a "lack of distance between Kinnel [*sic*] and his poems."[89] Writing for the *Georgia Review*, Peter Stitt seems grateful for the poet's departure from "the unrelenting seriousness, the pressure always to be deeply significant" that characterize the earlier poetry and "made Kinnell a poet best ingested in small doses." He notes that at times "Kinnell's very relaxation gets him in trouble," but mostly he concludes that "this is a volume of wonders" representing a "new departure for Galway Kinnell, on the whole a successful one."[90]

Two reviews in particular achieve what few others do: They maintain their focus on the work being reviewed, referring to other volumes only briefly and only to place the present work in context; they ground their discussion firmly in the poems themselves; and they explain clearly *why* they argue for or against the effectiveness of individual poems. Hank Lazer acknowledges in his introduction that "some readers will find [*Mortal Acts*] inferior to *The Book of Nightmares*, possibly because [it] is lighter, less unified, and looser," but he dismisses such a reading, arguing that "these two books are different. *Mortal Acts, Mortal Words* is a collection of poems. . . . *The Book of Nightmares* is a book of poems, a single sequence of poems intended to be read as a unified whole." The bulk of his essay explains why he finds many poems remarkable: their "perfect adjectives," their "resistance to metaphor and simile," their "specific, intense union with the physical world." And when he turns to those poems he regards as weakest in the volume, he points to specific passages and explains that they are "weakened and blurred by . . . many plurals and vague, general terms," such as use of the word "things."[91] In his remarks in the *Hawaii Review* Howard Nelson notes that "startling, deeply etched physical description, combining sharp detail and an intuitive apprehension of the presence of a thing, has always been one of Kinnell's strengths," and he points to poems in *Mortal Acts* that underscore that quality. He admits, though, that "Kinnell is also drawn to abstractions, discursiveness, the direct expression of ideas, and even didacticism in his poetry," and he offers two examples of the "discursive, philosophical manner" in poems from this collection.[92] Readers of poetry are grateful for reviewers like Lazer and Nelson whose purpose is to offer constructive criticism within the larger context of elucidating the poet's major concerns.

Other reactions to *Mortal Acts* range from high praise to harsh condemnation. Jerome Mazzaro faults this collection for eliciting "neither a social vision nor a concept of form more permanent or larger than its author" and finds that "the poems . . . act not as temporary stays so much as distractions from the struggle." Pointing out that the absence of women in the volume is evidence of the poet's need to "get beyond himself," Mazzaro nevertheless credits Kinnell with "technical feats" and the ability to "feel widely in words."[93] Vernon Shetly accuses the poet of arriving "at resolutions he ultimately falls short of earning" and of "too often [resorting] to rhetoric as a substitute for imaginative energy."[94] As if she had read a different book altogether from the one Shetly read, Sandra Prewitt Edelman contends that Kinnell's "lines breathe where lines ought to breathe" and "images are linked together organically, growing as they do out of an honest perception of underlying likenesses in things." Edelman finds repeatedly throughout the collection that "grace and healing are spun out together."[95] John Piller remarks simply that "the nightmare vision that gave [Kinnell's] early work its hauntingly defiant vigor" has given way in the 1980 volume to "a settled sense of the joy of reawakening."[96]

While finding much to praise about *Mortal Acts, Mortal Words,* Stephen Yenser was one of those reviewers who felt the need to explain why this volume differs so greatly from what proceeded it:

> [Kinnell] must find himself on easier terms with mortality partly because he finds it easier to see the universe as a whole. "Can it ever be true," he wonders in the *Nightmares,* "all bodies, one body, one light / made of everyone's darkness together?" Now he can answer more certainly in the affirmative. . . . Grand as it is, *The Book of Nightmares* could only, after all, be written once. Kinnell was determined not to repeat himself but to go on, and he has gone on.

Mortal Acts is less spectacular, perhaps, than *Nightmares* because it has moved beyond the "simultaneous fear of and desire for" death that the earlier work embodied. Passing through the nightmares has allowed the poet "to mitigate the fear of death" and produce what Yenser calls "testimonies to unicity."[97]

R. W. Flint argues that *Mortal Acts* is "a respectably solid, if restful, book, if anything richer in interest than *Flower Herding on Mount Monadnock* of 1964," so "Why," he wonders in his essay, "have critics sounded so disappointed with it?"[98] The answer lies, perhaps, in the fact that the 1980 volume is more subdued, less spectacular, less intense; it is more likely, though, that reviewers who expected Kinnell to continue his *Nightmares* performance in subsequent books had failed to understand fully the message in the final poem of that work. "Lastness" reminds us that "earth is all there is" and that the poem is an "earthward gesture." Having confronted the nightmare that is mortality, Kinnell is able to challenge his newborn son to "find / the one flea which is laughing,"[99] not merely to accept the limitations of humanity but to find the glory in it. Like Frost's persona who goes to the woods to prepare himself to return to the world, Kinnell could be true to the lessons of his nightmares only if he turned to the quotidian, to the commonplace that defines our lives and which he believes offers us our only means of transcendence.

Two critical studies appeared between the publication of *Mortal Acts* in 1980 and *Selected Poems* in 1982. The *Dictionary of Literary Biography* published an entry on Kinnell in 1980 in which Charles Frazier provides an overview of the poetry through *The Book of Nightmares*. Ironically, in the concluding paragraph Frazier notes that "it would be unreasonable to expect major departures or the opening of drastically new ground in the poetry following [*Nightmares*]." Kinnell's poetry, he asserts, "has not, over the years, developed through distinct major phases, nor has it undergone radical changes."[100] The publication of *Mortal Acts* certainly calls into question such an assertion. Frazier's overview is nonetheless valuable, though, in its attention to individual poems, its summary of major themes, and its biographical information. In a 1981 article in the *Literary Review: An International Journal of Contemporary Writing,* Joe Marusiak examines the retrospective volumes of Kinnell and William Everson (*The Avenue Bearing the Initial of Christ into the New World,* 1974, and *The Veritable Years,* 1978, respectively). While the essay is largely a rumination on both men's work, Marusiak centers his remarks on the idea that Kinnell and Everson "are *poets*—people whose outlet happens to be words first and foremost, but *people* just the same" who are "struggling with the questions of perception and expression and significance." Both, Marusiak argues, "are asking after the human situation in a pattern that is not exclusively poetic but also cosmic, historical, social, cultural, individual."[101]

One other critical essay on Kinnell's work was published in 1982, but its focus is on a single poem in *Body Rags* entitled "The Last River." Writing for the *Thoreau Society Bulletin,* Peggy Parris explicates that poem with particular emphasis on its connections to Thoreau's "Civil Disobedience" and *Walden*. Noting that the poem "grew out of Kinnell's experience in a Southern jail" when he was "arrested for his participation in voter registration activities," Parris argues that Kinnell's "portrayal of Thoreau, in 'The Last River,' is a homage to a man of ideals who lived by them in a less than ideal world."[102] The study is of interest to Kinnell's readers because "The Last River" is, as Hayden Carruth notes in the *Hudson Review,* "the strongest single piece of writing the [Civil Rights] Movement has produced."[103]

Despite the critical world's ambivalence regarding *Mortal Acts, Mortal Words,* nearly every reviewer of the 1982 *Selected Poems* was able to look back on Kinnell's career as a whole and speak with confidence about his prominence as an American poet. Only William Harmon, in his review for *Poetry,* finds little to compliment in Kinnell's work; he argues that "The Avenue Bearing the Initial of Christ into the New World" is "one absolutely magnificent piece of very great poetry indeed," but concludes that it "makes every other piece by Kinnell seem relatively insipid."[104] More frequent were comments like that of Phoebe Pettingell, who finds that "these *Selected Poems* shine with an intensity that encompasses death *and* life"[105] or Robert Hass's assertion that Kinnell's writing is "hard and clear, full of odd, original and physically palpable phrasings," and "musical."[106]

The publication of *Selected Poems* presented critics with an opportunity to evaluate Kinnell's entire career, and several did so in a rather predictable fashion. Kenneth Funsten, for example, comments that *"The Book of Nightmares* demonstrates Kinnell's full potential" and that *Mortal Acts, Mortal Words* is "clearly an intermediary collection."[107] Richard Tillinghast, like numerous critics before and after him, complains about the poet's "lapses into prosiness," but contends that "when Kinnell is at the top of his form, there is no better poet writing in America."[108]

On the other hand, having before them samplings from each of Kinnell's previously published works led some reviewers to make fresh observations. Reginald Gibbons points out the poet's ability to balance "intense intimacy on paper" with "an equally intense power of observation and distance from himself."[109] Writing for the *Philadelphia Inquirer,* L. M. Rosenberg claims that "Kinnell is not a poet who is easily reduced to review-size quotes. His power is immense, but cumulative." Rosenberg contends not only that *Nightmares* is "the best single work of poetry to appear in the latter half of this century" but also that one of the poems therein, "Little Sleep's-Head Sprouting Hair in the Moonlight," could "stand against any poem written at any time." Because that poem and "most of Galway Kinnell's best work is gathered under one cover in *Selected Poems,"* Rosenberg contends, "it is an important book."[110] Donald Hall, in a lengthy discussion about Kinnell's *Selected Poems* and Hayden Carruth's *The Sleeping Beauty,* addresses what he terms "the anomaly of Kinnell's reputation," responding in particular to the harsh comments of Donald Davie in "Slogging for the Absolute" (discussed earlier in this introduction). Critics fail to understand Kinnell, he concludes, because "the literary traditions of the American academy have deteriorated so much that most American academicians cannot hear poetry, have no sense of its *art,* lack a prosody or a notion of metaphor: our leading critics of the contemporary read without leg-muscles or tongues, read without bodies."[111] Charles Molesworth looks back over Kinnell's career and argues that the poet "has maintained many of the same features in his poetry that he first took from the Romantic legacy, and he is still recognizably the poet whom Donald Davie castigated . . ." Now, though, in light of Kinnell's more recent works and with the benefit of hindsight, Molesworth believes we can "go back and redraw our sense of what lay behind that earlier work." In so doing, he argues, "what we might hear is that the song of the 'Tenderness toward Existence,' as he put it near the end of *The Book of Nightmares,* was always the main melody while the preoccupation with pain and loss made up the grace notes."[112]

In his remarks for the *London Times Literary Supplement,* Jay Parini deems Kinnell "one of the strongest voices of his generation." He goes on to argue that while "many critics found a reduction of powers in Kinnell's last book, *Mortal Acts, Mortal Words,*" he believes only that "the ferocity is gone" and that "Kinnell, having explored the lyric sequence so successfully," has "return[ed] to the form that first drew him to poetry—the personal lyric." Noting that the edge of Kinnell's *Nightmares* has been replaced by a "luxurious wholeness, a sense of grace," Parini concludes that "Kinnell has become what no one could have foreseen: a poet of consolation."[113] In an essay in which he compares Kinnell to poet Mark Strand, Peter Stitt contends that "all of Kinnell's work is marked by thematic cohesion and rhetorical dignity" and that "*Selected Poems* is a powerful and memorable volume that ought to solidify his reputation as one of the major voices of our age."[114]

Morris Dickstein laments the inclusion in *Selected Poems* of so large a number of Kinnell's early poems, finding them rife with "hollow echoes of Yeats," but he finds in the more recent work evidence that Kinnell is "one of the true master poets of his generation and a writer whose career exemplifies some of what is best in contemporary poetry." In defense of *Mortal Acts, Mortal Words,* Dickstein maintains that its "unassuming charm . . . caused it to be undervalued, even ignored, by many critics." He believes, however, that in *Mortal Acts* "Mr. Kinnell managed to lower the volume without retreating to formalism or triviality" and that it is his "best book, a collection that prove[s] that at least one poet in the Whitman-Williams mode of the 60's had survived not only intact but triumphant."[115]

Selected Poems was awarded both the American Book Award (Kinnell was a cowinner with Charles Wright) and the Pulitzer Prize for Poetry in 1983, prompting an onslaught of critical attention. In that same year, the *Saturday Review* published an essay by Madeleine Beckman that touches on thematic concerns in the poetry but which is centered largely on biographical matters.[116] David Young provided a useful introductory essay on Kinnell, focusing on five of his poems selected to accompany it in the *Longman Anthology of Contemporary American Poetry 1950–1980.*[117] In the following year, Alan Williamson included a discussion of Kinnell's work in his book *Introspection and Contemporary Poetry.* Chapter 4, "Language Against Itself: The Middle Generation of Contemporary Poets," addresses the concern Kinnell and others have with "forcing language to transcend itself" in order to reach "our authentic experience—the experience of the body and of the unconscious—that do not express themselves directly in verbal terms."[118] The year 1984 also saw the publication of Tess Gallagher's essay titled "The Poem as a Reservoir for Grief," a large portion of which is devoted to Kinnell's "Goodbye." Gallagher asserts that poems offer "the best and oldest forms we have for attending and absolving grief, for bringing it into a useful relationship to those things we are about to do toward a future." Explicating "Goodbye"—

as well as William Heyen's "The Berries" and Michael Burkard's "Islands of Feeling"—Gallagher describes how poetry can enable "imaginative returns to the causes, the emblems of loss" and thus aid us in the grieving process.[119]

Cary Nelson and Charles Altieri both included discussions of Kinnell in their book-length works published in 1984. Nelson's *Our Last First Poets: Vision and History in Contemporary American Poetry* devotes an entire chapter to an exploration of "how the language of *The Book of Nightmares* is permeated with Kinnell's particular conception of death," but Nelson places that volume in the context of Kinnell's earlier work, thus allowing readers to trace the development of Kinnell's prevalent death theme throughout his career.[120] Although Altieri's mention of Kinnell in *Self and Sensibility in Contemporary American Poetry* is brief, it is noteworthy because of its rather unique reading of *Nightmares*. Altieri contends that the reason this volume's "strained rhetoric" is frequently the target of attacks is that Kinnell has set himself an impossible task:

> In order to sustain and to resolve the level of intense, theatricalized suffering of the poem's often brilliant nightmare visions, Kinnell must be able to elaborate a metaphysical scheme equal to his demonic moments and capacious enough to justify a fully bardic stance. But Kinnell's ideas are very thin, and so he is forced to rely on the verbal gestures of intense emotion grafted onto conventional romantic postures.

Citing a section of *Nightmares* and accusing it of bathos, Altieri concludes that Kinnell's "general Rilkean stance collapses into a Blakean version of 'Dover Beach'" and the reader is offered "mostly exercises in lyric sensibility masquerading as thought." The problem Altieri attempts to elucidate is not limited to Kinnell but is characteristic of poets writing in the late seventies; what happens, he asks, "when a poem is asked to carry the burden of restoring to a culture large religious visions, however secularized or psychologized"? Pointing to Kinnell's *Nightmares* and other contemporary works, he concludes that "in seeking to make dramatic situations essentially representative moments exemplifying the working of larger metaphysical properties, poems may end up doing too little."[121]

In her 1984 essay on *Mortal Acts, Mortal Words*, Lorrie Goldensohn brings a feminist perspective—among others—to Kinnell's poetry. Early in the study, she discusses the tension between Kinnell's prose statements about what she calls "poetry's limited reach" and the "sentimental compromises" she finds at times in his verse. Goldensohn points to "The Last Hiding Places of Snow" as one instance where the poet "refuses . . . to rest on the constitutive powers of language" and instead "skitters uncomfortably close to bathos"; she then adds that in this same poem Kinnell is also guilty of "other problematic exclusions and refusals," most of which "cluster around the treatment of women and children."[122] Ten years after this reading of *Mortal Acts,*

Goldensohn revisited her essay and incorporated a broader perspective, including Kinnell's depiction of women and the domestic in his 1994 volume, *Imperfect Thirst*. The revised version is included in this anthology under the title "Domestication of the Transcendental."

Seeing and Healing: A Study of the Poetry of Galway Kinnell, a book-length analysis by James Guimond, also appeared in 1984.[123] Although Guimond includes references to the more recent work, clearly *The Book of Nightmares* and the poetry leading up to it provide the focus for his discussion. First he provides an overview of themes in Kinnell's work, followed by a chapter on the poet's early development. He places Kinnell's particular nightmare vision in the context of "American Dreams and Nightmares" in chapter 3 before devoting an entire chapter to explaining how *The Book of Nightmares* represents "a more deliberate effort to confront the darker, more mysterious, and visionary side of human experience" within that peculiarly American historical context. The final chapter of the book explores the concept of poet as shaman and points to the healing message in *Nightmares* and in other works as well, particularly *Mortal Acts*.

Two more studies appeared prior to the publication of Kinnell's next volume of poetry. Julie Wosk mentions the poet in her essay "The Distancing Effect of Technology in 20th Century Poetry and Painting," highlighting "Vapor Trail Reflected in the Frog Pond" as one example of Kinnell's attempt to bridge the gap between humanity and the sophisticated technological advancements of this century.[124] In a particularly cogent essay, Andrew Hudgins focuses on Kinnell's struggle in *Nightmares* with "the separation of the conscious and unconscious aspects of the mind" and the ensuing dichotomies inherent in such a division: "rational and irrational, mind and body, and ultimately life and death." In opposition to those critics who have accused Kinnell of inconsistencies in his philosophy and poetics, Hudgins argues that Kinnell "honestly confronts both sides of the dichotomy, and never slides off into glib lyricism or the intellectual fuzziness of fashionable mysticism."[125]

The Past appeared in 1985. Reactions were generally positive, with the exception of two reviews. Writing from the point of view of one who had long admired Kinnell's work, Alice Phillips finds the poems in *The Past* at times immature, "lightweight," or "pure filler." She points out, however, that in the poems dedicated to the memory of Richard Hugo and James Wright "Kinnell transmutes his bereavement and gratitude into powerful images . . . and word music," and she praises the final poem, "The Seekonk Woods," as "what should have been happening all along."[126] James Finn Cotter accuses Kinnell of a "tendency to overexplain" and asks, "Why does the poet feel driven to prove himself to his readers; they already trust his sincerity." About the two elegies that even Phillips finds strong, Cotter laments, "Kinnell seems intent on making mythology out of gossip; his hero-worship sounds too exaggerated, as if straining for the epic moment while only half-believing it himself."[127]

In sharp contrast, Daniel L. Guillory describes the opening of *The Past* as depicting "moving evocations of [Kinnell's] life in Sheffield, Vermont some thirty years ago," concluding his remarks with the assertion that this is "a major book by a major poet."[128] Whereas Phillips criticizes Kinnell for philosophizing, L. M. Rosenberg praises Kinnell for being, "as all great poets must be, a philosophical poet." Admitting that the poet's "seriousness" is not always successful, Rosenberg calls this collection "a glorious one, certainly the strongest since *The Book of Nightmares*," adding that "The Fundamental Project of Technology" is "far and away the best poem we have on the bombings at Nagasaki and the dangers of the nuclear age."[129] Although finding much to commend in *The Past*, J. D. McClatchy nonetheless considers it a continuation of *Mortal Acts, Mortal Words*—a book in which the language "thickened a bit," one in which the "tone was bored, even sentimental" when held up to *The Book of Nightmares*.[130]

Several other reviews provide useful insights into *The Past* in particular and Kinnell's work in general. Indicative of Kinnell's popularity with audiences outside the academic arena is Cathleen Medwick's comment in *Vogue* magazine that his admirers "are an enraptured multitude." Despite the fact that Medwick is writing for a nonscholarly audience, the essay is of interest to scholars because it contains revealing excerpts from her interview with Kinnell—statements, for example, in which he expresses his views on the connections between love and death.[131] In a brief review in the *New Leader*, Phoebe Pettingell points out that *The Past* embodies Kinnell's "biological perception of the world," a "conviction that man is part of the animal kingdom, and must be stripped 'back down / to hair, flesh, blood, bone, the base metals,' to be seen for what he is."[132] Harold Beaver comments briefly on *The Past*, summing it up as a retrospective of the poet's "childhood, his first love, his growing children and the breakup of a marriage." He applauds Kinnell for displaying a "masterly economy" and for his landscapes that embody "emotion without a hint of pastoral extravagance or natural fallacy."[133] *New York Times* reviewer Michiko Kakutani explains that in later works like *Mortal Acts* and *The Past*, Kinnell has moved from *Nightmare*'s "fierce, post-Romantic terror" over humanity's "precarious condition" to a focus "on the undying spirit, on the possibility that death may mean not mere extinction, but a reconciliation with the universe's great ebb and flow."[134] Roger Mitchell admits that it is difficult to talk about any of Kinnell's work without comparing it to *The Book of Nightmares*, although he finds that he prefers the poems in *The Past* because they are "more human in scale, less committed to being rituals and myths and more to being responses to what—so it feels—is really there in Galway Kinnell's life."[135]

A year after the publication of *The Past*, David Kleinbard published a study of what he calls Kinnell's "poetry of transformation," *The Book of Nightmares*. He points out that when it first appeared, *Nightmares* "was praised as an evocation of a national trauma, the Vietnam war and its effects on this country," but that in 1986 "it seems more remarkable as an expression of private experience in visionary images."[136] That same year, Joyce Dyer's critical essay "The Music of Galway Kinnell's *Mortal Acts, Mortal Words*" provided a brief look at the music motif that "haunts all of Kinnell's volumes" but which appears in the 1980 volume "frequently and mysteriously." Dyer traces through *Mortal Acts* "chords of beauty and grace-notes of hope" that "urge us to accept our mortal state."[137]

Five more critical essays and two books about Kinnell's poetry appeared prior to the publication of his next volume of poetry in 1990. In 1987, the *Dictionary of Literary Biography Yearbook* provided an update on Kinnell, addressing major themes in his works from *Mortal Acts, Mortal Words* to *The Past* and examining the critical reception during that time.[138] Able to look back at nearly thirty years of Kinnell's poetry, critics writing in the late eighties converged on those concerns that are most central to Kinnell and that are most prevalent in his poetry. In 1987, Susan Weston published a study on Kinnell's poetics, emphasizing the poet's understanding of language—and therefore poetry—as a physical manifestation of the human body. In a clearly written essay that traces this theme throughout Kinnell's career, Weston argues that "Kinnell sees poetry as a product of and approach to the body, and the body itself as the vehicle of transcendence."[139] Catharine F. Seigel takes a look at Kinnell's role as a political activist and examines his more political poems, including "Vapor Trail Reflected in the Frog Pond" and "The Fundamental Project of Technology." Her essay, titled "Corso, Kinnell, and the Bomb," argues that especially in the latter poem Kinnell "succeeds at that difficult task of being both political and poetic."[140] Granville Taylor begins his analysis of Kinnell's poetry by stating, "To read the poetry of Galway Kinnell is to witness a poetic evolution." He argues that "Kinnell's poetry develops from Christian to natural theology, from irony to lyricism, and from pessimism to affirmation and joy" and that it "shows that the sacred dimension can be found in contexts which are not explicitly Christian and even explicitly non-Christian."[141] Finally, Thomas Gardner returns to *The Book of Nightmares* to examine Kinnell's efforts to "unpack the rich implications of . . . the single moment in Whitman in which the limitations of the embrace are exposed and the device is then reformulated." Kinnell, Gardner argues, "passes through his confrontation with human emptiness . . . and has transformed what he sees as the unstated sense of loss in 'Song of Myself' back into its obvious sense of power, splintered and brief, but directed outward toward the world."[142] Ranging in topic from the physical to the political to the spiritual, these essays constitute some of the most useful and important studies written to date on Kinnell's poetry.

Two books on Kinnell appeared in 1987. Howard Nelson edited a collection of critical essays and reviews as part of the University of Michigan's *Under Discussion* series. *On the Poetry of Galway Kinnell* includes seven original essays as well as a sampling of reviews and previously published studies of

Kinnell's work through *The Past*. Particularly useful are the essays on individual poems—explications, largely, that provide a depth of understanding not possible in studies with broader theses. Nelson's introduction is itself a study of one aspect of Kinnell's poetics: the weight of his words, which Nelson explores by examining not only the poetry but also the "assiduous and continuous" revisions through which Kinnell takes his work.[143] In his book *Intricate and Simple Things: The Poetry of Galway Kinnell*, Lee Zimmerman investigates dichotomies in Kinnell's work: isolation and belonging, the self and the world, desire for life and longing for death. Each chapter after the introduction is devoted to an individual volume of Kinnell's poetry, and throughout the study Zimmerman explores the poet's diverse literary influences.[144]

Galway Kinnell's tenth volume of poetry appeared in 1990, exactly thirty years after the publication of his first, *What a Kingdom It Was*. Sarah Cahill writes that *When One Has Lived a Long Time Alone* "is structurally taut, pared down to its essence, more economical" than his earlier collections of poems—qualities she attributes to the tremendous control the poet has now achieved in his voice. Comparing Kinnell to Irish poets, Cahill finds that, like them, Kinnell can be read on two levels: "for sound, during which you feel the heft of the line, like a collection of polished stones weighing pleasantly in the hand—and then for content, which then seems surprisingly like an extra bonus." Cahill includes a brief discussion of the volume's title poem, which, she asserts, ends "with a final moment of vulnerability, humility, and mortality." She concludes, "And that, as we all know, is what finally elevates all tragic figures."[145]

While Cahill finds Kinnell "especially successful when he turns his attention to erotic suggestion," *Publishers Weekly* notes that the poet's "language is sometimes too controlled to express the intensity of erotic love."[146] Reviewers registered other complaints as well. While conceding that "nearly every poem includes at least one passage that is tender or beautiful enough to redeem the poem and reward one's having read it," John Piller finds the "poems . . . of uneven accomplishment" and claims that at times Kinnell's "depth of emotion . . . verges on the sentimental." Piller is bothered by "Kinnell's proselike rhythms and flat declarative style," which he believes dissolves the tension in some poems.[147] John Shoptaw hears in these poems merely "a man speaking to men about themselves" and provides examples of the "limitations of Kinnell's masculinist mythology." Pointing to "Flower of Five Blossoms," for example, Shoptaw contends that "unnamed and unconscious, woman is merely the vehicle of a man's self-completion."[148]

Several reviewers focused on Kinnell's use of language in these poems. Pointing out that the poet has "always been a hungry lover of language at its basic level, where sound curls into meaning," Stephen Yenser finds that in reading these poems "one sometimes has the feeling [Kinnell] is *making* words out of sound as a potter shapes a pot from clay."[149] Mary Kinzie maintains that "one can scarcely avoid the metaphor of musical skill when admiring the highly organized array of verbal responses in these poems to the physical responses implied by their themes." She deems Kinnell "an accomplished navigator of the sensory" who, at this point in his career, "composes . . . with no suggestion of effort."[150] Writing in the *Chicago Tribune,* L. M. Rosenberg describes the volume as "a duet of conflicting musics, a split impulse between the dark, dire, laboring male and the life-giving, 'blisamous' female." The essence of his music, she claims, is "the old oppositions between death and love."[151] Claiming that Kinnell "surely possesses the most lyrical voice of his generation," Joyce Peseroff adds that in this volume one finds "the isolate self witnessing rejection, disappointment, and the shadow of death."[152] Samuel Hazo declares that "each poem has about it the authenticity of the word-carver's art" and that in Kinnell's poetry "life shines through without distortion."[153]

Between 1991 and 1994, I published four critical studies on Kinnell, explorations of his literary debts to Theodore Roethke, Robert Frost, and Walt Whitman. While each essay focuses on one of those three influences, together they attempt to understand Kinnell's brand of twentieth-century romanticism by pointing out how it is similar to and different from the poetics of each of these forebears.[154] In 1992, the fourth book-length study of Kinnell's work appeared. As part of Twayne's *United States Authors* series, Richard Calhoun's *Galway Kinnell* provides a helpful introduction to the poet's work while proposing that his "achievements as a poet are best seen as part of an evolution on his part, shared . . . with poets of his generation, from the modernism of Eliot and Pound to his own use of the postmodernist explorations into the personal of poets like Theodore Roethke and Robert Lowell."[155] Calhoun devotes one chapter to a biographical overview, one to a study of Kinnell's prose writings, and several to analysis of individual books of poetry.

Kinnell's most recent volume, *Imperfect Thirst,* appeared in 1994. In an advance review, *Publishers Weekly* applauds the astonishing "breadth in the volume."

[P]oems range from an expression of poetic resistance to the fashionable scholarly disinterment of language in "The Deconstruction of Emily Dickinson," to the delicate tableau he creates of a woman caring for her father in "Parkinson's Disease," to his gleefully erudite tribute to excrement in "Holy Shit." Primal themes—love, nature, mortality—emerge in newly compelling forms.

The reviewer concedes that while "at times Kinnell's remarks to himself seem needlessly self-referential," his voice is nonetheless "unsurpassable . . . when the poet speaks intimately to us."[156] In a review commissioned for this collection, Fred Moramarco observes how Kinnell uses language to "describe the reality of a world that may be completely illusory." Starting with "The Pen"— what Kinnell calls a "proem" in *Imperfect Thirst*—Moramarco traces the poet's frustration with a language that sometimes moves us "further from the emotional context of actual experience rather than closer to it." Carefully addressing a number of poems, this review has the depth of an essay written by one who has given thoughtful attention not only to this volume but to the poet's entire career.

While the purpose of *Critical Essays on Galway Kinnell* is to provide the most comprehensive overview of critical responses to date, it is, of course, impossible to include every review and scholarly essay. I have therefore used two criteria in deciding what to include: first, I considered whether a particular piece offered readers insight either into individual volumes of Kinnell's poetry or into the career as a whole. Second, I took into consideration the existence of Howard Nelson's fine collection of essays published in 1987; whenever I could avoid duplicating the commentary included therein without omitting an important point of view, I did so. The fact that at the age of sixty-nine Galway Kinnell is still vitally active as a creator, reader, commentator, and teacher of poetry means, of course, that this collection offers by no means the final word in Kinnell studies; instead, it is an attempt to make accessible to Kinnell's readers a representation of the critical opinions offered so far and to encourage them to continue the discussion of his immense contribution to American letters.

Notes

1. Galway Kinnell, "Only Meaning Is Truly Interesting," *Beloit Poetry Journal* 4 (Fall 1953): 1–2.

2. Galway Kinnell, "The Poetics of the Physical World," *Iowa Review* 2, no. 3 (Summer 1971): 116, 120.

3. Melvin Walker La Follette, "Kinnell's 'First Song,' " *Explicator* 14 (April 1956): item 48.

4. Gene H. Koretz, "Kinnell's 'First Song,' " *Explicator* 15 (April 1957): item 43.

5. John Logan, "Fine First Book," review of *What a Kingdom It Was,* by Galway Kinnell, *Commonweal,* 4 November 1960, 154.

6. Selden Rodman, "A Quartet of Younger Singers," review of *What a Kingdom It Was,* by Galway Kinnell, *New York Times Book Review,* 18 September 1960, 50.

7. Louise Bogan, "Verse," review of *What a Kingdom It Was,* by Galway Kinnell, *New Yorker,* 1 April 1961, 130.

8. Stanley J. Rowland Jr., review of *What a Kingdom It Was,* by Galway Kinnell, *Christian Century,* 22 February 1961, 248.

9. James Dickey, "Five First Books," review of *What a Kingdom It Was,* by Galway Kinnell, *Poetry* 97 (Fall 1961): 319.

10. Glauco Cambon, *Recent American Poetry,* Pamphlets on American Writers, no. 16 (Minneapolis: University of Minnesota Press, 1962), 31–33.

11. Joseph Bennett, "I've Got a Little List," *Hudson Review* 13, no. 3 (Fall 1960): 478–79.

12. Sherman Hawkins, "Galway Kinnell: Moments of Transcendence," *Princeton University Library Chronicle* 25, no. 1 (Autumn 1963): 56–70.

13. Mona Van Duyn, "Vision, Celebration, and Testimony," review of *Flower Herding on Mount Monadnock,* by Galway Kinnell, *Poetry* 105, no. 4 (January 1965): 264–66.

14. Herbert C. Burke, review of *Flower Herding,* by Galway Kinnell, *Library Journal* 89 (15 March 1964): 1251.

15. De Witt Bell, "Wonders of the Inner Eye," review of *Flower Herding,* by Galway Kinnell, *New York Times Book Review,* 5 July 1964, 5.

16. Fred Bornhauser, "Poetry by the Poem," review of *Flower Herding,* by Galway Kinnell, *Virginia Quarterly Review* 41 (14 November 1964): 146.

17. S. J. Rowland Jr., "Octet," review of *Flower Herding,* by Galway Kinnell, *Christian Century,* 22 July 1964, 939.

18. John Malcolm Brinnin, "Plath, Jarrell, Kinnell, Smith," review of *Flower Herding,* by Galway Kinnell, *Partisan Review* 34 (Winter 1967): 156–60.

19. Robert Pack, "The Muse Is Always Gay," review of *Flower Herding,* by Galway Kinnell, *Saturday Review of Literature* 14 November 1964, 60.

20. R.W. Flint, "Recent Poetry: Three American Poets," review of *Flower Herding,* by Galway Kinnell, *New York Review of Books,* 25 June 1964, 14.

21. Jane Taylor [McDonnell], "The Poetry of Galway Kinnell," *Perspective: A Quarterly of Literature* 15 (1968): 189–200.

22. Publisher's note, inside front dust jacket, *Black Light,* by Galway Kinnell (San Francisco: North Point, 1980).

23. Phoebe Adams, review of *Black Light,* by Galway Kinnell, *Atlantic,* May 1966, 132.

24. Anonymous, review of *Black Light,* by Galway Kinnell, *Virginia Quarterly Review* 42 (Summer 1966): xc.

25. Mona Van Duyn, "The Poet as Novelist," *Poetry* 109 (February 1967): 337–38.

26. Kenith Trodd, "Hell for Mum," review of *Black Light,* by Galway Kinnell, *New Statesman,* 1 September 1967, 261–62.

27. Gwendolyn Brooks, review of *Black Light,* by Galway Kinnell, *Book Week,* 10 July 1966, 17.

28. John Logan, "The Bear in the Poet in the Bear," review of *Body Rags,* by Galway Kinnell, *Nation,* 16 September 1968, 244.

29. Michael Benedikt, "Critic of the Month: IV," review of *Body Rags,* by Galway Kinnell, *Poetry* 113 (December 1968): 188.

30. Michele Murray, "*Body Rags* by Galway Kinnell," review of *Body Rags,* by Galway Kinnell, *New: American and Canadian Poetry* 8 (December 1968): 42.

31. Richard Dillard, review of *Body Rags,* by Galway Kinnell, *Virginia Quarterly Review* 44 (Summer 1968): ciii.

32. Dillard, ciii.

33. Laurence Lieberman, "New Poetry in Review," review of *Body Rags,* by Galway Kinnell, *Yale Review* 58 (October 1968): 137–38.

34. Ian Hamilton, "Declarations of Despair," review of *Body Rags,* by Galway Kinnell, *London Observer,* 21 September 1969, 34.

35. Alan Brownjohn, "Dark Forces," review of *Body Rags,* by Galway Kinnell, *New Statesman,* 12 September 1969, 346–47.

36. Jerome Judson, "Uncommitted Voices," review of *Body Rags,* by Galway Kinnell, *Saturday Review of Literature,* 1 June 1968, 33.

37. Hayden Carruth, "Making It New," review of *Body Rags,* by Galway Kinnell, *Hudson Review* 21, no. 2 (Summer 1968): 403–4.

38. Richard Howard, "Galway Kinnell: 'Everything That May Abide the Fire Was Made to Go Through the Fire,'" in his *Alone with America: Essays on the Art of Poetry in the United States since 1950* (New York: Atheneum, 1969), 258–71.

39. Ralph J. Mills Jr., "A Reading of Galway Kinnell: Part 1," *Iowa Review* 1, no. 1 (1970): 66–67.

40. Ralph J. Mills Jr., "A Reading of Galway Kinnell, Part 2," *Iowa Review* 1, no. 2 (1970): 121.

41. Galway Kinnell, "Author's Note" to *First Poems 1946–1954,* in *The Avenue Bearing the Initial of Christ into the New World* (Boston: Houghton Mifflin, 1974), 3.

42. Charles G. Bell, "Galway Kinnell," in *Contemporary Poets of the English Language,* 3d ed., ed. Rosalie Murphy (New York: St. Martin's, 1970), 601–4.

43. Robert Langbaum, "Galway Kinnell's *The Book of Nightmares,*" review of *The Book of Nightmares,* by Galway Kinnell, *American Poetry Review* 8, no. 2 (March–April 1979): 30–31.

44. Donald Hall, "A Luminous Receptiveness," review of *The Book of Nightmares,* by Galway Kinnell, *Nation,* 18 October 1971, 378.

45. Thomas Lask, "The Makers and Their Works," review of *The Book of Nightmares,* by Galway Kinnell, *New York Times,* 1 September 1971, 35.

46. Michael Benedikt, "The Apotheosis of Darkness Vs. Bardic Privilege," review of *The Book of Nightmares, Poetry* 121 (November 1972): 106–7.

47. Arthur Oberg, "The One Flea Which Is Laughing," review of *The Book of Nightmares,* by Galway Kinnell, *Shenandoah* 25 (Fall 1973): 85–86.

48. William Virgil Davis, " 'The Wasted Breath': Galway Kinnell's *The Book of Nightmares,*" review of *The Book of Nightmares,* by Galway Kinnell, *Montana Review* 3 (1982): 59.

49. Rosemary F. Deen, "*The Book of Nightmares* by Galway Kinnell," review of *The Book of Nightmares,* by Galway Kinnell, *Commonweal,* 24 December 1971, 308.

50. James Whitehead, "Leaping Ghazals and Inside Jokes Concealed in Tropes," review of *The Book of Nightmares,* by Galway Kinnell, *Saturday Review of Literature,* 18 December 1971, 40.

51. M. L. Rosenthal, "Under the Freeway, in the Hotel of Lost Light," review of *The Book of Nightmares,* by Galway Kinnell, *New York Times Book Review,* 23 November 1971, 77.

52. Richard Howard, "Changes," review of *The Book of Nightmares,* by Galway Kinnell, *Partisan Review* 38 (Winter 1971–72): 484–90.

53. Richmond Lattimore, "Poetry Chronicle," review of *The Book of Nightmares,* by Galway Kinnell, *Hudson Review* 24 (Fall 1971): 501–2.

54. Robert Peters, "On Climbing the Matterhorn: Monadnock," review of *The Book of Nightmares,* by Galway Kinnell, *Northeast Rising Sun* 1 (January 1976).

55. Lattimore, 501–2.

56. Jane Taylor McDonnell, review of *The Book of Nightmares,* by Galway Kinnell, *Carleton Miscellany* 12, no. 2 (Summer 1972): 153–156.

57. Galway Kinnell, "The Poetics of the Physical World," *Iowa Review* 2, no. 3 (Summer 1971): 113–14, 116, 119.

58. Galway Kinnell, "Poetry, Personality, and Death," *Field* 4 (Spring 1971): 65, 74.

59. Adrienne Rich, "Poetry, Personality and Wholeness: A Response to Galway Kinnell," *Field* 7 (Fall 1972): 11–18.

60. Howard, 487.

61. Galway Kinnell, "Whitman's Indicative Words," *American Poetry Review* 2, no. 2 (March–April 1973): 9–11. Reprinted in *Walt Whitman: Walt Whitman's Autograph Revision of the Analysis of "Leaves of Grass" (For Dr. R. M. Bucke's "Walt Whitman"),* ed. Quentin Anderson and Stephen Railton (New York: New York University Press, 1974), 53–63. A revised version appears in *Walt Whitman: The Measure of His Song,* ed. Jim Perlman et al. (Minneapolis, Minn.: Holy Cow!, 1981), 215–27.

62. Charles Molesworth, "The Rank Flavor of Blood: Galway Kinnell and American Poetry in the 1960's," *Western Humanities Review* 27 (1973): 225–39.

63. Patrick Keane, review of *The Avenue Bearing the Initial of Christ into the New World: Poems 1946–1964,* by Galway Kinnell, *New Republic,* 27 July and 3 August 1974, 24–25.

64. Vernon Young, review of *The Avenue Bearing the Initial of Christ into the New World,* by Galway Kinnell, *Hudson Review* 27 (Winter 1974–1975): 599–600.

65. Christopher Ricks, "In the Direct Line of Whitman, the Indirect Line of Eliot: *The Avenue Bearing the Initial of Christ into the New World*, by Galway Kinnell," *New York Times Book Review*, 12 January 1975, 2.

66. James Atlas, "Autobiography of the Present," review of *The Avenue Bearing the Initial of Christ into the New World*, by Galway Kinnell, *Poetry* 125 (February 1975): 295–302.

67. Terry Comito, "Slogging toward the Absolute," review of *The Avenue Bearing the Initial of Christ into the New World*, by Galway Kinnell, *Modern Poetry Studies* 6, no. 2 (1975): 189–192.

68. Jerome McGann, "Points of Departure in Recent Poetry," review of *The Avenue Bearing the Initial of Christ into the New World*, by Galway Kinnell, *Chicago Review* 27, no. 1 (1975): 161–64.

69. Donald Davie, "Slogging for the Absolute," *Parnassus* 3, no. 1 (1974): 9–22.

70. Donald Davie, "Reply to Ralph J. Mills, Jr.," *Parnassus* 3, no. 2 (1974): 291.

71. William E. Thompson, "Synergy in the Poetry of Galway Kinnell," *Gypsy Scholar* 1, no. 2 (1974): 52–69.

72. James F. Mersmann, *Out of the Vietnam Vortex: A Study of Poets and Poetry Against the War* (Lawrence: University Press of Kansas, 1974), 23, 237–39.

73. John Hobbs, "Galway Kinnell's 'The Bear': Dream and Technique," *Modern Poetry Studies* 5, no. 3 (Winter 1974): 237–50.

74. Linda Wagner, " 'Spindrift': The World in a Seashell," *Concerning Poetry* 8 (Spring 1975): 5–9.

75. J. T. Ledbetter, "Galway Kinnell's 'The Bear,' " *Explicator* 33 (April 1975): item 62.

76. Conrad Hilberry, "The Structure of Galway Kinnell's *The Book of Nightmares*," *Field* 12 (Spring 1975): 28–46.

77. William Virgil Davis, " 'The Rank Flavor of Blood': Galway Kinnell's 'The Bear,' " *Notes on Contemporary Literature* 7, no. 2 (1977): 4–6.

78. Glauco Cambon, "Dante on Galway Kinnell's 'Last River,' " in *Dante's Influence on American Writers 1776–1976*, ed. Anne Paolucci (New York: Griffin House for Dante Society of America, 1977), 31–40.

79. Andrew Taylor, "The Poetry of Galway Kinnell," *Meanjin* 36 (1977): 228–41.

80. Geoffrey Thurley, "Devices Among Words, Kinnell, Bly, Simic," chap. 12 in *The American Moment: American Poetry in the Mid-Century* (New York: St. Martin's, 1977), 210–28.

81. Takako U. Lento, "The Deathwish and the Self in Contemporary American Poetry," *Kyushu American Literature* 19 (1978): 17–27.

82. J. Boening, review of *Walking Down the Stairs*, by Galway Kinnell, *World Literature Today* 53, no. 3 (Summer 1979): 572.

83. Susan Weston, review of *Walking Down the Stairs*, by Galway Kinnell, *Iowa Review* 10, no. 1 (1979): 95–98.

84. Galway Kinnell, preface to *Walking Down the Stairs* (Ann Arbor: University of Michigan Press, 1978), xii.

85. Anonymous review of *Mortal Acts, Mortal Words*, by Galway Kinnell, *Publisher's Weekly*, 28 March 1980, 40.

86. Katha Pollitt, "Two Poets: Run-on Lines," review of *Mortal Acts, Mortal Words*, by Galway Kinnell, *Nation*, 5 July 1980, 26–27.

87. Robert B. Shaw, "Utensils Down the Dream," review of *Mortal Acts, Mortal Words*, by Galway Kinnell, *Nation*, 8 November 1980, 477.

88. Harold Bloom, "Straight Forth Out of Self," review of *Mortal Acts, Mortal Words*, by Galway Kinnell, *New York Times Book Review*, 22 June 1980, 13.

89. Peter Serchuk, "Confessions of Travelers and Pilgrims," review of *Mortal Acts, Mortal Words*, by Galway Kinnell, *Sewanee Review* 89 (April 1981): 271–78.

90. Peter Stitt, "Dimensions of Reality," review of *Mortal Acts, Mortal Words*, by Galway Kinnell, *Georgia Review* 34, no. 4 (Winter 1980): 887–94.

91. Hank Lazer, "That Backward-Spreading Brightness," review of *Mortal Acts, Mortal Words,* by Galway Kinnell, *Ironwood* 16, no. 2 (Fall 1980): 92–100.

92. Howard Nelson, review of *Mortal Acts, Mortal Words,* by Galway Kinnell, *Hawaii Review* 12 (Fall 1981): 113–16.

93. Jerome Mazzaro, "At the Start of the Eighties," review of *Mortal Acts, Mortal Words,* by Galway Kinnell, *Hudson Review* 33 (Autumn 1980): 455–58.

94. Vernon Shetly, "Take But Degree Away," review of *Mortal Acts, Mortal Words,* by Galway Kinnell, *Poetry* 137 (February 1981): 298–99.

95. Sandra Prewitt Edelman, "The Poet as Healer," review of *Mortal Acts, Mortal Words,* by Galway Kinnell, *Southwest Review* 66 (Spring 1981): 215–19.

96. John Piller, review of *Mortal Acts, Mortal Words,* by Galway Kinnell, *Virginia Quarterly Review* 56 (Autumn 1980): 146.

97. Stephen Yenser, "Recent Poetry: Five Poets," review of *Mortal Acts, Mortal Words,* by Galway Kinnell, *Yale Review* 70, no. 1 (October 1980): 105–28.

98. R. W. Flint, "At Home in the Seventies," review of *Mortal Acts, Mortal Words,* by Galway Kinnell, *Parnassus* 8, no. 2 (1980): 51–62.

99. Galway Kinnell, "Lastness," *The Book of Nightmares* (Boston: Houghton Mifflin, 1971), 71–75.

100. Charles Frazier, "Galway Kinnell," in *Dictionary of Literary Biography,* vol. 5: *American Poets since World War II,* ed. Donald J. Greiner (Detroit: Gale, 1980), 397–402.

101. Joe Marusiak, "Where We Might Meet Each Other: An Appreciation of Galway Kinnell and William Everson," *Literary Review: An International Journal of Contemporary Writing* 24, no. 3 (Spring 1981): 355–70.

102. Peggy Parris, "Rags of His Body: Thoreau in Galway Kinnell's 'The Last River,' " *Thoreau Society Bulletin* 161 (Fall 1982): 4–6.

103. Carruth, 400.

104. William Harmon, "Kumin and Kinnell (and Kilmer)," review of *Selected Poems,* by Galway Kinnell, *Poetry* 142 (April 1983): 50–52.

105. Phoebe Pettingell, "Sane and Sacred Death," review of *Selected Poems,* by Galway Kinnell, *New Leader,* 20 September 1982, 16–17.

106. Robert Hass, review of *Selected Poems,* by Galway Kinnell, *Book World,* 5 September 1982, 6.

107. Kenneth Funsten, "To Accept Death as an Appreciation of Life," review of *Selected Poems,* by Galway Kinnell, *Los Angeles Times,* 6 February 1983, 2.

108. Richard Tillinghast, review of *Selected Poems,* by Galway Kinnell, *Boston Review* 8 (February 1983): 36.

109. Reginald Gibbons, "Three Diverse Voices on Nature, Domesticity, Society," reviews of *Selected Poems,* by Galway Kinnell, *Chicago Tribune Arts and Books,* 24 April 1983, section 7, 3–4.

110. L. M. Rosenberg, "A Poet with the Flame of Greatness," review of *Selected Poems,* by Galway Kinnell, *Philadelphia Inquirer,* 13 February 1983, 6.

111. Donald Hall, "Text As Test: Notes On and Around Carruth and Kinnell," *American Poetry Review* 12 (November–December 1983): 27–32.

112. Charles Molesworth, " 'Backward-spreading brightness': Career's End in Contemporary American Poetry," *LIT* 1, no. 3 (1990): 183–89.

113. Jay Parini, "From Scene to Fiery Scene," review of *Selected Poems,* by Galway Kinnell, *London Times Literary Supplement,* 1 March 1985, 239.

114. Peter Stitt, "Stages of Reality: The Mind/Body Problem in Contemporary Poetry," review of *Selected Poems,* by Galway Kinnell, *Georgia Review* 37, no. 1 (Spring 1983): 201–10.

115. Morris Dickstein, "Intact and Triumphant," review of *Selected Poems,* by Galway Kinnell, *New York Times Book Review,* 19 September 1982, 12, 33.

116. Madeleine Beckman, "Galway Kinnell Searches for Innocence," *Saturday Review of Literature* 9 (September-October 1983): 14–16.

117.   David Young, "Galway Kinnell," in *The Longman Anthology of Contemporary American Poetry: 1950–1980,* ed. David Young and Stuart Friebert (New York: Longman, 1983), 241–44.

118.   Alan Williamson, "Language against Itself: The Middle Generation of Contemporary Poets," in his *Introspection and Contemporary Poetry* (Cambridge, Mass.: Harvard University Press, 1984), 65–92.

119.   Tess Gallagher, "The Poem as a Reservoir for Grief," *American Poetry Review* 13 (July–August 1984): 7–11.

120.   Cary Nelson, "Ecclesiastical Whitman: Galway Kinnell's *The Book of Nightmares,*" in his *Our Last First Poets: Vision and History in Contemporary American Poetry* (Urbana: University of Illinois Press, 1984), 187–90.

121.   Charles Altieri, *Self and Sensibility in Contemporary American Poetry* (New York: Cambridge University Press, 1984), 44–45.

122.   Lorrie Goldensohn, "Approaching Home Ground: Galway Kinnell's *Mortal Acts, Mortal Words,*" *Massachusetts Review* 25 no. 2 (Summer 1984): 303–21.

123.   James Guimond, *Seeing and Healing: A Study of the Poetry of Galway Kinnell* (New York: Associated Faculty Press, 1984).

124.   Julie Wosk, "The Distancing Effect of Technology in 20th Century Poetry and Painting," *San Jose Studies* 11, no. 2 (Spring 1985): 22–41.

125.   Andrew Hudgins, " 'One and Zero Walk Off Together': Dualism in Galway Kinnell's *The Book of Nightmares,*" *American Poetry* 3, no. 1 (Fall 1985): 56–71.

126.   Alice Phillips, "Past Imperfect," review of *The Past,* by Galway Kinnell, *Village Voice,* 11 April 1985, 56–57.

127.   James Finn Cotter, "Poetry's Need to Name," review of *The Past,* by Galway Kinnell, *Hudson Review* 39 (Spring 1986): 153–60.

128.   Daniel L. Guillory, review of *The Past,* by Galway Kinnell, *Library Journal* 110 (15 November 1985): 100.

129.   L. M. Rosenberg, "Four Dark Volumes That Manage to Shine," review of *The Past,* by Galway Kinnell, *Chicago Tribune,* 2 February 1986, section 14, 40.

130.   J. D. McClatchy, "A Pulitzer Poetry Winner Offers a Volume of Memories," review of *The Past,* by Galway Kinnell, *Philadelphia Inquirer,* 23 March 1986.

131.   Cathleen Medwick, "Poetry in Motion," review of *The Past,* by Galway Kinnell, *Vogue,* November 1985, 280–81.

132.   Phoebe Pettingell, "Songs of Science," review of *The Past,* by Galway Kinnell, *New Leader,* 16–30 December 1985, 19–20.

133.   Harold Beaver, "Refuge in the Library, on the Farm, and in Memories," review of *The Past,* by Galway Kinnell, *New York Times Book Review,* 2 March 1986, 14–15.

134.   Michiko Kakutani, "Mortality and Love," review of *The Past,* by Galway Kinnell, *New York Times,* 2 November 1985, 13.

135.   Roger Mitchell, "That's It," review of *The Past,* by Galway Kinnell, *American Book Review* 9, no. 2 (March–April 1987): 23.

136.   David Kleinbard, "Galway Kinnell's Poetry of Transformation," *Centennial Review* 30, no. 1 (Winter 1986): 41–56.

137.   Joyce Dyer, "The Music of Galway Kinnell's *Mortal Acts, Mortal Words,*" *Notes on Contemporary Literature* 16, no. 3 (May 1986): 5–8.

138.   Nancy Tuten, "Galway Kinnell," *Dictionary of Literary Biography Yearbook: 1987,* ed. Matt Brook (Detroit: Gale, 1988), 257–64.

139.   Susan Weston, "To Take Hold of the Song: The Poetics of Galway Kinnell," *Literary Review: An International Journal of Contemporary Writing* 31, no. 1 (Fall 1987): 73–85.

140.   Catharine F. Seigel, "Corso, Kinnell, and the Bomb," *University of Dayton Review* 30, no. 1 (Winter 1987): 95–103.

141.   Granville Taylor, "From Irony to Lyricism: Galway Kinnell's True Voice," *Christianity and Literature* 37, no. 4 (Summer 1988): 45–54.

142. Thomas Gardner, "The Wages of Dying Is Love: Galway Kinnell's *Book of Nightmares*," in his *Discovering Ourselves in Whitman: The Contemporary American Long Poem* (Urbana: University of Illinois Press, 1989), 59–77.

143. Howard Nelson, ed., *On the Poetry of Galway Kinnell: The Wages of Dying* (Ann Arbor: University of Michigan Press, 1987).

144. Lee Zimmerman, *Intricate and Simple Things: The Poetry of Galway Kinnell* (Urbana: University of Illinois Press, 1987).

145. Susan Cahill, "A Hundred Verses of Solitude," review of *When One Has Lived a Long Time Alone*, by Galway Kinnell, *Express Books* 13, no. 16 (February 1991): 6–7.

146. Anonymous review of *When One Has Lived a Long Time Alone*, by Galway Kinnell, *Publishers Weekly* 7 September 1990, 80.

147. John Piller, review of *When One Has Lived a Long Time Alone*, by Galway Kinnell, *Virginia Quarterly Review* 67, no. 2 (Spring 1991): 65.

148. John Shoptaw, "Kinnell's Manhood Quartet," review of *When One Has Lived a Long Time Alone*, by Galway Kinnell, *Princeton Alumni Weekly*, 6 March 1991, 24.

149. Stephen Yenser, review of *When One Has Lived a Long Time Alone*, by Galway Kinnell, *Poetry* 158 (July 1991): 217–21.

150. Mary Kinzie, "Meaning in Place: A Moral Essay," review of *When One Has Lived a Long Time Alone*, by Galway Kinnell, *American Poetry Review* 21, no. 1 (January–February 1992): 7–14.

151. L. M. Rosenberg, "Of Love and Death: Galway Kinnell's Stark, Obsessive, Conflicting Musics," review of *When One Has Lived a Long Time Alone*, by Galway Kinnell, *Chicago Tribune*, 3 February 1991, section 14, 4.

152. Joyce Peseroff, review of *When One Has Lived a Long Time Alone*, by Galway Kinnell, *Ploughshares* 17, no. 1 (Spring 1991).

153. Samuel Hazo, "Poetry's View of Life," review of *When One Has Lived a Long Time Alone*, by Galway Kinnell, *Pittsburgh Press*, 16 December 1990.

154. Nancy Tuten, "Theodore Roethke and Galway Kinnell: Voices in Contemporary American Romanticism," *Northwest Review* 29, no. 2 (May 1991): 126–142; " 'The Seekonk Woods': Kinnell's Frostian 'Directive' to the Wilderness," *Robert Frost Review* (1992): 45–51; "The Language of Sexuality: Walt Whitman and Galway Kinnell," *Walt Whitman Quarterly Review* 9, no. 3 (Winter 1992): 134–141; " 'For Robert Frost': Form and Content in Galway Kinnell and Robert Frost," in *His 'Incalculable' Influence on Others: Essays on Robert Frost in Our Time*, ed. Earl Wilcox (Victoria, Canada: University of Victoria Press, 1994), 97–104.

155. Richard Calhoun, *Galway Kinnell* (New York: Twayne, 1992), x.

156. Anonymous review of *Imperfect Thirst*, by Galway Kinnell, *Publishers Weekly*, 26 September 1994, 57.

REVIEWS

From A Quartet of Younger Singers

SELDEN RODMAN

Twelve years ago, introducing a selection of American poems from Edward Taylor to Robert Lowell, I expressed misgivings about the horde of young academics then bent upon assuming the mantle of Henry James. I predicted that the future of American poetry, if it had a future, lay in the footsteps of Walt Whitman. No Whitmans, or even Whitmaniacs, appeared. Of the elder poets still active today, only Frost and Cummings seem able to continue making poems—by which I mean personal statements having moral as well as rhythmic fervor; and in my own generation, who but Stanley Kunitz? Once more the hope, if there is hope, is with the young poets. Ted Hughes, Alastair Reid, George Starbuck, Allen Ginsberg have something to say—and now Galway Kinnell.

Kinnell like Ginsberg (and unlike the other three who are lyric, dazzling us with words) is a rhapsodist of the Open Road. Avenue C may not be a road Walt would have recognized, but the easy gait of the sloucher, his familiarity with familiar types, and his capacity to identify rather than intellectualize, would certainly have warmed that great heart. The early poems tend to be allusive and elusive, but in "Freedom, New Hampshire," a very moving and direct elegy for a dead brother, Kinnell hits his stride. And in the last and longest poem of the book [*What a Kingdom It Was*], "The Avenue Bearing the Initial of Christ Into the New World," he literally goes to town. I do not hesitate to call this the freshest, most exciting, and by far most readable poem of a bleak decade. . . .

From I've Got a Little List

JOSEPH BENNETT

. . . Galway Kinnell's volume [*What a Kingdom It Was*] seems to lack
direction and shape until one reaches his long poem "The Avenue Bearing the
Initial of Christ Into the New World." "The Avenue" is a memorable poem.
Set these lines against Mr. Auden's deciduous mumblings at Clio's expense,
or Mr. Moss's ultra-violet and infra-red clichés:

> Fishes do not die exactly, it is more
> That they go out of themselves, the visible part
> Remains the same, there is little pallor,
> Only the cataracted eyes which have not shut ever
> Must look through the mist which crazed Homer.

> These are the vegetables of the deep,
> The Sheol-flowers of darkness, swimmers
> Of denser darknesses where the sun's rays bend for the last time.

Mr. Kinnell uses a surface realism that is effective and spare, never gaudy, to
express the classical imagination. The locale is pin-pointed, realized; it blooms.
The efficient images—"A propane- / gassed bus makes its way with big, airy
sighs"—exist not for themselves but for the increment, the march of the poem.
With its swarming masses of concrete detail, expressionist in technique, sensual, it is finely picked over and assembled. The result gleams with a strange
chilling beauty; a work of art; frightening and cold. Mr. Kinnell is every bit the
craftsman. And what he has crafted has life, has a horrible finality.

He has been with Stetson in the ships at Mylae, in the *fourmillante cité*,
but he has learned the essential rule that so few grasp while lessoning there:
handle the language, make it serve you. The poem is eclectic, carefully edited.
It springs from Baudelaire and *The Waste Land* in a rigorous sort of way. It's
not derivative, but it couldn't have been done without mad Hieronymo:

> On the Avenue, through air tinted crimson
> By neon over the bars, the rain is falling.

Reprinted by permission from *The Hudson Review* 13, no. 3 (Autumn 1960), 478–79. Copyright © 1960
by The Hudson Review, Inc.

> You stood once on Houston, among panhandlers and winos
> Who weave the eastern ranges, learning to be free . . .

The poet seems to be influenced by Eliot wearing the mask of W. C. Williams. He tries to work a bit of Williams into the surface; it comes out *Waste Land*, as it should, since what is good in Williams is *Waste Land* Eliot. *J'oïs la cloche de Serbonne*, Kinnell tells us. It's what Eliot got in turn from Laforgue.

Baudelaire, Laforgue, Eliot—*fourmillante cité, L'Hiver Qui Vient, What the Thunder Said*—all at work on Manhattan's Lower East Side.

How many people have not tried to do this, if not to Manhattan, to Metropolis in America—to bring Baudelaire's Metropolis, its fogs, to America's shores. Kinnell comes near to succeeding:

> That night a wildcat cab whined crosstown on 7th.
> You knew even the traffic lights were made by God,
> The red splashes growing dimmer the farther away
> You looked, and away up at 14th, a few green stars;
> And without sequence, and nearly all at once,
> The red lights blinked into green,
> And just before there was one complete Avenue of green,
> The little green stars in the distance blinked.
>
> It is night and raining. You look down
> Towards Houston in the rain, the living streets,
> Where instants of transcendence
> Drift in oceans of loathing and fear, like lanternfishes,
> Or phosphorus flashings in the sea, or the feverish light . . .

Perhaps he succeeds. He almost succeeds. He needs a bit of purification, to get at the root of the problem, slough off the excess. A poetry of essences, really, he should aim at. This is a remarkable and exciting work. . . .

[Review of *What A Kingdom It Was*]

STANLEY J. ROWLAND

From the fields and back streets of America, Mr. Kinnell gives us a voice that is lyrical and exuberant, if sometimes uneven, in this first book of poems. As one of the younger poets (born in 1927), he has a feeling for the meaningfulness of human experience that many of his contemporaries share, and which is replacing the themes of despair in poetry and reasserting its capacity for wonder.

This capacity is found in the pastoral "First Song," with its controlling image of "the towering Illinois twilight," and the sense of wonder in being alive grows through the book. The pastoral images remain primary until the final poem on Avenue C, though the pastoral feeling is gradually deepened and merged into subtler perceptions. The major perceptions and concerns of the poetry revolve, sometimes at quite a distance, around a Christian sense of the human being sustained by "Being-itself." (Tillich's phrase is especially apt here.) Not that the poems are those of a religious formalist; in the lines on "First Communion," for example, the speaker contrasts that experience with the joy of nature life, and asserts:

> Jesus, it is a disappointing shed
> Where they hang your picture
> And drink juice, and conjure
> Your person into inferior bread . . .

As the book proceeds, the sense of faith occurs subtly and more richly in the poetry, and is radically tested. Man's destruction of life is examined in "Burning" and "The Wolves," in which men become worse than beasts. Both poems are good illustrations of Mr. Kinnell's ability to create miniature fables—in Marianne Moore's words, "imaginary gardens with real toads in them." A fairly successful effort is made to place man's destructiveness in Christian perspective in the poem "To Christ Our Lord," which concludes with the couplet:

Reprinted by permission from *The Christian Century* 78, 22 February 1961, 248. Copyright © 1961 by the Christian Century Foundation.

Then the Swan spread her wings, cross of the cold north,
The pattern and mirror of the acts of the earth.

In "Easter," Mr. Kinnell meditates on a death resulting from human depravity: a woman "raped, robbed, weighted, drowned." The "disinfected voice of the minister" is overtly rejected, yet helps to intimate a future for the dead woman. She is seen working loose from the mud, then floating down-river, and the poem concludes with these lines addressed to her:

It is as you thought. The living burn.
In the floating days may you discover grace.

A feeling of hope seems almost equally balanced by resignation and a note of bitterness in this and others of the volume's poems that deal with death, such as the slightly tangled "Supper after the Last" and the moving if occasionally prosaic "Freedom, New Hampshire." Quite often the poetry seems to fling us at the abyss of despair, depravity and nihilism, but always we are miraculously sustained. There is, in other words, an underlying sense of trust. And this sense allows Mr. Kinnell's poetry to range more widely and joyfully than that of a number of his contemporaries, even though they too are concerned with the value and meaningfulness of human experience.

Mr. Kinnell's poems don't generally show the subtlety and structural tightness found in the work of a very good contemporary such as W. D. Snod-grass, but his potential seems broader. His ability to make us glimpse the wonder of being repeatedly transforms the rubble and slums of New York's Avenue C, which he celebrates in a long, loosely knit and beautifully lyrical poem called "The Avenue Bearing the Initial of Christ into the New World." It concludes:

In the nighttime
Of the blood they are laughing and saying,
Our little lane, what a kingdom it was!

It is quite a kingdom when, despite the depravity and ruin, we can recognize its real beauty—which Mr. Kinnell's perception and art help to show us.

From The Muse Is Always Gay

ROBERT PACK

. . . Galway Kinnell's first volume of poems, *What a Kingdom It Was,* published only four years ago, contained a long poem, "The Avenue Bearing the Initial of Christ Into the New World," which in many ways replied to Eliot's wordly pessimism. At moments it clearly parodies Eliot: "Behind the Power Station on 14th, the held breath / Of light, as God is a held breath, withheld . . ." This poem, I believe, can stand comparison with the more famous "The Waste Land" in coherence, verbal richness, controlled evocation through images and mythic reference—in every way, in fact, but one: it is not an attempt to break from a particular tradition. Thus it lacks the fascination of innovation, but this does not mean that Kinnell lacks a distinctive voice. The history of art is filled with both consolidators and innovators; surely Yeats is not inferior to Eliot, nor Mozart to Beethoven. And both Yeats and Mozart were individuals without shifting radically from the traditional means of their art. Yeats's leaning toward colloquial speech while holding to strict forms is at the very heart of the tradition of English poetry, from Wyatt through Wordsworth. I labor this point here because of the current infatuation with innovation, change, and revolution. Not all men need to slay their fathers in order to achieve manhood.

What matters finally is the integrity that guides the artist's use of his chosen means so that it reflects his personality and makes full use of his talent. Kinnell possesses this integrity. "The Avenue" has not gone unnoticed, but neither has it been acknowledged for the marvelous poem it is. Has the ordinary reader even heard of it? (Imagine if Tennyson were its author!) Let me quote a section here for the delight of it and because I would like to suggest that in his latest book Kinnell has tended to become more inward, mystical, and visionary:

> First Sun Day of the year. Tonight,
> When the sun will have turned from the earth,
> She will appear outside Hy's Luncheonette,
> The crone who sells the *News* and the *Mirror,*
> The oldest living thing on Avenue C,

Reprinted from *The Saturday Review of Literature,* 14 November 1964, 60.

Outdating much of its brick and mortar.
If you ask for the *News* she gives you the *Mirror*
And squints long at the nickel in her hand
Despising it, perhaps, for being a nickel,
And stuffs it in her apron pocket
And sucks her lips. Rain or stars, every night
She is there, squatting on the orange crate,
Issuing out only in darkness, like the cucarachas
And strange nightmares in the chambers overhead.
She can't tell one newspaper from another,
She has forgotten how Nain her dead husband looked,
She has forgotten her children's whereabouts
Or how many there were, or what the *News*
And *Mirror* tell about that we buy them with nickels.
She is sure only of the look of a nickel
And that there is a Lord in the sky overhead.
She dwells in a flesh that is of the Lord
And drifts out, therefore, only in darkness
Like the streetlight outside the Luncheonette
Or the lights in the secret chamber
In the firmament, where Yahweh himself dwells.
Like Magdalene in the Battistero of Saint John
On the carved-up continent, in the land of sun,
She lives shadowed, under a feeble bulb
That lights her face, her crab's hands, her small bulk on the crate.

In the context of the entire poem, the image of the crone has many meanings, many overtones, related as she is to the mother of Christ: but what is most important is the intensity of her visualized, literal presence. Kinnell's initial commitment is to the look of things, the landscape, the scars and details of city streets. Kinnell takes the greatest care to present the physical details. And he accomplishes this without ever sounding merely factual or assuming the protected posture of detachment; his narrator's voice always manages to remain lyrical. His commitment to the world he describes is thus always felt by the reader.

In his new book, *Flower Herding on Mount Monadnock,* he becomes more meditative, more philosophical. This new voice sometimes takes him further from his main concern, the theme of pain, for he abandons the look of the world for the meaning of the world; that is to say, he becomes mystical and abstract. But at his best, the object of his meditation is the place of pain in the spectacle of life, someone's pain in a specific setting.

A man stands on the pier.
He has long since stopped wishing his heart were full
Or his life dear to him.
(*From "The River that is East."*)

Her shoulder shrugs as though
To drive away birds which, anyway, weren't intending
To alight. In the harbor the conscript bugler
Blows the old vow of acceptance into the night—
It fades, and the wounds of all we had accepted open.
(From "The Homecoming of Emma Lazarus.")

While the face wheezes for grub,
And sweat skips and splashes from hummock down to hummock,
And inconceivable love clasps the fat of life to its pain.
(From "Hunger Unto Death.")

A Bengal poet, disciple of Tagore,
His tongue flickering through his talk like a serpent's,
Looks from his window on the city. He says
Each day he has to transcend its pain anew.
His face darkens by the window and gives nothing away.
It is his pain, by the love that asks no way out.
(From "Calcutta Visits.")

On a street crossed by fading songs
I held you in my arms
Until you slept, in these arms,
In rags, in the pain of a little flesh.
(From "To a Child in Calcutta.")

Kinnell's sense of pain seems to me real and unmitigated, and yet there is nothing shrill in its expression, nothing hysterical in the rhythms of his speech. I find something strangely soothing in his easy rhetoric, his natural cadences, and wonder if Kinnell's gentleness comes too close to softness, to sentimentality.

I should try to make clearer what I mean by Kinnell's gentleness, for I think it is one of his distinctive qualities. In the face of pain, without making evil paradoxical and necessary to the good, without diminishing its immediate reality, Kinnell always rises to an affirmation. He makes this affirmation firmly but *sotto voce*, not by a trumpet blast with its questionable bravado. So in the last section of "Spindrift":

What does he really love,
That old man,
His wrinkled eyes
Tortured by smoke,
Walking in the ungodly
Rasp and cackle of old flesh?

The swan dips her head
And peers at the mystic
In-life of the sea,
The gull drifts up
And eddies towards heaven,
The breeze in his arms . . .

Nobody likes to die
But an old man
Can know
A kind of gratefulness
Towards time that kills him,
Everything he loved was made of it.

In the end
What is he but the scallop shell
Shining with time like any pilgrim?

Beautiful as I find this poem, something in me holds back. There is an invisible presence that Kinnell perceives, as in "the mystic / In-life of the sea," that he has not really made visible to me, and for that reason I am not consoled as he seems to be. To speak of the old man as a "pilgrim" detracts from the more convincing reality of the "Rasp and cackle of old flesh." Does Kinnell assume that the mystery of things is in some way benevolent? Or is he simply less afraid of old age and death than I am? Perhaps Kinnell will go on to render the mystery he believes in more palpably to others' senses, or perhaps he will show what it is within himself that bestows benevolence on what he beholds of human anguish. It is the virtue of his art that he evokes in his reader a personal response and a demand for even further revelation of who he is and what he sees. . . .

The Bear in the Poet in the Bear

John Logan

Each generation looks about to see who the great ones are in the arts, and in our time we can single out Galway Kinnell as one of the few consummate masters in poetry. His third book, *Body Rags,* is uniformly strong beside *What A Kingdom it Was* (1960) and *Flower Herding on Mount Monadnock* (1964), and it takes some risks those books do not. In two of the three poems in the final section of the new book, "The Porcupine" and "The Bear," there is some of the best poetry to be found any place today while the long, civil rights–concerned poem, "The Last River," which makes up the entire second section, is one of the most pertinent and ambitious poems of the time.

The latter poem turns the situation of a jail in the deep South into a Dantesque drama and reflection of considerable complexity. One should know that Kinnell was in fact jailed for civil rights activities in Selma. Although I admire it, I do not find the poem entirely successful because the elements of formal repetition and of classical allusion sometimes appear too heavy-handed. For example this:

> He comes out of the mist.
> he tells me his name is Henry David.
> He takes my hand and leads me over the plains of crushed asphodel.

However, if one is going to seek an analogue to Virgil as a guide through the hell of Selma, it would be difficult to better the choice of Henry David Thoreau who, in a planned act of civil disobedience during the Mexican War, refused to pay taxes to a government he considered abstract.

"The Last River" repeats many of the images of the nineteen (mainly short) poems which constitute the first section of the book. There is a good deal of specifically religious symbolism ("Let's go I say, a big / salty wafer of spit in my mouth") and there are wings, flowers and flames employed in connection with a Roethke-like motif of opening and/or being transformed. But the longer poem, understandably in a poem of the South, lacks the snow that frequently falls in the shorter ones—sometimes in a climate a bit like that of Robert Bly:

> *Soon it will be spring,*
> *again the vanishing of the snows,*
> *and tonight*
> *I sit up late, mouthing*
> *the sounds that would be words*
> *in this flimsy jew's-harp of a farmhouse.*

The farmhouse, by the way, is a real one near Sheffield, Vt., red, windy, on top of a beautiful hill at the end of an isolated, unimproved road, and it has for some years been a site of inner and outer lookings and of labors which Galway Kinnell has turned into poetry.

"The River" also contains the title motif:

> *A man of noble face*
> *sits on the iron bunk, wiping*
> *a pile of huge blades clean*
> *in the rags of his body.*

This is varied twice in the descriptions of the horrid Charon-figure in the poem: "limbs tied on with knots and rags," and once in "The Porcupine" where the title phrase "body-rags" occurs directly. The title is perhaps meant to echo the famous "aged man" passage from Yeats's "Sailing to Byzantium," possibly as prefigured by Pound (Yeats's secretary at the time) in a letter to Viola Baxter, October 24, 1907: "This body-rag thing tattered on my soul."

The two poems "The Porcupine" and "The Bear" I think the best in the book. They make up a pair on related subjects having finally to do with the poet and with poetry. There is a strong identification of the poet-speaker with the animal in each case, and the animals themselves share certain qualities— ponderousness, voraciousness and resilient, brute strength.

Kinnell details seven (highly ironic) points in which the porcupines resemble man in general and poets in particular. In his bear poem, the identification of the poet and the bear is made extraordinarily close—in the first place, through the starving speaker's subsistence on the blood-soaked turds of the bear he hunts, so that that which has passed through the bear passes also through the poet, and in the second place, through the fact that the poet cuts open the warm carcass of the bear and takes shelter there against the vicious wind and cold.

> *. . . lumbering flatfooted*
> *over the tundra,*
> *stabbed twice from within,*
> *splattering a trail behind me*

He is born out of the body of the bear again, having thought in his dream that he "must rise up and dance"—and he writes his poem. But first he makes an agonized step, infantlike and bearlike as well (it is a "hairy-soled trudge"), and like the ancient mariner he wanders the rest of his days wondering "what anyway . . . was that sticky infusion, that rank flavor of blood, that poetry, by which I lived." The present poem is to be seen as the fruit of that wondering, and it is a remarkable one in its re-enactment of the existential loneliness, the sense of abandonment before the elements and the dual role of hunter and hunted under which we all live out our lives.

The image of poetry itself as a "sticky infusion" of bloody bear shit must make us reflective when we find it in the work of one of our best poets. The figure of the poet-as-bear is familiar from the work of Theodore Roethke and Delmore Schwartz. Roethke's bear, like Kinnell's, dances: "O watch his body sway! This animal remembering to be gay." Schwartz, Roethke and Kinnell are all big men, and they have projected their size into an image whose emotional dynamics all poets share to a certain extent, beginning with their disbelief in the likelihood of a creature such as melancholy, flesh-heavy man bursting into song.

The element of bearlike ponderousness or awkwardness we are familiar with in the image of the poet, for it relates to his (no doubt justified) feeling of being "out of his element" like Baudelaire's albatross on the deck of a ship.

Voraciousness is another element in this image, for the poet gluts himself with reading and experience out of which to write, and it contributes to the concept of ponderousness, particularly in those constipated times when one produces nothing. Kinnell's porcupine is voracious as the bear—and on a diverse diet as if for making poems:

> *Fatted*
> *on herbs, swollen on crabapples,*
> *puffed up on bast and phloem, ballooned*
> *on willow flowers, poplar catkins, first*
> *leafs of aspen and larch,*
> *the porcupine*
> *drags and bounces his last meal through ice,*
> *mud, roses and goldenrod, into the stubbly high fields.*

The last line reminds us of Eliot's line adapted from Mallarmé's description of poetry: "Garlic and sapphires in the mud."

The resilient strength of bear and porcupine is a quality the poet desperately needs in order to counterbalance his (killing) sensitivity and which, like them, he sometimes possesses sufficiently to survive.

But neither the bear nor the porcupine in Kinnell's poems *does* survive. They die slow, terrible deaths, the first from the inner stabbing of a sharpened stick coiled in his food and the other from being shot three times and falling to unwind his guts from a tree limb.

Seeing the poet as imaged by the bear returns one to the image of poetry itself as the excretion of the wounded animal: "that sticky infusion, that rank flow of blood, that poetry by which I lived." The visceral connotation is not of itself arresting for again it is part of the general image of poetry which, when it is any good, comes certainly from the inner depths—and the sexual ring of "sticky infusion" is predictable and right. But there is an aura of violence (self-destructive, dying) to the visceral imagery of the poems and to the phrase "rank flavor of blood" which stops me, and I want to comment on it.

In the porcupine poem the self-pain is quite specific:

> In my time I have
> crouched, quills erected,
> Saint
> Sebastian of the
> sacred heart, and been
> beat dead with a locust club
> on the bare snout.

And in the bear poem the figure of the poet's dream (himself) is "stabbed twice from within" (compare the "self-stabbing coil / of bristles reversing" in the porcupine poem) while the trail of generative blood behind the dying bear is related to the umbilical cord or life line of the producing poet. This figure of the agonized generative trail is repeated in "The Porcupine" and in the third poem which makes up this final section of the book, "Testament of a Thief." In the latter poem it takes the form of a pewkworm whose path, as it is drawn out of the body "by winding him up on a matchstick / a quarter turn a day for the rest of your days" creates a "map of my innards," that is, a poem of the interior life. In the former poem it is figured in the strung-out intestines of the shot porcupine who "paying out gut heaved / and spartled through a hundred feet of goldenrod" before dying.

Poetry is a wandering trail of blood and bear shit. It is a pewkworm wound through a hole in the buttocks or cheeks of a man. It is the tree-hooked entrails of a porcupine. The images are all repulsive and they are all figures of the slow destruction of the self. They remind specifically of George Barker's description of poetry: "I give you the image of the captive of the Gaels whose torture was to . . . unwind his intestines around a tree, for this is the poet . . . whose bowels are wound around Eden tree in coils at once agonizing and glorious. I mean each turn is a poem." Kinnell writes very similarly, "I have come to myself empty, the rope / strung out behind me / in the fall sun / suddenly glorified with all my blood."

The idea of the poet as masochist emerges. Sartre levels the accusation tellingly in *Literature and Existentialism*. But I would insist that poetry is not a record of self-destructive experiences. Rather, it is often a record of recovery from them. It is not the blood-soaked shit of a dying bear. Rather, it is the gold into which that stuff is turned by the magus gift of the poet. Thus the horse droppings in a poem of James Wright's "blaze into golden stones." But perhaps this is basically what Kinnell means by putting his poetics inside a poem, like a hunter inside a bear which shelters and transforms him into something fecund, dreaming.

On the other hand, if the content of Kinnell's bear poem does really have a masochistic bias to it, then this emphasis is (quite brilliantly and purposefully) weakened by the choice of a form in which the material is repeated from a dream inside the poem. For the meaning of the dream-within-the-dream Freud has said is often to put down the significance of the content so displayed, to say in effect "it was only a dream."

These two poems are very rich and mind-seizing and might be seen in other ways. I want finally to mention two other angles of vision: One might look at the images of porcupine gut, pewkworm and bear trail simply as derivative from or extensions of the figure of the poet into something quite real (the poem). And one might look at the immersion of the hunter in the warm, colorful vitals of the bear as a figure of the contemporary poet who, withdrawn at last from libraries and from psychoanalysis (the book of himself), steeps himself instead in the pied field of human experience, partly revolting, partly serene and beautiful—like the porcupine amid the mud and the goldenrod.

From Joyful In the Dark

Michael Goldman

Galway Kinnell's third volume adds to his growing reputation as a superior lyric poet. There are many fine poems in "Body Rags," and the most impressive thing about them is the distance they travel inward from beginning to end. Sometimes there are vaguenesses or rhetorical flourishes (and one poem, "The Correspondence School Instructor . . ." goes on nine lines beyond its natural and brilliant conclusion), but the poems move deeper line by line, without any heavy breathing on the poet's part. We are kept in an easy commerce with the outer world—until we discover that the inner world has spoken.

Throughout the book, Kinnell's attention focuses on our painful attachment to the minimal shreds of our mortality, our "body rags." In our last moments, and even in those instants when we have intuitions of harmony, peace or transcendence, we are involved with the decaying and desiring body. "Last" is Kinnell's favorite word in these poems, and the great thing about them is not that he is concerned with ideas about last things, but that he leads us toward the emotional mysteries that rise out of our deepest apprehensions of mortality.

Reprinted from *The New York Times Book Review*, 18 February 1968, 12. Copyright © 1960, 1964, 1968, 1975 by The New York Times Company. Reprinted by permission.

Galway Kinnell's *The Book of Nightmares*

ROBERT LANGBAUM

Published in 1971, Galway Kinnell's *The Book of Nightmares* (Houghton Mifflin) emerges as one of the best long poems of recent years. It represents an unforeseeable leap forward for Kinnell. Although the earlier work prepares us for it through its imagery and concern with nature, there is nothing on this scale, nothing that extends man's spiritual dimensions so high and so low, nothing that extends the range of man's connections so far into biological and cosmic process—though such connections are made in the earlier poetry: "In bed at night there was music if you listened, / Of an old surf breaking far away in the blood" ("Freedom, New Hampshire"). *The Book of Nightmares* is Kinnell's *Divine Comedy*, a *Divine Comedy* without God but with soul, a soul inseparable from body and from man's life in nature. Unlike Dante but like the romantic poets to whose tradition he belongs, Kinnell tries to pull an immortality out of our mortality.

The earlier poetry prepares us for *The Book of Nightmares* in that it shows Kinnell as one of our best nature poets. "Leaping Falls" is another version of Wordsworth's "Tintern Abbey." The poet returns to a falls where he has had a boyhood experience of rushing water, but now the falls is frozen over. He utters a word (of memory, imagination?) and the water breaks loose again:

> *A topmost icicle came loose*
> *And fell, and struck another*
> *With a bell-like sound, and*
> *Another, and the falls*
> *Leapt at their ledges, ringing*
> *Down the rocks and on each other*
>
> *Like an outbreak of bells*
> *That rings and ceases.*

The present reality, the silence, returns. The falls are frozen over again, but with a difference; for now the icicles burn: "A twigfire of icicles burned pale

"Galway Kinnell's *The Book of Nightmares*" reprinted from *The American Poetry Review* 8, no. 2 (March / April 1979): 30–31.

blue." Internal burning informs Kinnell's nature imagery; so does the murderousness of nature and the creative power of death. "The invisible life" of a
flower

> *Goes up in flames that are invisible*
> *Like cellophane burning in the sunlight.*
>
> *It burns up. Its drift is to be nothing.*

("Flower Herding on Mount Monadnock")

The flower's dying is its life.

Kinnell's most ambitious poem prior to *The Book of Nightmares* is the title
poem of his collected *Poems 1946–64,* "The Avenue Bearing the Initial of
Christ into the New World." This is a poem about the life of orthodox Jews
on Avenue C in New York's lower East Side. The poem does not quite come
off, because the subject matter is too external to Kinnell. Significantly, the
best section is No. 11, on the killing and cleaning of a carp, where Kinnell
can show the murderousness of our life in nature. The most spectacular example of this theme is "The Bear," the last poem in *Body Rags* (1968). The
speaker, starving in his mad seven-day trek down the blood-splattered trail of
a dying bear, comes upon the bear as he dies. He eats the bear's flesh, drinks
his blood, rips him open, climbs inside him and sleeps, dreaming he is that
dying bear, dying into the speaker's stomach. "I awaken I think," says the
speaker in the end. The line makes us wonder whether the whole experience
of the bear has been a dream. The whole experience is dreamlike, surrealist;
yet it has the immediacy of direct observation. The speaker spends the rest of
his days

> *wandering; wondering*
> *what, anyway,*
> *was that sticky infusion, that rank flavor of blood, that poetry, by which I lived?*

Poetry for Kinnell is regression, and he uses the nightmarish ingestion of animal life as an image of regression. The imagery of regression has since
Wordsworth been a way of achieving intensity in nature poetry, and nature
poetry has been a way of talking about the unconscious. That is how nature
imagery turns surrealist in Kinnell, Merwin, Bly, Strand, Wright, Tate, and
the other so-called "new surrealist poets" of the late Sixties and the Seventies.
Ingestion and the mixing of nightmare and reality are important themes in
The Book of Nightmares. Of all Kinnell's earlier poems, only "The Bear" equals
The Book of Nightmares in intensity.

Like all Kinnell's longer poems, *The Book of Nightmares* is a sequence. It is
a sequence made up of poems that are in themselves sequences of disparate
lyrics or even sometimes prose passages. In his recent book *Sailing Into the*

Unknown, M. L. Rosenthal speaks of the poetic sequence as "our characteristic form of the long poem." For in combining disparate lyrical passages, the sequence combines intensities without the need for slack transitions; and intensity is our main criterion of excellence. In all its seventy-five pages, *The Book of Nightmares* hardly ever declines from the highest pitch of intensity. Its few weak spots are the places where Kinnell strains after an intensity that does not come off—as in the lines, "inward-swirling / globes biopsied out of sunsets," which are spoiled by the failure of the adventurous word "biopsied."

The Book of Nightmares is, like so many recent poems, autobiographical and confessional. Yeats said that he used traditional meters in order to universalize personal experience: "If I wrote of personal love or sorrow in free verse, or in any rhythm that left it unchanged, amid all its accidence, I would be full of self-contempt because of my egotism and indiscretion." Like most his contemporaries, Kinnell uses free verse; but he universalizes his experience through an imagery that connects it with cosmic process:

> *I walk out from myself,*
> *among the stones of the field,*
> *each sending up its ghost-bloom*
> *into the starlight, to float out*
> *over the trees, seeking to be one*
> *with the unearthly fires kindling and dying*
>
> *in space—*

Poem I, about the birth and infancy of his daughter Maud, introduces three themes that run through the book—the road or journey; Maud, whose infancy is an event on the road; and nightmare, here it is Maud's nightmares of the future. Her birth is stunningly described: "she skids out on her face into light." But it is also a kind of death; for as they cut

> *her tie to the darkness*
> *she dies*
> *a moment, turns blue as a coal,*
> *the limbs shaking*
> *as the memories rush out of them.*

His singing to her she will remember unconsciously as an ancestral voice:

> *you will remember,*
> *in the silent zones*
> *of the brain, a specter, descendant*
> *of the ghostly forefathers, singing*
> *to you in the nighttime—*

The end echoes "Tintern Abbey" as the poet, looking forward to his daughter's future the way Wordsworth looks forward to Dorothy's, even uses the word "sister":

> And in the days
> when you find yourself orphaned,
> emptied
> of all wind-singing, of light,
> the pieces of cursed bread on your tongue,
>
> may there come back to you
> a voice,
> spectral, calling you
> sister!
> from everything that dies.
>
> And then
> you shall open
> this book, even if it is the book of nightmares.

Kinnell has a big voice. This is lyricism in the great tradition.

Poem II, about the killing and ingestion of hens, has the curious title "The Hen Flower," suggesting that the process is fruitful. The beginning is startling:

> Sprawled
> on our faces in the spring
> nights, teeth
> biting down on hen feathers, bits of the hen
> still stuck in the crevices—if only
> we could let go
> like her, throw ourselves
> on the mercy of darkness, like the hen

if only we, like the hen, could give ourselves up to death and thus to the perpetuation of life. The hen wing the poet is eating is "a hen flower," one with his bones, veins, with "my flesh / hairs lifting all over me in the first ghostly breeze / after death." That wing will recur throughout the poem; for he and the hen share an immortality in their biological connection. A passage on the "sucked carcass" of a hen killed by weasels illustrates perfectly the romantic trick of transcendentalizing the real:

> And when I hoisted
> her up among the young pines, a last
> rubbery egg slipping out as I flung her high, didn't it happen
> the dead
> wings creaked open as she soared
> across the arms of the Bear?

The hen shares also the poet's fear of death; for Kinnell will die on a mattress of hen feathers, where "even the tiny crucifix," symbol of the hen's sacrificial death, "drifting" like a feather "face down at the center of the earth / even these feathers freed from their wings forever / are afraid."

In "The Shoes of Wandering," Poem III, the poet continues his journey in old Salvation Army shoes with which he walks "on the steppingstones / of someone else's wandering." *"The first step,"* he writes, echoing Eliot's *Four Quartets, "shall be / to lose the way."* Now he is attempting to make connections with other human beings rather than with nature. Like all nature poetry, *The Book of Nightmares* is about the attempt of the lonely soul, existing in a world where community has broken down, to reforge connections. Lying in a sordid hotel room "on bedclothes gone stiff / from love-acid, night-sweat," he imagines that the shoes belonged to a drunk who died in this room:

> *his self-mutterings worse*
> *than the farts, grunts, and belches*
> *of an Oklahoma men's room,*
> *as I shudder down to his nightmare*

Poem III is tremendous in the way it magnifies man's spiritual dimensions by generating the highest spiritual intensity from the most sordid circumstances. The road becomes an icon:

> *The witness trees*
> *blaze themselves a last time: the road*
> *trembles as it starts across*
> *swampland streaked with shined water . . .*
> *. . . . .*
> *shoes rising and falling*
> *through the dust, wings of dust*
> *lifting around them, as they flap*
> *down the brainwaves of the temporal road.*

This last line, too, echoes *Four Quartets.*

Poem IV, "Dear Stranger," which is somewhat less successful because less intense, establishes the poet's estrangement from his wife. He can make connections through biological links (with his daughter, with the ingested hen) and through imagination, but not through social community. Poem V, "In the Hotel of Lost Light," returns to the poet lying on the hotel bed where he imagines a drunk died. He watches, as the dying man must have watched, a fly dying in a spider's web, shrivelling

> *in the gaze*
> *from the spider's clasped forebrains, the abstracted stare*
> *in which even the nightmare spatters out its horrors*
> *and dies.*

and he thinks of the crab lice in the dying man's pubic hair. The comparison of the fly's death to Roland's is too literary; it spoils the integrity of the scene. But this poem, where the murderousness of nature is so sordid that nightmare overwhelms reality, is the book's nadir, its inferno. "In the Hotel of Lost Light, under the freeway," with the Vietnam war raging outside, the poet writes "by the light / from the joined hemispheres of the spider's eyes."

Poem VI gives us terrifying scenes of the Vietnam war and terrible indictments of the present: "In the Twentieth Century of my nightmare / on earth, I swear on my chromium testicles" to "my iron will, my fear of love, my itch for money, and my madness"; and of the future:

> *To the last man surviving on earth*
> *I give my eyelids worn out by fear, to wear*
> *In his long nights of radiation and silence.*

Nevertheless, this poem is called "The Dead Shall Be Raised Incorruptible"; the resurrection theme is expressed in the refrain: *"Lieutenant! / This corpse will not stop burning!"* which suggests, like the internally burning flower I have already discussed, that living is dying and that there is a principle of renewal in death. It is through this organic principle, which is the point of romantic nature poetry, that nature poetry gets applied to human life.

We see this in the next poem where the biological link between the poet and his infant daughter, Maud, compensates for the nightmares just portrayed. She wakes up screaming from a nightmare, but father and daughter offer healing to each other:

> *I think*
> *you think*
> *I will never die, I think I exude*
> *to you the permanence of smoke or stars,*
> *even as*
> *my broken arms heal themselves around you.*

In a lovely passage he wishes for her the immortality she envisions: "I would blow the flame out of your silver cup / . . . I would scrape the rust off your ivory bones, / . . . I would let nothing of you go, ever," until "lovers no longer whisper to the presence beside them in the dark, *O corpse-to-be.*" He then wonders whether mortality is her nightmare, "being forever / in the pre-trembling of a house that falls." She will learn about dying even as she learns about sexual love; for "the wages / of dying is love," he concludes as the answer to all the nightmares. This poem is pure song.

The theme of love is complicated in Poem VIII, where the poet and his wife are "two mismatched halfnesses lying side by side in the darkness," though they are linked when he feels with his hand the "fishy thrash" of the new foetus within her. He explains their estrangement by citing Plato's myth of the sexes as torn halves of an original hermaphroditic being; and he adduces as another example of estrangement the (homosexual?) Southern sheriff who, after jailing and cursing him, took his hand with an "almost loving / animal gentleness." All nature is, according to the title, a "Call Across the Valley of Not-Knowing." Poem VIII is remarkable in the way it ranges from the sexual to the spiritual, combining in the stately final section, which returns to the theme of the journey, the romantic and metaphysical styles:

> *We who live out our plain lives, who put*
> *our hand into the hand of whatever we love*
> *as it vanishes,*
> *as we vanish,*
> *and stumble toward what will be, simply by arriving,*
> *a kind of fate,*
>
> *some field, maybe, of flaked stone*
> *scattered in starlight*
> *where the flesh*
> *swaddles its skeleton a last time*
> *before the bones go their way without us,*
>
> *might we not hear, even then,*

even at this moment of death, he asks, accomplishing a breathtaking transition back to nature,

> *the bear call*
> *from his hillside—a call, like ours, needing*
> *to be answered—and the dam bear*
> *call back across the darkness*
> *of the valley of not-knowing*
> *the only word tongues shape without intercession,*
>
> *yes . . . yes . . . ?*

Echoing Lawrence on tortoise calls and Eliot in *Ash Wednesday* and *Four Quartets,* the poem discovers the rhythm that connects this world with the dim frontier of the next—the next conceived as, in Keat's phrase, our "happiness on Earth repeated in a finer tone." Poem VIII is the book's climax.

The last two poems are less intense. Poem IX, "The Path Among the Stones," continues the theme of the journey, connecting it with the evolution of life and the stars. In Poem X, "Lastness," the poet's son Sancho Fergus is born. The poet reiterates the book's central question: "Is it true / the earth is all there is, and the earth does not last?"; and the book's central point: "Living brings you to death, there is no other road." Stated so baldly, these seem rather banal observations. It is right, we are told, that "the tenth poem" should be "the last, that one / and zero" should

> *walk off the end of these pages together,*
> *one creature*
> *walking away side by side with the emptiness.*

This makes us realize that Kinnell's concern for connections stems from his loneliness. He recalls a Bach concert that expressed the composer's belief in immortality. *The Book of Nightmares,* instead, is a

> *concert of one*
> *divided among himself,*
> *this earthward gesture*
> *of the sky-diver,*

who aspires to immortality, but "obeys the necessity and falls." The poet's inner division is reflected in the contradictory admonitions: "Sancho Fergus! Don't cry! / or else, cry"; and in the irony with which the poem ends: when the corpse is "laid out, see if you can find / the one flea which is laughing." The reference is probably to the statement in Poem VII that men should "feel as free on earth as fleas on the bodies of men," that we ought to enjoy our mortality as the fleas enjoy it. These last lines are ironical because only the flea is having a good time.

The irony makes a trivial ending after so long a stretch of passion and positive vision. Yet the irony, if it represents all Kinnell could come up with as a final statement, is at least honest; it is better than bombast. It seems anti-climatic just because Kinnell, at a time when so many poets are content to be skillful and trivial, speaks with a big voice about the whole of life—though society appears only as nightmare: the social filtered through the private nightmare. Even with its weak spots, its few lapses in intensity, *The Book of Nightmares* is major poetry.

"The Wasted Breath":
Galway Kinnell's *The Book of Nightmares*

WILLIAM VIRGIL DAVIS

If, as Galway Kinnell has suggested, "The dream of every poem is to be a myth," perhaps it is equally true that the myth behind every poem is a dream. Certainly, several of Kinnell's most memorable poems inhabit a realm of unreality on the borderline between sleep and waking and take as their theme the curious complicity between dream and waking reality. In poems such as "The Porcupine" and "The Bear" the speaker finds himself stunned to speech by a realization of his own identification with an animal. In each case this identification leads him to a vision in which he sees how human experience transforms itself as it becomes the stuff of poetry. Likewise, he sees that poetry, even during periods of unconscious "waking," becomes the stuff of life. Such realizations provide both vision and curse since they demand that one spend the rest of his life "Wandering: wondering / what anyway, / was that sticky infusion, that rank flavor of blood, that poetry by which I lived."

"Death, / the whole of death,—even before life's begun." This is Rilke, epigraph to Kinnell. *The Duino Elegies* stand beside and support *The Book of Nightmares*. Kinnell himself has attested to both the thematic and structural genesis of his book in Rilke's powerful poem, but it is only one of many threads in Kinnell's complicated cloth. Since this is a fabric which critics will pick at for a long time to come, what I propose here is to pull out some of the most brightly-colored threads, hold them up to the light, see how they shine.

Kinnell's poem begins in the midst of a journey, the poet eternal itinerant. In "Under the Maud Moon," beside a "wet site / of old fires" the speaker stops, bends, lights "a small fire in the rain." This is a personal ceremony in praise of the birth of the poet's daughter, and it is also an impersonal ritual celebrating life itself, birth not of daughter but of "girlchild." As the dead wood reddens in the flame, corpses come back to life. As the poet sits singing before his fire, somewhere out ahead of him "a black bear sits alone / on his hillside, nodding from side / to side" in his own way of making music. In "Lastness," when the poem ends, even then the journey will continue. The fire lighted at the beginning of the poem "in the dying world" for the

Reprinted from the *Montana Review* 3 (1982): 57–64. Published by Owl Creek Press.

speaker's daughter just born, continues to burn at the end of the poem, "no matter, now, whom it was built for." The black bear still sits alone, but now he sees that "a death-creature / watches from the fringe of the trees" and even he understands that he is that creature, that bear watching himself.

In this "long rustle / of being and perishing" which is the world, the only proper gift worth giving is a gift of words which tell the truth.

> And in the days
> when you find yourself orphaned,
> emptied
> of all wind-singing, of light,
> the pieces of cursed bread on your tongue,
>
> may there come back to you
> a voice,
> spectral, calling you
> *sister!*
> from everything that dies.
>
> And then
> you shall open
> this book, even if it is the book of nightmares.

The seventh section of the poem, "Little Sleep's-Head Sprouting Hair in the Moonlight," opens with the awakening of the poet's infant daughter Maud, who screams as she rouses from her nightmare. The poet, called by her crying, "sleepwalks" into her room to comfort her, even though he already knows that he can give her nothing but another version of the nightmare vision. He speaks to her saying "Little Maud,"

> I would blow the flame out of your silver cup,
> I would suck the rot from your fingernail,
> I would brush your sprouting hair of the dying light,
> I would scrape the rust off your ivory bones,
> I would help death escape through the little ribs of your body,
> I would alchemize the ashes of your cradle back into wood

The process of life begun, there is no way to reverse it, even if the father would. This is the nightmare of the waking world, "the pre-trembling of a house that falls." When he recognizes this—for himself, as father to his daughter—he hopes, in the face of such knowledge, that his daughter will "learn to reach deeper / into the sorrows" to the "still undanced cadence of vanishing." As the poet holds his daughter in his arms, himself intermediary in the chain of life ("I can see in your eyes / / the hand that waves once / in my father's eyes"), he sees that she already knows what he must tell her.

Because this is the case and because there is nothing further even a father can do, he puts her back in her crib to dream on in her nightmare, to dream her nightmare out to its end. As the hours "begin to sing" for her as she sleeps, he promises to return, to take her for a walk.

> Little sleep's-head sprouting hair in the moonlight,
> when I come back
> we will go out together,
>
> we will walk out together among
> the ten thousand things,
> each scratched too late with such knowledge, *the wages*
> *of dying is love.*

"Little Sleep's-Head," seventh poem of ten poems each in seven parts, is the thematic and structural center of this "bridge which arcs" across a landscape of nightmare; it points both forward and back. In the catalogue of blessings which the poet intones over his daughter he promises up to death and even beyond it, until "hens scratch their spell across hatchet blades" and "men fell as free on earth as fleas on the bodies of men." Here we go back to the beginning and forward to the final flea on the corpse.

"I have glimpsed / by corpse-light." Death illuminates life. "The Hen Flower" is framed by sections in which the speaker, restless insomniac, sees, in his vision of the death of a hen, symbol of "the wages of dying." The death of the bird is so real, so fully realized, that the identification between bird and man, like the identification between man and animal in "The Porcupine" and "The Bear," merges in such a way that the man becomes the bird for the sake of his seeing.

The identification forces the recognition of the parallel between bird and man: "Wing / of my wing, / of my bones and veins, / of my flesh . . . wing / made only to fly . . . and unable / to fly." This identification forces the inescapable realization that death must be met and made use of for life to be worth love. Like the hen "longing only / to die," we must be able to "let go / like her, throw ourselves / on the mercy of darkness." These are hard words, hard to hear, hard in our culture to understand. They cut below the life surfaces and force us to face the nightmare. This is what keeps us awake. What we see and try to avoid seeing all around us, "the cosmos spelling itself, / the huge broken letters / shuddering across the black sky and vanishing."

We must hold to what is vanishing—as it vanishes. This is the ultimate paradox of existence which the hen, as flower, symbolizes. It is, in itself, symbol of bloom, birth, life. At the end of this poem the speaker assumes again his personal presence, names his own name to be certain he hears what he has said.

> Listen Kinnell,
> dumped alive
> and dying into the old sway bed,
> a layer of crushed feathers all that there is
> between you
> and the long shaft of darkness shaped as you,
> let go.

To say this is not to say that it is easy. Lying in his room, on his pillow of hen feathers, he knows that "even these feathers freed from their wings forever / are afraid." It is not easy, but it is necessary. Life is informed by death, this is the sleep which the insomniac must accept, this the glimpse by corpselight, beacon in the nightmare world. Having had this vision definitively impressed upon him, the speaker relinquishes, in fear, his hold on earth and gives himself over to the truth of the vision, even if it is still a nightmare.

The pursuit through this landscape of nightmare is a "path / inventing itself / . . . stumbling on," a journey each man must make. The poet chooses his shoes from the rack in the Store of the Salvation Army and walks out "in dead shoes, in the new light." When he has to stop he stays at the Xvarna Hotel of "hidden light," identifying with others who have come before him, stumbling the way.

"The Shoes of Wandering" describes the early stages of the journey each man must make. When he has found the shoes which fit him "down to the least knuckle and corn" of his already deformed feet, "the eldershoes of my feet," the poet knows he is on the right way. Even so,

> I long for the mantel
> of the great wanderers, who lighted
> their steps by the lamp
> of pure hunger and pure thirst,
>
> and whichever way they lurched was the way.

A crone warns him with a cryptic warning: "*poor fool, / poor forked branch / . . . you will feel all your bones / break / over the holy waters you will never drink.*" Like Lear, he runs the risks of madness, despair, in this world "photographed with tragedy."

When one opens himself to the nightmare world, he must expect the worst. The next three sections of the poem are a descent into a kind of hell of the imagination, a dredge through the pit of memory. The poet "drives down, grain / after grain, into the last, / coldest room, which is memory," there to visit the terror within the rooms of his own imaginings, there to "listen for the maggots" which "break into the brain and cut / the nerves which keep the book of solitude."

The book of solitude: another name for the book of nightmares; for the book of death. In an essay on "Poetry, Personality, and Death" Kinnell says, "The death of the self I seek . . . is a death, yes, but a death out of which one might hope to be reborn." Therefore, "if there is one more love / to be known, one more poem / to be opened into life, / you will find it there / or nowhere." This poem will be called "Tenderness toward Existence."

> The self is the least of it.
> Let our scars fall in love.

One wonders, "Can it ever be true— / all bodies, one body, one light / made of everyone's darkness together?" The fifth, central section of the book, "In the Hotel of Lost Light," fills with "music blooming with failure" written in a "languished alphabet" as "the carnal / nightmare soars back to the beginning" but forward ahead too in time. Here the poet records the dreams of his own death, identifying himself in his death with the outcasts of society as he has been identifying with them throughout his vision. Until now, the poet has lived with time-bound terrors; now, with the loss of time, his nightmare mind caught in the final flickers of vanishing light spins through time and history fusing with the nightmares of others, both anonymous and named. Here, clearly, is "the absolute spell / of departure."

"The Dead Shall Be Raised Incorruptible" is the blackest pit of all. The horrors of war symbolize the horrors of the world at large. The poem begins with a corpse burning. The corpse will not stop burning. The irony of the title mocks at facile answers to a world in which man's inhumanity tests even his own ingenuity. Among the many recent anti-war poems published in this country perhaps only Robert Bly's "Counting Small-Boned Bodies" is more graphic than "The Dead Shall Be Raised Incorruptible." A soldier keeps calling, "*Lieutenant! / This corpse will not stop burning!*" A man in death is no longer even a man; he is a dead body, a corpse to be burnt. The man having been burnt, the corpse cannot be put out. The poem ends with the corpse still burning.

In the midst of such a world become nightmare, the poet makes out man's last will and testament, giving "the emptiness my hand" while "the fly, / the last nightmare, hatches himself." Finally, it has been too much. The Horror has lasted too long; it is "the Twentieth Century of my nightmare / on earth," the twentieth-century of man's trespass on the land. The final vision is of the earth scorched, the men dead, smoke rising from flesh and bones. "A few bones / lie about in the smoke of bones."

What is left? What is possible? "*The wages of dying is love.*" "The Dead Shall Be Raised Incorruptible" is followed by "Little Sleep's-Head Sprouting Hair in the Moonlight" and this is followed by "The Call Across the Valley of Not-Knowing."

At the end of "The Dead Shall Be Raised Incorruptible" there is one hope left: "a wind holding / the cries of love-making from all our nights and days / moves among the stones, hunting / for two twined skeletons to blow its last cry across." What is left, even in the world of nightmare, is the breath of love, the breath of the poet speaking of love, the breath of the poet speaking. "The Call Across the Valley of Not-Knowing" opens with the poet in bed with his wife, twined skeletons, available for the breath which will be, will make, love.

The last three poems, "The Call Across the Valley of Not-Knowing," "The Path Among the Stones," and "Lastness," make a muted chorus of celebration. They are the least successful parts of the poem, probably because Kinnell is trying too hard for a sense of affirmation here at the end of his poem. "*Yes*" is, the poet says at the end of "The Call Across the Valley of Not-Knowing," "the only word tongues shape without intercession."

Patchwork of all he has been, the poet, in "old shoes / flowed over by rainbows of hen-oil" stands "here, between answer / and nothing." At least he knows that the answer is not nothing. "Lastness / *is* brightness. . . . It lasts." Here where "witness trees heal / their scars" at flesh fires and flames still rise from bones, the poet sees that the scapegoat can become celebrant. "Somewhere / in the legends of blood sacrifice / the fatted calf / takes the bonfire into his arms, and *he* / burns *it*."

"Lastness" goes back to beginnings. The fire in the rain, the bear, his fur glistening, appear again here. In place of the daughter, the girlchild of the opening poem, here a boychild, a son, is born. The nightmare vision is passed on from generation to generation. As the father dies into his son so the son is born into the vision of nightmare which the father has lived through. Not yet completely born, caught in the birth canal, the baby takes on the burden of the vision he has inherited and accedes to it: "he squinted with pained, / barely unglued eyes. . . . And almost / smiled, I thought, almost forgave it all in advance." To his son the father bequeaths his final words:

> Sancho Fergus! Don't cry!
>
> Or else, cry.
>
> On the body,
> on the blued flesh, when it is
> laid out, see if you can find
> the one flea which is laughing.

This is the book of nightmares, "poem / if we shall call it that, / or concert of one / divided among himself / . . . this free floating of one / opening his arms into the attitude / of flight, as he obeys the necessity and falls."

But even in the face of the inevitability of death there is still hope:

> the dead lie,
> empty, filled, at the beginning,
> and the first
> voice comes craving again out of their mouths.

In his tenth *Elegy* Rilke said, "Someday, emerging at last from this terri-fying vision, / may I burst into jubilant praise to assenting Angels!" Galway Kinnell cannot be so optimistic, cannot hope so much, at least not here.

> This is the tenth poem
> and it is the last. It is right
> at the last, that one
> and zero
> walk off together,
> walk off the end of these pages together,
> one creature
> walking away side by side with the emptiness.

The poem ends in the grip of the same vision of nightmare with which it began. In his essay, "The Poetics of the Physical World" Kinnell wrote:

Poetry is the wasted breath. This is why it needs the imperfect music of the human voice, this is why its words have no higher aim than to press themselves to us, to cling to the creatures and things we know and love, to be the ragged garments.

In the—"long rustle of being and perishing" which is the world, *The Book of Nightmares* will not soon stop echoing.

A Luminous Receptiveness

DONALD HALL

When Galway Kinnell puts his feet into old shoes, bought at the Salvation Army, he does not fill them; the shoes fill him. He is possessed by the shoes, as he is possessed by bears and chickens and children. Though the voice of *The Book of Nightmares* is Galway Kinnell's voice, the poet is without *identity*, as in Keats's wonderful passage. Identity comes from the ego. *Some* good poetry comes from identity; bad poetry is cursed by it.

There is the danger of possession without return (and without poetry). All connection with the body and the world fades out. Everything becomes impalpable. In *The Book of Nightmares*, "Virginia" incurs this loss, "Virginia," who writes "Dear Galway" a letter signed, "Yours, faithless to this life." Though Kinnell has written a book of death, he is faithful to this life, after his fashion. He feels the lure of the vacuum but he returns bringing images. Death is the underside of everything living, and the skull shines beneath the skin; but, equally, there is no death without the image of resurrection. Man is the house that falls, but to the Catholic imagination there is no fall that does not summon the rise again; we see, "by corpse-light, in the opened cadaver / of hen, the mass of tiny, / unborn eggs. . . ." (*Mass?*) The eggs will remain unborn, ". . . each getting / tinier and yellower as it reaches back toward / the icy pulp / of what is. . . ." But there were eggs in the dead hen.

> And when I hoisted
> her up among the young pines, a last
> rubbery egg slipping out as I flung her high, didn't it happen
> the dead
> wings creaked open as she soared
> across the arms of the Bear?

The wings made a cross, then.

Crosses are more common than bears, and *The Book of Nightmares* is the last medieval poem, saturated with the Eastern moment of the Church.

Reprinted with permission from *The Nation*, 18 October 1971, 377–78. Copyright © by The Nation Co., Inc.

("One image crossed the many-headed . . ." in Yeats.) The Church of possession, and neither of possessions nor of possessing others. It is not the Church of intelligence or of information but of intuition, a passive luminous receptiveness. Kinnell shares this quality of mind with the more Protestant Roethke and Whitman. But Kinnell's death is not Whitman's death nor Roethke's death. It is Calvary, continual and unavoidable. Even to mention avoidance is to be foreign to Kinnell's character; is to summon consciousness or ego or intellect. One does not avoid the particles that make the universe; one receives them.

Peter, "apostle of stone," lives in this book, and "the last grails of light." Bones and skeletons, the "witness tree," "blood sacrifice," and "in the graveyard / the lamps start lighting up, one for each of us, / in all the windows / of stone." When the sky-diver falls, he falls crossed, "opening his arms into the attitude / of flight"—and Kinnell becomes the modern man in the medieval woodcut—"as he obeys the necessity and falls. . . ." But the idea of obedience brings to the scientific news a religious attitude.

The nightmare is the continual fear: maggots in the corrupt flesh; death for the self experienced through the selves of others; death for the simple self in its nakedness; fear of the continual crucifixion and of the possession which is introduced by images of crosses. There is also the joy which death illuminates. "Death is the mother of beauty," said Stevens. Kinnell says, "*the wages / of dying is love,*" which puts a considerable reversal upon the motto of another church. Orthodoxy of any kind would not occur to Kinnell; orthodoxy is belief and belief relies on theology. Kinnell's intuitive assemblage takes its materials from a religion but its structure is the flow of experience— which is to say that the structure does not matter; we swim in *The Book of Nightmares* as in a sea without shores. (Or we do not read it at all.) But this sea is huge and contains all of Kinnell's life that he can bring to the poem; everything that has flowed in him comes to this sea.

The love of Kinnell's line is most specifically for the poet's children, but also for the animals and objects of the world. There is the love that is empathy or compassion; there is "the dream / of all poems and the text / of all loves—'Tenderness toward Existence' "; there is also erotic love, but the book as a whole lacks Eros. Its body is more skull than skin. The love that is the wages of dying includes sensual love only in its wholeness. In this integrated universe, Eros brings about the birth that ends in the death that pays us with love.

The Book of Nightmares is fantastic, yet it is still a book in which the experience is wholly real to the intuition of the reader. It is Kinnell's experience, dreamed for its wholeness, aged in that dream, and set out plainly and passionately. It is not an exercise in surrealism, like much of the bad poetry being written now—mechanical irrationalism.

If the reader accepts the lure and the fear of possession, follows Kinnell and hesitates with him, he will have no difficulty with the presences of the poem: children, hotels, war, a sheriff, an airplane, the henyard, stars; and he will accept the impelling presence of the imagination I call medieval and Catholic—for lack of a word which would specify the saturated untheological church of Kinnell's reception of the *other*. We accept because Kinnell's transformations compel us, and the hypnosis of his rhythm possesses us. We do not rebel at doctrine because the poem has no doctrinal design on us. We do not enter *The Book of Nightmares;* it fills us up. The loss of ego is the greatest gain; it is *poetry*.

[Review of *The Book of Nightmares*]

Jane Taylor McDonnell

Much of this book should be familiar to readers of Galway Kinnell—the easy accumulative style, the long poems in several mutually-reflecting parts, the wilderness and slum settings, the preoccupation with violence, the loneliness of the wanderer-poet. The newness comes with the "gothic" folklore and the eschatology. *Book of Nightmares* draws heavily on the imagery of astrology, witchcraft, spells, the fear of "possession," and the concoction of potions; but it also (and this goes beyond the merely gothic imagery) is concerned with "last things," with death and the nightmare images of death which must be lived with.

As in his earlier books, Kinnell writes poems of wandering and exploration, where the meaning is allowed to accumulate through several parts (each of these poems is in seven parts and the poems are themselves continuous). But here a new mythology replaces, or rather supplements, the natural imagery, the "myth" of the land its creatures found in the earlier books. These poems are not primarily poems of exploration and discovery in which a place or thing is well seen, experienced, and understood, as in Kinnell's first two volumes, nor are they exactly like the more remarkable poems of *Body Rags* ("The Bear" and "The Porcupine," for example) where the lives of wild animals are used emblematically as images for the deepest fears of the poet. Now the poems are united, quite simply, by the consciousness of death. Here we see children just born, moving towards death; a hen killed and its entrails read; the poet buying the shoes of some dead stranger and lying in beds old men have died in. We also see opened cadavers and corpses burning in Vietnam.

The poems are in many ways a deliberate descent into the underworld, a deliberate psychological risk-taking—the entertaining of visions for the sake of exorcizing them. This is certainly not to say they are "insincere." But Kinnell does hold the visions up for his (and our) steady gaze: "do not let this last hour pass, / do not remove this last, poison cup from our lips." I think, however, that much of the effectiveness of the poems depends not upon indulgences of the *memento mori* sort, but upon a folk-lore of fear sometimes very personally felt.

Reprinted from *The Carleton Miscellany* 12 (Spring 1972): 153–56.

Book of Nightmares is not without sensationalism, however. The deliberate excesses of some of the imagery ("the languished alphabet / of worms," "the sweet, excremental / odor of opened cadaver," snakes crawling "cool paths / over the rotted thigh," etc.) accounts for the over-stated and embattled tone of some of the poems. For this reason, the two central poems, "In the Hotel of Lost Light" and "The Dead Shall be Raised Incorruptible," are the least effective in the book. The broad social satire involved in the bitterly ironic last testament of the Christian Man in "The Dead Shall be Raised Incorruptible" fails because of the obviousness of its targets:

> In the Twentieth Century of my trepass on earth,
> having exterminated one billion heathens,
> heretics, Jews, Moslems, witches, mystical seekers,
> black men, Asians, and Christian brothers,
> every one of them for his own good,
>
> a whole continent of red men for living in unnatural community
> and at the same time having relations with the land,
> one billion species of animals for being sub-human,
> and ready to take on the bloodthirsty creatures from the other planets,
> I Christian man, groan out this testament of my last will.
>
> (page 42)

The poet may be "right" in his anger, but the hysteria of some of the poems seems merely modish.

But, of course, these two poems are planned as the ultimate nightmare images of the sequence, the central images of death, hatred, destruction, and war, before the poet, or the speaker, comes to terms with his fears. The last, as well as the first, poems in the book are more effective partly because they are Kinnell's personal assumption of the common nightmare (his public and declamatory voice has always been his least successful), and partly because of their remarkable combination of affection and tenderness with anguish, of wonder and forgiveness with horror. He strives for the affectionate understanding which was also the special achievement of the earlier poetry: here he says "a poem writes itself out: its title—the dream / of all poems and the text / of all loves—'Tenderness towards Existence.' " It is, however, in this book far more difficult for him to reach this simple affirmation and he must pass through much more harrowing experiences to get there:

> 1.
> You scream, waking from a nightmare.
>
> When I sleepwalk
> into your room, and pick you up,
> and hold you up in the moonlight, you cling to me
> hard,

as if clinging could save us. I think
you think
I will never die, I think I exude
to you the permanence of smoke or stars,
even as
my broken arms heal themselves around you.

2.
I have heard you tell
the sun, *don't go down,* I have stood by
as you told the flower, *don't grow old,*
don't die. Little Maud,

I would blow the flame out of your silver cup,
I would suck the rot from your fingernail,
I would brush your sprouting hair of the dying light,
I would scrape the rust off your ivory bones,
I would help death escape through the little ribs of your body,
I would alchemize the ashes of your cradle back into wood,
I would let nothing of you go, ever,
until washerwomen
feel the clothes fall asleep in their hands,
and hens scratch their spell across hatchet blades,
and rats walk away from the cultures of the plague,
and iron twists weapons toward the true north,
and grease refuses to slide in the machinery of progress,
and men feel as free on earth as fleas on the bodies of men,
and lovers no longer whisper to the presence beside them in the dark,
   O corpse-to-be . . .

And yet perhaps this is the reason you cry,
this the nightmare you wake screaming from:
being forever
in the pre-trembling of a house that falls.

(pp. 49–50)

This passage, from "Little Sleep's-Head Sprouting Hair in the Moonlight," is typical of the best poems in the volume. The poem has an occasion, not just a set of abstract feelings; it combines the fear of death quite naturally with affection and tenderness for the child; the incantation and formulaic verse is effective in showing the anguished wishfulness of the father. Finally, the *memento mori* suggestion of the skull beneath the sprouting hair is an unobtrusive and simple "truth." Certainly Kinnell has achieved a new sort of success in this poem and in others in *Book of Nightmares.* This book is different from his others not only in its greater density and continuity of imagery, in its emphasis on horror rather than wonder, but also in its convincing personal assumption of our common nightmare.

In the Direct Line of Whitman, the Indirect Line of Eliot: *The Avenue Bearing the Initial of Christ into the New World*

CHRISTOPHER RICKS

In the old days, when T. S. Eliot was an American poet, he saw the point of English humor: "Humor is distinctively English. No one can be so aware of the environment of Stupidity as the Englishman. . . . Wit is public, it is in the object; humor (I am speaking only of *real* humor) is the instinctive attempt of a sensitive mind to protect beauty against ugliness; and to protect itself against stupidity" (1918). Yet American humor has burgeoned since then. (Did America get helpfully stupider?) In films, plays, novels, poems, songs, the visual arts, jokes, and in the daily give-and-take, American humor has been a glory. And, of course, a challenge. The American artist who cuts himself off from humor, or is no good at it, may be cut off, not just from some valuable ways of looking at life but from a national source of energy, the hiding-places of the best American power. . . .

Kinnell began with a keen gratitude to William Carlos Williams, about whom he wrote a bad poem (its humor curdles to sarcasm), and likewise with a gratitude to Frost (ditto), and so to the most enduring of his gratitudes, to "the mystical all-lovingness of Walt Whitman." For Richard Howard's recent anthology, "Preferences," Kinnell chose to pair with one of his own poems some of "Song of Myself." Whenever Kinnell is doing the hushed bated-breath thing, all portentous self-attentive first-personry ("I wake in the night," or "I sit listening / To the surf"), the importance comes on as winsome self-importance, or "Song of My Self-Importance." The cosmic browbeats the comic. Yet from the start—"Two Seasons," the very first poem in the book—there were fine poems in which self-importance, the intelligent *exclusion* of humor, was dramatically right because the poems were about rapt young lovers and how they manage temporarily to exclude so much and are fearful of humor. And from the start, again (the second poem, "A Walk in the Country"), there was the glint of apt humor, delicate, wistful but wiry, in the two kinds of touchingness:

> *And I thought, is it only me such*
> *Beauty refuses to touch?*

The best of Kinnell, which is very good, comes when he resists the expected humorlessness of rural-piety poetry (which often disguises its humorlessness behind wisps of whimsy), and when he is not claiming to be either a sensitive plant or a sarcastic cactus. There are such penetratingly humorous poems as the parable, half-town and half-country, "Indian Bread"; or the gruff aggrievedness of "Duck-Chasing"; or the teeming townscape, humane, fascinated and therefore fascinating, of "The Avenue Bearing the Initial . . ."; or the miniature country vignette, "Spring Oak":

> *Above the quiet valley and unrippled lake*
> *Where woodchucks burrowed new holes, and birds sang,*
> *And radicles began downward and shoots*
> *Committed themselves to the spring*
> *And entered with tiny industrious earthquakes,*
> *A dry-rooted, winter-twisted oak*
> *Revealed itself slowly. And one morning*
> *While the valley underneath was still sleeping*
> *It shook itself and it was all green.*

The poem is itself a tiny industrious earthquake, committing itself to the spring and revealing itself, all with affectionate banter and without any of the pomposity which the American Mother Earth sometimes gets from her poetic children. The concluding poem, "Flower Herding on Mount Monadnock," gets up, having wised up:

> *I can support it no longer.*
> *Laughing ruefully at myself*
> *For all I claim to have suffered*
> *I get up. Damned nightmarer!*

[Review of *The Avenue Bearing the Initial of Christ into the New World*: *Poems 1946–1964*]

PATRICK KEANE

In the decade and a half since his first book appeared, Galway Kinnell has emerged as one of the most powerful and moving poets of his generation. His is an elementary poetry—a poetry of dark woods and snow; of wind and fire and stars; of bone and blood. His subjects are perennial: love illumined and made more precious by the omnipresence of death. He said recently:

> *It is through something radiant in our lives that we have been able to dream of paradise, that we have been able to invent the realm of eternity. But there is another kind of glory in our lives that derives precisely from our inability to enter that paradise or to experience eternity. That we last only for a time, that we know this, radiates a thrilling, tragic light on all our loves, all our relationships, even on those moments when the world, through its poetry, becomes almost capable of surprising time and death.*

Almost; for Kinnell has posed the most anguished of all our questions: "Is it true / the earth is all there is, and the earth does not last?" If it does not, it can still be irradiated and somehow made sacred, if not by God then by the poet.

Best known for *Body Rags* (1968), *The Book of Nightmares* (1971) and the two volumes preceding these, *What a Kingdom It Was* (1960) and *Flower Herding on Mount Monadnock* (1964), these are now brought together in this new volume. (The remarkable title derives from the no less remarkable, life-charged poem in which Kinnell, back in 1960, celebrated New York City's teeming Avenue C.)

The new book is valuable for a number of reasons. First it offers us an opportunity for comparison. An exceptional performer, Kinnell has in recent years given many readings. Often, standing before an audience, he would feel a definite reluctance to say a line as written, a reluctance he gradually came to trust. These on-the-spot excisions and alterations now appear for the first time in print, and those who wish to examine the process of revision—and

Reprinted by permission from *The New Republic*, 27 July and 3 August 1974. Copyright © 1974 by The New Republic, Inc.

incidentally, to note one effect of public readings on the poet himself—need only consult the poems as they originally appeared in *Kingdom* and *Flower Herding*.

Second, the new volume brings together in an attractive and inexpensive format all of the poetry prior to *Body Rags*. This is especially useful since *First Poems 1946–54* was published in a limited edition, while *Kingdom* and *Flower Herding* have been out of print for several years. As a result all of Kinnell's published poetry is now conveniently available in three volumes.

Third, while the large audience attracted by *The Book of Nightmares* may initially turn to this new collection as a sort of prolegomenon, few, after reading, will be inclined to question the earlier work's intrinsic merit. For what really matters are the poems themselves, and many of these are splendid. Several must serve for many.

In "To Christ Our Lord," a *Bildungsroman* in six stanzas, a boy reluctantly eats for Christmas dinner the bird he has killed earlier in the day. The sound of its wing-beat "had stirred his love," yet he fired. "Now the grace praised his wicked act." Yet "he ate as he had killed, with wonder." The poem began in snow ("The legs of the elk punctured the snow's crust. . . .") and ends there: "At night on snowshoes on the drifting field / He wondered again, for whom had love stirred? / The stars glittered on the snow and nothing answered. / Then the Swan spread her wings, cross of the cold north, / The pattern and mirror of the acts of earth."

The movement and structure of this early poem are typical of much of the best of Kinnell's work: the rondure, or reversion of a poem's end upon its beginning; the movement from a closely observed particular to the ("almost") transcendent emblem. If there are moments when we feel that the things of this world have been too quickly transformed to emblems, we have those other poems in which Kinnell's eye is glued to the particular. The most famous instance is the "Avenue C," with its plethora of people, vegetables, rust-water icicles, storefronts and bedbugged mattresses. But that poem, too, in what Kinnell elsewhere calls a "saprophytic blossoming," flames out in the shining of the shook foil on all those loving notations: "In the nighttime / Of the blood they are laughing and saying. / Our little lane, what a kingdom it was! / oi weih, oi weih."

In Kinnell's moving elegy for his brother Derry, we have another saprophytic blossoming, moving from the dead cow and dung that make grass green to the "grass green for a man," and on to a peroration reminiscent, and worthy, of Yeats: "It is true / That only flesh dies, and spirit flowers without stop / For men, cows, dung, for all dead things; and it is good, yes— / But an incarnation is in particular flesh / And the dust that is swirled into a shape / And crumbles and is swirled again had but one shape / That was this man. When he is dead the grass / Heals what he suffered, but he remains dead, / And the few who loved him know this until they die."

There is a glory in Kinnell's best poetry, and the temptation, to paraphrase Coleridge in his lecture on *The Tempest,* is to stop reviewing and simply recite. One last example. Here is the concluding section of the title poem from *Flower Herding on Mount Monadnock,* a movement illustrative of the pattern we've noted, and poetry almost as lucid and beautifully elegaic as Prospero's speech in *The Tempest:*

> In the forest I discover a flower.
>
> The invisible life of the thing
> Goes up in flames that are invisible
> Like cellophane burning in the sunlight.
>
> It burns up. Its drift is to be nothing.
>
> In its covertness it has a way
> Of uttering itself in place of itself,
> Its blossoms claim to float in the Empyrean,
>
> A wrathful presence on the blur of the ground.
>
> The appeal to heaven breaks off.
> The petals begin to fall, in self-forgiveness.
> It is a flower. On this mountainside it is dying.

From Autobiography of the Present

JAMES ATLAS

. . . It is good to have Galway Kinnell's early poems collected into a single volume, not only so that we can have before us the lineaments of his development, but because so many of these poems are brilliant in themselves. The present collection takes its title from a long poem that has been much anthologized in recent years, the extraordinary range and energy of which became apparent to me on reading it over after nearly a decade's lapse. *The Avenue Bearing the Initial of Christ into the New World* is one of the most vivid legacies of *The Wasteland* in English, building its immense rhetorical power from the materials of several dialects, litanies of place, and a profound sense of the spiritual disintegration that Eliot divined in modern urban life. And like Eliot's, Kinnell's is a religious poem, in which the chaotic forces of survival (in this instance, the turbulent, jumbled life of New York's lower East Side, along Avenue C) ultimately preside over the terror latent in our late stage of civilization. Since it is impossible to isolate any single passage from the magnificent sprawl of this poem, I can only suggest its importance by stressing that my comparison of it to *The Wasteland* was intended to be less an arbitrary reference than an effort to estimate the poem's durable achievement.

The very early poems of his apprenticeship distinguish themselves from most such offerings in the quality of their feeling, their naturalness and depth of insight. Kinnell is in possession of a gift that so few poets have now, with their emphasis on subdued, laconic diction. Almost any stanza from his first two books yields the fierce vision refined later on:

> The sunlight streams through the afternoon
> Another parable over the sloughs
> And yellowing grass of the prairies.
> Cold wind stirs, and the last green
> Climbs to all the tips of the season, like
> The last flame brightening on a wick.

He is so close to his subject, the natural world in all its tyranny and splendor, that his sympathies are readily translated into the richness of cadence and lan-

Reprinted by permission from *Poetry* 125 (February 1975): 295–302.

guage that poetry should always have. He echoes Wordsworth's inclination for the sublime, the generalizing of emotion from nature, combined with the passionate eye of Hopkins; and in the later poems, an awareness of the American landscape in both its political and pastoral dimension:

> Under
> The rain the continent wheeled, his own land
> Electric and blind, farmlights and cities'
> Blazes—points, clusters and chains—
> Each light a memory and the whole of darkness
> Memory.

There is a wonderful variety in these poems; reading through them all at once, one becomes aware of how much he has struggled to exercise his imagination, writing out of the deepest sources of contemplation, sketching in the temper of an afternoon with a few fine strokes, recording his immense love of the texture of experience, awaking in a forest "half alive in the world," and knowing "half my life belongs to the wild darkness." As a companion to the diffuse and dream-like experiments of *The Book of Nightmares* and *Body Rags,* the publication of a Selected Poems is well-deserved; what is so remarkable is that these earlier poems should constitute in themselves such a major work. . . .

Straight Forth Out of Self

Harold Bloom

Tis 20 years now since Galway Kinnell published his first book of poems, "What a Kingdom It Was." The glory of that volume was a long poem, "The Avenue Bearing the Initial of Christ Into the New World," an overtly Whitmanian celebration and lament that remains one of the major American visions of New York City. Rereading it alongside Mr. Kinnell's new book confirms the sense I remember experiencing two decades ago, that here was another phantasmagoria of the city worthy of its ancestry, in that line that goes from Poe's "The City in the Sea" through Whitman on to its culmination in Hart Crane's "The Bridge." Galway Kinnell had made a magnificent beginning, and held a remarkable promise.

Whether his subsequent work as yet has vindicated that promise is problematic, though there have been very good poems in all of his books, including his new "Mortal Acts, Mortal Words:" His poetic virtues have remained constant enough, and have won him a deserved audience. Of his contemporaries, only the late James Wright and Philip Levine have been able to write with such emotional directness, without falling into mere pathos, the usual fate of American poets who speak straight forth out of the self. Mr. Kinnell is able to avoid the difficulties whose overcoming is necessary when we read John Ashbery, James Merrill and A. R. Ammons, among current poets, but whether his eloquent simplicities have the discipline of Mr. Levine's best poems is open to some question.

The poet and critic Richard Howard once characterized Galway Kinnell's poetry as being an Ordeal by Fire, which is to give him a generous accolade he may not have earned, or not fully as yet. The characterization points not only to Mr. Kinnell's most pervasive metaphor, the flame of Pentecost, but also to his largest poetic flaw, a certain over-ambition that makes of each separate poem too crucial an event. One must be Hart Crane to sustain a poetry in which each broken interval carries with it open question of spiritual survival. Mr. Kinnell's gifts, whatever they will yet be, do not gracefully sustain such enormous tensions. Some of his best earlier poems, such as "The River That Is East" and "The Bear," had design and diction firm enough to outlast their own intensities, but most of the more recent verse does not.

Reprinted by permission from *The New York Times Book Review,* 22 June 1980, 13. Copyright © 1980, 1982, 1985 by The New York Times Co., Inc. Reprinted by permission.

Much of "The Book of Nightmares" (1971) is devoted to a frontal assault upon the American Sublime that only an American Rilke could now attain, and Mr. Kinnell, despite his formidable will and courage of sheer being, is not yet such a poet.

But I grow a little uneasy at my own ingratitude as a reader, when confronted by a lyric meditation as beautiful and gentle as "Wait" in this new volume. It is difficult not to be grateful for a poem as generous, honest and open as "There Are Things I Tell to No One," or for a lyrical closure as precise as that in "The Gray Heron":

> It stopped and tilted its head,
> which was much like
> a fieldstone with an eye
> in it, which was watching me
> to see if I would go
> or change into something else.

Something also has to be said for Mr. Kinnell's descriptive powers, which are increasing to a Whitmanian amplitude. The last poem in the book, "Flying Home," will convey an authentic shock of recognition to anyone who has shared recently in that experience. But to sum up, this does seem to me the weakest volume so far by a poet who cannot be dismissed, because he seems destined still to accomplish the auguries of his grand beginnings. Any just review of him could end by quoting Mr. Kinnell's version of a Fire Sermon, from "The Avenue Bearing the Initial of Christ Into the New World":

> Children set fires in ashbarrels,
> Cats prowl the fires, scraps of fishes burn.
>
> A child lay in the flames.
> It was not the plan. Abraham
> Stood in terror at the duplicity.
> Isaac whom he loved lay in the flames.
> The Lord turned away washing
> His hands without soap and water
> Like a common housefly.

That Backward-Spreading Brightness

HANK LAZER

In "The Age of Criticism," Randall Jarrell writes that "most people understand that a poet is a good poet because he does well some of the time." That
certainly is the case with Galway Kinnell's writing and with Kinnell's latest
book. I'm sure that some readers will find it inferior to *The Book of Nightmares*,
possibly because *Mortal Acts, Mortal Words* is lighter, less unified, and looser.
But these two books are different. *Mortal Acts, Mortal Words* is a collection of
poems, in fact, of several different kinds of poems. *The Book of Nightmares* is a
book of poems, a single sequence of poems intended to be read as a unified
whole.

At their finest, Kinnell's new poems, as with many of his earlier poems,
are testaments of faith. The second section of "There Are Things I Tell to No
One," one of the best poems in *Mortal Acts, Mortal Words*, is the heart of Kinnell's faith:

> I say "God"; I believe,
> rather, in a music of grace
> that we hear, sometimes, playing to us
> from the other side of happiness.
> When we hear it, when it flows
> through our bodies, it lets us live
> these days lighted by their vanity
> worshipping—as the other animals do,
> who live and die in the spirit
> of the end—that backward-spreading
> brightness. And it speaks in notes struck
> or caressed or blown or plucked
> off our own bodies: *remember*
> *existence already remembers*
> *the flush upon it you will have been,*
> *you who have reached out ahead*
> *and taken up some of the black dust*
> *we become, souvenir*
> *which glitters already in the bones of your hand.*

This essay first appeared in *Ironwood* 16, no. 2 (Fall 1980): 92–100. Reprinted by permission.

It is fair to say that, like the previous passage, much of Kinnell's best poetry is Rilkean. It is *not* fair to say, therefore, that Kinnell is derivative. It just so happens that Rilke helped to stake out some rather elemental, crucial territory in the life / death interface. And Kinnell enters that territory too, but by his own vision or, as might be said, by his own lights.

There are, throughout this book, happy, glorious, celebratory lines. The poet takes a great and rich joy in this world: "no matter what fire we invent to destroy us, / ours will have been the brightest world ever existing." And there is still the death-hiss, still the world of dread and dissolution. But the advance that *Mortal Acts, Mortal Words* marks is in Kinnell's greater certainty of those impermanent but perfect moments of celebration. In this book the poet can say with conviction that "I have always felt / anointed by her love," and he can declare that "I am in the holy land."

But, again, to return to "There Are Things I Tell to No One," it is the earned sureness of this poetry that I admire: "In this spirit / and from this spirit, I have learned to speak / of these things, which once I brooded on in silence." Like Walt Whitman, Kinnell's great service is to show us that life, our life, is holy:

> Yes, I want to live forever.
> I am like everyone. But when I hear
> that breath coming through the walls,
> grace-notes blown
> out of the wormed-out bones,
> music that their memory of blood
> plucks from the straitened arteries,
> that the hard cock and soaked cunt
> caressed from each other
> in the holy days of their vanity,
> that the two hearts drummed
> out of their ribs together,
> the hearts that know everything (and even
> the little knowledge they can leave
> stays, to be the light of this house),
>
> then it is not so difficult
> to go out, to turn and face
> the spaces which gather into one sound, I know now, the singing
> of mortal lives, waves of spent existence
> which flow toward, and toward, and on which we flow
> and grow drowsy and become fearless again.

I am proud to be corny and say that Kinnell, with such poetry, can deepen our appreciation of that great, brief gift: life. And he can also help us in that Rilkean task: to read the word "death" without negation.

The key fact for Kinnell is the uniqueness of each creature, life, moment, love. That is, as he writes in "52 Oswald Street," Kinnell draws his strength "from unrepeatable life." He writes with a great eye for the specific, particular beauty of this world:

> the pelvic bones of a woman
> lying on her back, which rise
> smoothed by ten thousand years
> on either side of the crater
> we floated in, in the first life,
> that last time we knew
> more of happiness than of time.

For Kinnell, moments of epiphany and transcendence occur only by our becoming deeply familiar with the world. We transcend, that is, move to the realm of floating, first life, and that last time, only by being joined to the physical world.

That specific, intense union with the physical world must be accomplished by more than mere sight or vision. In his essay, "Poetry, Personality, and Death," which originally appeared in *Field* and is now available in *A Field Guide to Contemporary Poetry and Poetics,* Kinnell explains:

> Don't we go sightseeing in cars, thinking we can experience a landscape by looking at it through glass! A baby takes pleasure in seeing a thing, yes, but seeing is a first act. For fulfillment the baby must reach out, grasp it, put it in his mouth, suck it, savor it, taste it, manipulate it, smell it, physically be one with it. From here comes our notion of heaven itself. Every experience of happiness in later life is a stirring of that ineradicable memory of once belonging wholly to the life of the planet.

Yes, for Kinnell in his poetry too, seeing is but a first act, and no poem better illustrates that fact in his new book than "Saint Francis and the Sow," which, with its single, long, gorgeous sentence, requires quotation in its entirety:

> The bud
> stands for all things,
> even for those things that don't flower,
> for everything flowers, from within, of self-blessing;
> though sometimes it is necessary
> to reteach a thing its loveliness,
> to put a hand on its brow
> of the flower
> and retell it in words and in touch
> it is lovely
> until it flowers again from within, of self-blessing;
> as Saint Francis

put his hand on the creased forehead
of the sow, and told her in words and in touch
blessings of earth on the sow, and the sow
began remembering all down her thick length,
from the earthen snout all the way
through the fodder and slops to the spiritual curl of the tail,
from the hard spininess spiked out from the spine
down through the great broken heart
to the blue milken dreaminess spurting and shuddering
from the fourteen teats into the fourteen mouths sucking and
    blowing beneath them:
the long, perfect loveliness of sow.

"Saint Francis and the Sow" is a remarkable poem, fit to join company with Kinnell's finest animal poems of bear and porcupine. At the heart of Kinnell's work is the understanding that "sometimes it is necessary / to reteach a thing its loveliness." It is by way of hand and word, touch, snout, tail, spine, heart, and teat that the poet's, and our own, sacramental relationship to the world is achieved.

Aside from the perfect adjectives—creased forehead, thick length, earthen snout, spiritual curl, great broken heart, and blue milken dreaminess—there are several other features that intrigue me about this poem. The first is the long sentence and the adventurous, correct line breaks—both features of this entire volume. In other poems of the single long sentence, as in "The Rainbow," Kinnell is able to give us a compressed, united experience. If a moment can be said to have duration, Kinnell gives us a long moment. And in the musical elaboration of a single sentence, Kinnell allows the moment to labor, dance, and play toward its fit and powerful conclusion. When Kinnell's long sentences click, as in "Saint Francis and the Sow," "After Making Love We Hear Footsteps," "The Last Hiding Places of Snow," and "Flying Home," the long sentences convey the beauty of Kinnell's reading voice and the poems sound like rich, even-tempered blessings. An additional feature of the poem, and a feature worth noting in general about Kinnell's work, is the way, especially in the last line, Kinnell resists the impulse to create metaphors or similes out of the physical world.

I think that this resistance to metaphor and simile is one feature that sets Kinnell's work apart from some of the contemporaries—Robert Bly, especially—with whom Kinnell's work is often linked. In an interview with Wayne Dodd and Stanley Plumly, to be found in *Walking Down the Stairs,* a collection of interviews with Kinnell recently released from the University of Michigan Press's fine Poets on Poetry Series, Kinnell is asked what it is that he mistrusts about simile. His answer:

I don't think things are often really like other things. At some level all things *are* each other, but before that point they are separate entities. Also, although they are common, as you say, in surrealist poetry, similes perhaps have the effect of keeping the irrational world under rational supervision. Perhaps the words "like" and "as if" draw a line through reality and say in effect, "Here we are no longer speaking of the real world—here we indulge our imaginations."

Kinnell, as in "Saint Francis and the Sow," insists on the perfection and uniqueness of the world that is. Thus, a difference between Kinnell and Bly, analogous to a difference between Whitman and Thoreau. Bly, like Thoreau, through metaphor and simile, or through what we now more loosely refer to as the image, creates symbols for the inner, spiritual world of man. Bly and Thoreau side more closely with Emerson's maxims in "Nature":

> Particular natural facts are symbols of particular spiritual facts. Nature is the symbol of spirit. . . . The use of natural history is to give us aid in supernatural history; the use of the outer creation, to give us language for the beings and changes of the inward creation.

Kinnell's sense of correspondence and symbolism in nature is closer to the side of Whitman when, at the end of section 13 of "Song of Myself," he cautions,

> And do not call the tortoise unworthy because she is not
>   something else,
> And the mocking bird in the swamp never studied the gamut,
>   yet trills pretty well to me,
> And the look of the bay mare shames silliness out of me.

If anything, Kinnell is more rigorous than Whitman in respecting the integrity and otherness of the creature world.

Thus, at the end of "The Gray Heron," where Kinnell even allows himself to throw in a "like," our dominant impression is of the difference between the lizard world and the human world. The poet, where he expected to find the heron he had seen, instead finds

> . . . a three-foot-long lizard
> in ill-fitting skin
> and with linear mouth
> expressive of the even temper
> of the mineral kingdom.
> It stopped and tilted its head,
> which was much like
> a fieldstone with an eye
> in it, which was watching me
> to see if I would go
> or change into something else.

In the finest short poem in *Mortal Acts, Mortal Words,* "Daybreak," which I quote in its entirety, Kinnell does allow himself a very precise comparison:

> On the tidal mud, just before sunset,
> dozens of starfishes
> were creeping. It was
> as though the mud were a sky
> and enormous, imperfect stars
> moved across it as slowly
> as the actual stars cross heaven.
> All at once they stopped
> and as if they had simply
> increased their receptivity
> to gravity they sank down
> into the mud; they faded down
> into it and lay still; and by the time
> pink of sunset broke across them
> they were as invisible
> as the true stars at daybreak.

But the more important analogy, between terrestrial and celestial heavens, is resisted. That correspondence (or contrast) remains outside the poem. Again, it is Kinnell's judicious adjectives—enormous, imperfect, actual, and true— that do so much in this poem, and that finally link together the opposite worlds of mud and sky, sunset and daybreak, imperfect starfish and true stars, our world and the other world. And the linking takes place so quickly, "all at once." It is just what Robert Frost says of the true poem in "A Figure a Poem Makes": "Like a piece of ice on a hot stove the poem must ride on its own melting." But what dominates Kinnell's poem, and Kinnell's poems through- out his career, is precision of description. The realm of correspondence is usu- ally only implied.

Part of this wonderful particularity throughout Kinnell's career comes from his insistence on bringing to life old, nearly dead words. In *Mortal Acts, Mortal Words* Kinnell gives us the gritty substance of certain special verbs: wastreled, dismouthed, moil, and curvetting, among the most arresting in the text. Like his brother, Whitman, who in a key line in "Song of Myself" uses "athwart" ("You settled your head athwart my hips and gently turned over upon me") and later in the poem says, "My foothold is tenoned and mor- tised in granite," Kinnell too has a special fondness for the tangible but unusual verb.

The main weakness with *Mortal Acts, Mortal Words* is that there are a fairly large number of poems that feel like filler. Many of these weaker poems—poems with humor, or extensive word-play, or poems rooted in domestic life—add range to Kinnell's work, but they simply do not stand up to re-reading. Though they add a necessary contrast or counterpoint to the overall collection, finally, poems such as "Angling, A Day," "In the Bamboo Hut," "Lava," "Crying," "Les Invalides," "On the Tennis Court at Night," and "Looking at Your Face," for this reader, don't make it.

In terms of the occasional failings in *Mortal Acts, Mortal Words* a pertinent poem to take a look at is "The Still Time." It is a poem weakened and blurred by its many plurals and vague, general terms: those summer nights, the steps of my life, everything that drove me crazy, and all the old voices. There are still beautiful moments in the poem, as when at the end of the next to the last stanza Kinnell writes,

> as though a prayer had ended
> and the changed
> air between the palms goes free
> to become the glitter
> on common things that inexplicably shine.

In this passage it is "*a* prayer," but even that release of air gets a bit blurred by the plural "things." Kinnell concludes the poem by saying,

> And all the old voices
> which once made broken-off, choked, parrot-incoherences,
> speak again,
> this time on the palatum cordis, all of them
> saying there is time, still time,
> for those who can groan
> to sing,
> for those who can sing to heal themselves.

It is the whole choir of old voices that weakens the specific, odd beauty of "broken-off, choked, parrot-incoherences." *A* voice singing to heal itself, *one* parrot-incoherence carefully listened to, would be much more effective.

I belabor this point because such a weakness in the lesser poems casts into some doubt the strength of Kinnell's writing. That strength is his bold and beautiful endings. In the weaker poems the big endings feel more like rhetorical habit than the earned or urgent necessity of the poem itself. More often, though, in *Mortal Acts, Mortal Words,* the poem seems to rise naturally and easily to its strong ending. In already strong poems, such as "Saint Francis and the Sow," "There Are Things I Tell to No One," "The Sadness of Brothers," or "The Rainbow," the ending simply takes the poem one notch higher.

At the end of "Fisherman," a poem consisting of words to a friend whose wife has died, obviously an inherently risky topic in terms of the subject's potential for sentimentality, Kinnell's last stanza is:

I don't know how you loved
or what marriage was and wasn't between you—
not even close friends understand anything of that—
but I know ordinary life was hard
and worry joined your brains' faces in pure, baffled lines
and therefore some deepest part of you has gone
with her, imprinted into her—imprinted now
into that world which only she doesn't fear any longer,
which you too will have ceased fearing—
and waits there to recognize you into it
after you've lived, lived past the sorrow,
if that happens, after all the time in the world.

This ending attains an eloquence as it labors upstream, battling all its qualifications, its obstacle course of buts, therefores, and whiches. But what rescues and exalts the ending is the qualification present in the last line: "if that happens." It is such a qualification that makes this ending feel at once moving and comforting, lofty and judicious.

So, too, in the marvelous poem "The Apple Tree." Kinnell speaks earlier in the poem about the moment

When the fallen apple rolls
into the grass, the apple worm
stops, then goes
all the way through and looks out
at the creation unopposed, the world
made entirely of lovers.

And Kinnell ends the poem by saying,

The one who holds still and looks out,
alone
of all of us, that one may die mostly of happiness.

Again, I suggest that it is the double sense of "may" and the qualification implied by "mostly" that deepens this ending.

There is a more important point to be made about these endings than their employment of careful qualifications. Kinnell's strong endings are tied to a more comprehensive vision: his own special vision of death. As in "The Apple Tree," where the apples "fail into brightness" and where Kinnell explains that "we die / of the return-streaming of everything we have lived," Kinnell's own endings to poems are part of a backward-spreading brightness. As Kinnell points out in "There Are Things I Tell to No One," endings are a way of tying us to beginnings:

> Just as the supreme cry
> of joy, the cry of orgasm, also has a ghastliness to it,
> as though it touched forward
> into the chaos where we break apart, so the death-groan
> sounding into us from another direction carries us back
> to our first world . . .

By the very nature of endings we learn how inextricably and closely linked are those seeming opposites, life and death, which by our fear we mistakenly wish to keep apart. As in "The Choir," where "eyes, nostrils, mouth strain together in quintal harmony / to sing Joy and Death well," Kinnell's own endings present an analogy for Kinnell's vision of our own ending. The glorious, humane, fine-sounding conclusions to Kinnell's poems are, finally, to be linked to the "return-streaming" and to "that backward-spreading / brightness" that Kinnell has spent a career pointing out to us.

Mortal Acts, Mortal Words presents us with a passionately moral poetry, but it is not priggish nor self-righteous. In this book we get the sense of a man saying directly, eloquently, and emotionally the things he knows. He tells us the few repeated facts and conjectures that he believes matter. Toward the end of "Flying Home," the last poem in the book, we land in an "imponderable world." And I believe that Kinnell's humility, the admission of a word such as "imponderable," is not the last bit phony. In the finest poems of *Mortal Acts, Mortal Words,* as in "Daybreak," we witness the perfect correctness of the slow starfish who moves through the mud and is suddenly receptive to gravity.

From Recent Poetry: Five Poets

Stephen Yenser

. . . Galway Kinnell has had to face a problem that Hass, Pinsky, and Schuyler, to the extent that their long poems seemed comprehensive and were preoccupying, must also be familiar with. In an interview in 1971, he had this to say about *The Book of Nightmares,* the superb long poem published earlier that year:

> I thought of that poem as one in which I could say everything that I knew or felt. . . . I didn't want to let that poem go. I felt I could spend the rest of my life writing it—revising and perfecting it. . . . Eventually I had to force myself to get rid of it, though I knew I would feel an unsettling emptiness for a long time afterward. I hope I feel as totally consumed again.

"Wait," in *Mortal Acts, Mortal Words,* seems written out of that very complex of feelings. One might even hear overtones of Rilke, who meant so much to Kinnell when he was writing the *Nightmares,* in its closing lines:

> Only wait a little and listen:
> music of hair,
> music of pain,
> music of looms weaving all our loves again.
> Be there to hear it, it will be the only time,
> most of all to hear
> the flute of your whole existence,
> rehearsed by the sorrows, play itself into total exhaustion.

The connection made in the last lines characterizes this new book even as it did the preceding volume. While suffering and song are tied up for any poet, Kinnell more than most has made that relationship an explicit subject. At times, song remedies suffering, as in "The Still Time," where all of his "old voices" return to tell him that "there is time, still time / for those who can groan / to sing, / for those who can sing to heal themselves." At other, more distinctive moments, sorrow and music seem one, as they do also in the fifth section of the last of the *Nightmares,* where so many of the elements in the

Reprinted by permission from *The Yale Review* 70, no. 1, 105–28.

poem come together: when "the violinist / puts the irreversible sorrow of his face / into the opened palm / of the wood, the music begins." That music is "the sexual wail / of the back-alleys and blood strings we have lived / still cry-ing, / still singing, from the sliced intestine / of cat." It is as though crying *were* singing. As he puts it in "Brother of My Heart," "the bravery / of the crying turns it into the true song."

What then saves Kinnell's poetry—as something assuredly does—from being melodramatic and maudlin? For one thing, for all his talk about sorrow, he never makes it appear that his sorrow differs from anyone else's. Respond-ing to an interviewer's question about Sylvia Plath, he once noted that "She thinks her own woes are the only ones and ceases to understand that other people suffer. . . . Also, it often seems she doesn't want to understand her misery so much as to intensify and perfect it. . . . But you see, I respond very much to her poems, and it is these elements in myself, as much as in Plath, that I'm trying to be clear about. All criticism is self-criticism." The last remarks suggest more strongly than the comments on Plath ever could the importance to Kinnell of recognizing his bonds with others. That recognition encourages a poetry that, however personal in its references, continually expands into larger statements. "You're tired," he tells himself in "Wait," but his next thoughts are, "But everyone's tired. / But no one is tired enough." His need to see his own feelings in a larger context can lead him into inflation and platitude, as I think it does in "Flying Home," in a long passage about his wife: "Very likely she has always understood / what I have slowly learned / and which only now . . . can I try to express: / that love is hard, / that while many good things are easy, true love is not, / because love is first of all a power, / its own power. . . ." But usually his generalizations rise out of striking images and crystallize in aphorisms, as in "Wait":

> Second-hand gloves will become lovely again;
> their memories are what give them
> the need for other hands. And the desolation
> of lovers is the same: that enormous emptiness
> carved out of such tiny beings as we are
> asks to be filled; the need
> for the new love *is* faithfulness to the old.

Then, too, rather than trying "to intensify and perfect" his sorrow, Kin-nell tries to understand its relationship to joy. For him as for Yeats the two seem interdependent: "It is written in our hearts, the emptiness is all. / That is how we have learned, the embrace is all." If true song involves crying, it also entails laughing, as it did even for Amos, the old hobo in "Memory of Wilmington," who, happy to have eaten a stolen chicken he cooked just beyond rawness, "sang, or rather laughed forth a song or two, his voice / creaking out slower and slower, / like the music in old music boxes, when time slows itself down in them." (Kinnell tries to keep his free verse line taut as a fishing line, paying it out or reeling it in, in accordance with pace and inflection.) Suffering, happiness, song: it sometimes seems that all of life might be summed up in a single utterance, as in "There Are Things I Tell to No One":

> Just as the supreme cry
> of joy, the cry of orgasm, also has a ghastliness to it,
> as though it touched forward
> into the chaos where we break apart, so the death-groan
> sounding into us from another direction carries us back
> to our first world. . . .

That cry or groan—they are really "one sound"—reverberates throughout this book, often in onomatopoetic forms, as Kinnell, who has sent us to the Oxford English Dictionary as often as any contemporary poet, resorts to the most primitive exclamations in order to get to the heart of the matter. In "The Choir" some "Little beings" (either children or figures in, say, a Giotto painting) sing for joy and pain at once as they "stand in rows, each suspended / from a fishing line / hooked at the breastbone, being hauled up / toward the heavenly gases" and, "their mouths gaping," say " 'Ah!' for God, / 'O!' for an alphabet of O's." "Crying" begins in tears and ends in wild laughter—"Happiness / was hiding in the last tear! / I wept it! Ha ha!"—and it seems no accident that the transcription of laughter simply inverts the letters in "ah." "Lava," a stunningly original marriage of the whacky and the deadly earnest, comprises a set of variations on that most expressive of noises. It recurs throughout in the aa (pronounced ä.ä), lava solidified in blocks and fragments, which Kinnell contrasts with pahoehoe (pā.hō.ā.hō.ā), lava flows hardened in smooth shapes. "I want to be pahoehoe, / swirled, gracefully lined, / folded, frozen where I flowed," he thinks at first, but soon he wants "even more . . . to be, ah me! aa, a mass of rubble still / tumbling after I've stopped," a surface that anyone in bare feet would cross while "groaning 'aaaah! aaaah!' at each step." It is an eerie, wonderful music that this poem makes:

> When I approach the dismal shore
> all made, I know, of pahoehoe,
> which is just hoi polloi of the slopes,
> I don't want to call, 'ahoy! ahoy!'
> and sail meekly in. Unh-unh.

He wants instead to "look back / at that glittering, black aa" he climbed across with a lover and to see and hear their revenants crying "'ah! ah!' to a heiau's stone floor" and the stone answering "'aaaaaah,' in commiseration /

with bones that find the way very long / and 'aaaaaah' in envy of yet unbroken bones." Occurring twice in both the title and the key word, the sound stands as it were in the first place for pain and in the second for joy. Indisputably, A = A.

The aa is to the pahoehoe much as Yeats's "blind man's ditch" is to Byzantium. If Kinnell cannot cast out remorse altogether ("I know now there are regrets / we can never be rid of: / permanent remorse"), he still finds himself "blessing the misery" and able to imagine that "the last cry in the throat . . . will be but an ardent note / of gratefulness." This attitude differs slightly but significantly from that in the *Nightmares.* The earlier book attests to what he once observed in Whitman, "the double thought of death," the simultaneous fear of and desire for it. As Whitman grew older, Kinnell thinks, "he was able to transfigure both the fear and the desire into a willingness to die and an even purer wish to live," and something of the same change has taken place in his work.

He must find himself on easier terms with mortality partly because he finds it easier to see the universe as a whole. "Can it ever be true," he wonders in the *Nightmares,* "all bodies one body, one light / made of everyone's darkness together?" Now he can answer more certainly in the affirmative. He has admired the way that "Song of Myself" takes the reader "through one person into some greater self," and he thinks the end of that poem, "where Whitman dissolves into the air and into the ground. . . . one of the great moments of self-transcendence in poetry." To put it perhaps too succinctly, to feel that the universe is a whole is to begin to transcend the self, and to go beyond the self is to mitigate the fear of death. Or even to redefine death. In "The Milk Bottle" he starts to say that a sea anemone sucking harmlessly at his finger nonetheless means "to kill," then checks himself: "no, / it would probably say, to eat / and flow, for all these creatures / even half made of stone seem to thrill / to altered existences." To the extent that we feel the same "thrill," we can believe that "any time / would be OK / to go, to vanish back into all things." In "The Still Time," "the wind blowing / the flesh away translates itself / into flesh and the flesh / streams in its reveries on the wind." The passage is no less beautiful for being itself a translation of "I depart as air . . . I effuse my flesh in eddies, and drift it in lacy jags." Whitman's lines might also lie behind the phrase "the flesh's waters" in "There Are Things I Tell to No One," which arrives at one of the volume's loveliest testimonies to unicity:

> . . . it is not so difficult
> to go out, to turn and face
> the spaces which gather into one sound, I know now, the singing
> of mortal lives, waves of spent existence
> which flow toward, and toward, and on which we flow
> and grow drowsy and become fearless again.

This view of things has permitted some of the finest poems that Kinnell has ever written. In one way or another it has let him write, in addition to poems quoted above, "Fergus Falling" (a little tale of death and continuity that includes a catalogue in which the details link and contrast so nicely that somewhere Whitman himself nods and smiles), "On the Tennis Court at Night," and "The Apple." Just look at this last poem's final stanza if you think it unlikely that this book can equal the *Nightmares*. Or look even at "The Gray Heron," a short, modest poem built of nuances. Kinnell goes searching in the brush for a heron he has glimpsed but finds only "a three-foot-long lizard / in ill-fitting skin." What a wonderful touch that skin is, especially in conjunction with the light rhyme of "bird" and "lizard." At the poem's end, yet another metamorphosis begins. The implications verge on the hylozoic:

> It stopped and tilted its head,
> which was much like
> a fieldstone with an eye
> in it, which was watching me
> to see if I would go
> or change into something else.

As surely as the observing poet has merged with the bird / lizard now changing before our eyes into a watching stone, Kinnell has changed into something else in this book. American literature is richer and stranger for the transformation. Grand as it is, *The Book of Nightmares* could only, after all, be written once. Kinnell was determined not to repeat himself but to go on, and he has gone on. It took him about nine years to write these poems, but if it had taken him thirty, none of the time could have been counted lost. *Mortal Acts, Mortal Words* might just give its title the lie. It is certainly one of the chief indications that all is well in American poetry.

From Dimensions of Reality

PETER STITT

. . . Galway Kinnell's feeling about life's meaning and value, as expressed in *Mortal Acts, Mortal Words,* is quite similar to that of Wayne Dodd. There is a rather portentous poem here called "The Apple"—it ends with this beautiful stanza:

> Yes, and leaves
> its leaves where they fall
> with fatalistic compliance on grass
> which long ago gave its stitchmarks away
> to the bodies of lovers
> who no longer exist, or exist
> as leaves that have rotted back into the apple
> still brightening its bitter knowledge above us
> which only needs to be tasted without fear
> to be the philosopher's stone and golden fruit of the risen world.

Again we find a surprise towards the end—the language and rhythm both intensify to yield a statement that glows with wisdom and stands at the conceptual heart of this book.

Galway Kinnell once said, according to Donald Hall, that he had no use for any poem upon which the poet did not bring to bear the weight of his entire life. The results of such a standard are there to see in Kinnell's earlier books—the unrelenting seriousness, the pressure always to be deeply significant. It is exhausting sometimes, and has made Kinnell a poet best ingested in small doses. This book is different; its relaxed tone is apparent from the start and results in a number of lighthearted poems, poems one feels Kinnell could not have written before. He is now capable, for example, of poems like "On the Tennis Court at Night," a kind of elegy for all the good times, times of friendship and youth. The last stanza:

This review first appeared in *The Georgia Review* 34, no. 4 (Winter 1980): 887–94. Reprinted by permission of the author.

> Clouds come over the moon;
> all the lines go out. November last year
> in Lyndonville: it is getting dark,
> snow starts falling, Zander Rubin wobble-twists
> his worst serve out of the black woods behind him,
> Stan Albro lobs into a gust of snow,
> Don Bredes smashes at where the ball theoretically
> could be coming down, the snow blows down
> and swirls about our legs, darkness flows
> across a disappearing patch of green-painted asphalt
> in the north country, where four men,
> half-volleying, poaching, missing, grunting,
> begging mercy of their bones, hold their ground,
> as winter comes on, all the winters to come.

This is both effective and affective, part of what may be the best tennis poem in existence. But where is that lumbering hermit, that hunter-poet, willing to eat blood-soaked bear turds in his quest for the ultimate poem?

He may appear briefly towards the end of the book, where Kinnell seems to give over much of this wonderful physical specificity in favor of a series of relatively abstract, relatively theoretical poems. Although much more ambitious than the earlier poems, these are also less successful—partly because their abstractness pales beside the earlier poems' love of physical detail, and partly because their complexity is at times confusing—as in these lines from "Pont Neuf at Nightfall":

> Just now a sprinkling
> of rain begins. It brings with it
> an impression of more lasting existence—
> brings it by removal, by the swiftness
> of each drop's drying from the stone.
> (Soon the stone will be completely wet.
> When *our* stone became wet, that·was
> when desolation came into the world.)

The general idea—perhaps—comes through, but the details, the images, are not at all well-handled. Ideas, in these later poems, dominate things in an unfortunate violation of the doctrine expressed at the end of "The Apple."

Elsewhere Kinnell's very relaxation gets him in trouble; a stanza like this—on his dead mother's love—leaves me gasping for breath:

> So lighted I have believed
> I could wander anywhere,
> among any foulnesses, any contagions,
> I could climb through the entire empty world
> and find my way back and learn again to be happy.

There is this kind of thing here, but mostly not; mostly this is a volume of wonders, of poems like "Kissing the Toad":

> Somewhere this dusk
> a girl puckers her mouth
> and considers kissing
> the toad a boy has plucked
> from the cornfield and hands
> her with both hands;
> rough and lichenous
> but for the immense ivory belly,
> like those old entrepreneurs
> sprawling on Mediterranean beaches,
> with popped eyes,
> it watches the girl who might kiss it,
> pisses, quakes, tries
> to make its smile wider:
> *to love on, oh yes, to love on.*

There is an endless pleasure in such poems. *Mortal Acts, Mortal Words* is a new departure for Galway Kinnell, on the whole a successful one. It is permeated by an expressed love for the created world—love for nature, love for family, love for woman. This is Kinnell's answer to set against the mortal winds that always are ready to blow across the face of this earth. . . .

[Review of *Mortal Acts, Mortal Words*]

HOWARD NELSON

In a 1971 interview Galway Kinnell commented, "It would be nice if in a single poem one could resolve a given problem forever—come to terms with it once and for all." But if ever a poet was unable to achieve such a resolution of his given problem, it is Kinnell. He has instead pursued his compelling theme through poem after poem to the border of obsession; then crossed the border and dealt with it again and again. Anyone who has read Kinnell's poetry over the years can be sure of his major theme. The title of his latest collection spells it out: *Mortal Acts, Mortal Words*.

The awareness of mortality has colored Kinnell's poetry from the beginning, and as one reads through it one finds many explicit attempts to focus this awareness in a single clear statement and attitude. "Spindrift," in *Flower Herding on Mount Monadnock* (1964), ends with these lines: "Nobody likes to die / But an old man / Can know / A kind of gratefulness / Towards time that kills him, / Everything he loved was made of it." The final phrase of "Little Sleep's-Head Sprouting Hair in the Moonlight," in *The Book of Nightmares* (1971), probably comes as close as anything could to paraphrasing the sense of mortality Kinnell has evolved: "*the wages / of dying is love*." And there are many passages in *Mortal Acts, Mortal Words* one could cite to carry on the illustration, as these lines from "Goodbye": "It is written in our hearts, the emptiness is all. / That is how we have learned, the embrace is all." As these quotations suggest, Kinnell is an elegist who finds consolation and a measure of glory in the fact of mortality itself. It is because we die, and because we know that this is unavoidably so, that human life is worthy of a unique intensity. Angels and non-human animals on their different levels no doubt experience much that we cannot, but it is the human lot and privilege to live a little while knowing our own end. Kinnell has expressed it well in one of his essays: "That we last only for a time, that everyone and everything around us lasts only for a time, that we know this, radiates a thrilling, tragic light on all our loves, all our relationships, even on those moments when the world, through its poetry, becomes almost capable of spurning time and death."

This review first appeared in *The Hawaii Review* 12 (Fall 1981): 113–16. Reprinted by permission of the author.

It is interesting that often writers of the strongest elegiac sense—Whitman, Willa Cather, and Keats would be examples—are also remarkable for the intensity and luminous quality of their sensory descriptions. Startling, deeply etched physical description, combining sharp detail and an intuitive apprehension of the presence of a thing, has always been one of Kinnell's strengths, and continues to be in *Mortal Acts, Mortal Words,* as in the wonderful "Saint Francis and the Sow":

> . . .
> as Saint Francis
> put his hand on the creased forehead
> of the sow, and told her in words and in touch
> blessings of earth on the sow, and the sow
> began remembering all down her thick length,
> from the earthen snout all the way
> through the fodder and slops to the spiritual curl of the tail,
> from the hard spininess spiked out from the spine
> down through the great broken heart
> to the blue milken dreaminess spurting and shuddering
> from the fourteen teats into the fourteen mouths sucking and
>   blowing beneath them:
> the long, perfect loveliness of sow.

On the other hand, Kinnell is also drawn to abstractions, discursiveness, the direct expression of ideas, and even didacticism in his poetry. The description which evokes and celebrates the sow, for example, is preceded by a sort of lesson on the often forgotten beauty that even the lowliest things contain. Another poem, "Wait," is precisely a piece of advice—a moving counsel against suicide. The discursive teaching mode can be fine, anchored to the physical as it is in "Saint Francis and the Sow," or nourished by a steady, level-voiced eloquence and the music of verbal repetitions, as in "Wait." But there are places in *Mortal Acts, Mortal Words,* mainly in the second half of the book, where even readers who have a taste for Kinnell's discursive tendencies and his persistent weaving of the theme of mortality may find the going heavy.

Perhaps the discursive, philosophical manner makes a background against which problems in the language stand out more severely. However that may be, the earnestness with which the profound issues and feelings are discussed sometimes becomes ponderous. The didactic quality can wear rather thin, as it does in the book's final poem, "Flying Home." Kinnell's way of stringing out long, complex sentences in ragged, enjambed lines usually creates marvelous cadences that have become one of the signatures of his poetry, but those sentences can also seem just too wordy and convoluted, as happens in "The Rainbow," for example. He loves dense, elaborate lines and phrasings, which are often magnificent, but sometimes are simply over-done—I've yet to meet anyone who can work up any enthusiasm for "parabola of bear-transcendence," a sore-thumb phrase from Kinnell's famous poem "The Bear." When such problems occur too frequently, the poetry becomes clotted, bogged down. When I read "the slow- / given sighs of post-coitum bliss" or "the carcass expels / defeated desire in one final curve / of groaning breath, the misery-arc / farewelling hands have polished / before each face . . . ," the poem reminds me of a boat that is taking on water.

But I need to add at once that it is a part of Kinnell's poetic stance and personality to risk melodrama and to push language to extremes in what he knows sometimes seems a "slogging for the absolute"—to use a phrase of his own somewhat out of context. But this is also his effort to write poetry that will reach deeply and honestly, and that will have some true intensity and magnificence to it. He succeeds often enough to make one willing to forgive a good bit of poetry that strains and buckles under the weight of its own language and compulsions.

In the respect that *Mortal Acts, Mortal Words* carries on Kinnell's favorite theme so persistently, the book offers the opposite of surprise; there is a sense of inevitability as he returns to it again and again. But within this thematic unity, a number of poems contain tones and shades of feeling which seem to me to be attractive developments in the evolution of his work. I am thinking of "Fergus Falling," "After Making Love We Hear Footsteps," "Angling, A Day," "Lava," "Blackberry Eating," "On the Tennis Court at Night"—poems, all in the first half of the book, which are relaxed, anecdotal, at times song-like. They are warmer and more easy-going and given to humor than we have come to expect from Kinnell. No doubt "developments" is not quite the right word in the sentence above; "returns" or "recurrences" would be more accurate. I notice that James Dickey, reviewing *What A Kingdom It Was* in 1961, described Kinnell as "a natural poet: humanly likeable, gentle, ruminative"—a combination of qualities that seems new now, twelve years after "The Bear," nine years after *The Book of Nightmares*.

Kinnell wrote memorably of his children in *The Book of Nightmares*. The three poems in *Mortal Acts, Mortal Words* about his son Fergus may not have the intensity of what he wrote there, but they compensate for this with a sense of simple human warmth—and by giving pleasure. It is the pleasure of listening to a person talk in an affectionate, unpretentious, concrete way about his life: a poem about his small son's habit of waking at the sound of his parents' love-making and running to their room and hopping into the bed with them; a somewhat wandering meditation centered around Fergus' fall from a tree; an account of a day's fishing which yielded almost nothing in the way of fish but produced a batch of sights, sayings, and moods that will stick oddly in the memory a long time.

Kinnell is enough at ease in these poems to make occasional asides—to make a joke about Fergus' baseball pajamas, or in the middle of narrating the fall from the tree to compare the marks his electric saw would have made in a plank it had been working, to "dark circles under eyes / when the brain thinks too close to the skin." He shifts gracefully into and out of a lovely long-lined catalogue of people who have lived and died in his valley. As always, he keenly senses the physical world, noticing "the slow spondees" of a wood-cutter's ax and a pond "giving off / its little steam in the afternoon," and the physical world where it is most deeply tangled in the world of human emotion: a small boy, as he falls asleep between his parents, "his little, star-tlingly muscled body," "his face gleaming with satisfaction at being this very child." *The Book of Nightmares* went through personal experience and reached for a sense of mythic ritual. These new poems seem satisfied to express a man's life on a more modest level, in more conversational tones, but in the end they touch something timeless just as surely.

Some of the longer, heavier poems in the book, such as "The Sadness of Brothers," "The Last Hiding Places of Snow," and "There Are Things I Tell to No One," are no doubt in some senses more important than the ones I've been praising. They contain much that is strong, but I want to follow my feeling that some of the "lighter" poems offer the finest, freshest moments in the collection, and close with a short poem I particularly like.

> BLACKBERRY EATING
>
> I love to go out in late September
> among the fat, overripe, icy, black blackberries
> to eat blackberries for breakfast,
> the stalks very prickly, a penalty
> they earn for knowing the black art
> of blackberry-making; and as I stand among them
> lifting the stalks to my mouth, the ripest berries
> fall almost unbidden to my tongue,
> as words sometimes do, certain peculiar words
> like *strengths* or *squinched*,
> many-lettered, one-syllabled lumps,
> which I squeeze, squinch open, and splurge well
> in the silent, startled, icy, black language
> of blackberry-eating in late September.

Small pleasures like going out and eating blackberries from their wands in the September air may not seem at first to be "mortal acts," but of course they are. It is a playful, serious poem about the savor that is in the physical world and in language, which itself sometimes can become a live, nearly physical thing, as it does in this poem. Certainly "Blackberry Eating" is not representative of the whole of Kinnell's work; it leaves out many aspects and ambitions that are crucial elements in the total picture. But it does demon-strate his peculiar genius for speaking the language of the physical and the physicalness of language. I think it is largely these powers that give his poetry its distinctive force and beauty.

From From Scene to Fiery Scene

JAY PARINI

Galway Kinnell writes in the tradition of the American sublime, and remains one of the strongest voices of his generation. His *Selected Poems,* which recently won a Pulitzer Prize, is culled from six volumes written over a span of nearly four decades, and represents Kinnell at his best; the poems convey the jagged innocence and elemental power for which he has become famous. The poet of the American sublime seeks, as ever, to become Emerson's famous "transparent eyeball," seeing everything and nothing, feeling the currents of "Universal Being" circulate through him. Kinnell stands directly in the line of American poet–seers from Emerson and Whitman to Roethke and Ammons.

He has brought to this tradition, though, his own special intensity. Unlike most of his contemporaries in the late 1940s and 50s, Kinnell is unselfconsciously expansive, and sometimes prolix. His most important poem of this period, included in *What a Kingdom It Was* (1960), is "The Avenue Bearing the Initial of Christ into the New World," a rich evocation of life along Avenue C in New York's lower East Side. Kinnell uses multiple dialects, a variety of verse forms, and a sonorous rhetoric in pursuit of his theme, survival through purgation. He declares that "everything / That may abide the fire was made to go through the fire / And it was clean." This poem is one of *The Waste Land*'s distant cousins, of course; Kinnell's Fire Sermon, like Eliot's, looks forward to the possibility of redemption: "I don't know what you died of", says a character in *Black Light,* Kinnell's only novel; "Whatever it was, that is what will bring you alive again."

Kinnell's first two books anticipate the major phase represented by *Body Rags* (1968) and *The Book of Nightmares* (1971). The poet-hero of these poems, which are usually long sequences of narrative lyrics, walks out in a northern, primitive landscape that, especially in *The Book of Nightmares,* becomes a dream landscape. He is a prophet, staring wide-eyed at a natural world full of emblems, as in "The Bear," his most famous poem, which recounts in graphic detail the tracking and eating of the totemic animal by a primitive hunter. Few poems written in the post-war period equal "The Bear" for sheer cumu-

Reprinted from *The London Times Literary Supplement,* 1 March 1985, 239. Reprinted by permission of the author.

lative power. It is a poem about death and resurrection, the transformations of flesh into spirit and reincarnation.

"The Bear" is excellent, and so are "The Porcupine," "The Last River" and "Under the Maud Moon," among other lyric sequences from this period. Like others in search of the American sublime, Kinnell finds this genre attractive because it allows for intense "lyric" moments within a more ambitious framework. What Kinnell adds to the form is a forceful narrative drive, taking his "hero," who is usually quite explicitly Kinnell himself, from scene to fiery scene. The quest normally ends in a death that frees the "body rags" from their corporeal chains.

Many critics found a reduction of powers in Kinnell's last book, *Mortal Acts, Mortal Words* (1980). The ferocity is gone, certainly. Kinnell, having explored the lyric sequence so successfully, returns to the form that first drew him to poetry—the personal lyric. In place of ferocity and narrative acceleration one finds a luxurious wholeness, a sense of grace. Kinnell has become what no one could have foreseen, a poet of consolation: "Distrust everything if you have to. / But trust the hours. Haven't they carried you everywhere, up to now?" He abandons the extremities of "The Bear" and its cousin sequences for domesticity. The finest of these poems is "After Making Love We Hear Footsteps," in which a married couple benignly receive a small visitor to their bed;

> In the half darkness we look at each other
> and smile
> and touch arms across his little, startlingly muscled body—
> this one whom habit of memory propels to the ground of his making,
> sleeper only the mortal sounds can sing awake,
> this blessing love gives again into our arms.

Another poem, of equal gracefulness, is "Blackberry Eating," which celebrates "the silent, startled, icy, black language / of blackberry-eating in late September." Oddly missing from this *Selected* is Kinnell's "On the Tennis Court at Night," which treats the sadness and mystery of ageing in a haunting way. . . .

Intact and Triumphant

MORRIS DICKSTEIN

At the Donnell Library in Manhattan some 10 years ago, I witnessed a poetry reading so charged with high emotion and bardic intensity it left me both excited and exhausted. I could only imagine how it left the poet, Galway Kinnell, who, scarcely looking down at the page, had chanted his way through the whole of "The Book of Nightmares," his book-length Rilkean sequence that remains one of the most ambitious works in contemporary poetry. This book, which exemplified Mr. Kinnell's belief that it is "the dream of every poem to be a myth," used material from his own life, such as the birth of his children, in ways that transcended autobiography and seemed to confront directly the rhythms of existence from birth to death. Especially as read aloud in one fell swoop, the poem gave powerful expression to the hopes and fears of a parent, husband and lover adrift in his own sense of mortality.

Later I came to feel that this remarkable book was less successful on the page than it had been in that momentous performance. But even in its special oral impact it could be seen as a culmination of the poetic revolution of the 1960's: the shift from formal poetry, with rhyme and regular meter, to a freer, more prosaic verse that follows the contours of the speaking voice; the turn from wit and irony to a more naked emotional urgency; the pursuit of sublimity through heightened language, memory and meditation; and a projection into nature. Even the book's profound anguish and sense of fatality placed it in the high Romantic vein that the poetry of the 60's had boldly revived.

Literary revolutions can prove just as transient or tyrannical as political ones. Once established, new styles can become routinized, timid and vulnerable to the mockery of the next avant-garde. The poets who gave up conventional form for the existential vagaries of inspiration found that even the language of passion, the alphabet of the sublime, could be mechanically simulated, or could fall imperceptibly into self-imitation. The literary landscape of the 70's is littered with the remains of poets who tried to wing it on affect or sincerity alone; by and large they produced shapeless poems that tot-

Reprinted from *The New York Times Book Review*, 19 September 1982: 12, 33. Copyright © 1980, 1982, 1985 by The New York Times Company. Reprinted by permission.

ter from experience to experience, written either in oracular bombast or a flat, ungainly language innocent of wit, imagery, rhythm and ideas.

The extremity of the new poetry, the reckless, even suicidal intensity of living and feeling it sometimes demanded of its creators, seemed by the early 70's to have induced a crisis in Galway Kinnell's career. The very achievement of "The Book of Nightmares" (1971) put a period to the kind of poetry it represented. Within a year he was telling an interviewer that "a door has been closed on something. It would be foolish to go on in the same way."

It was nine years before Galway Kinnell's next book of new poems, "Mortal Acts, Mortal Words," appeared. Here Mr. Kinnell managed to lower the volume without retreating to formalism or triviality. Though the book shows his continuing preoccupation with death, especially in poems about his late mother and long-dead brother, much of its wry humor, anecdotal directness and quiet simplicity reminded one more of Robert Frost (one of Mr. Kinnell's early models) than of the intensity of "The Book of Nightmares." He had concluded the earlier book with a stunning evocation of his son's birth, which led him to imagine his own death. In these later poems we glimpse the same boy, Fergus, discovering a pond, going on a fishing trip or trundling in on his parents after they have made love. The unassuming charm of this book caused it to be undervalued, even ignored, by many critics, especially by academic critics who had never really accepted the great shift in contemporary poetry. Yet, to my mind, it was Mr. Kinnell's best book, a collection that proved that at least one poet in the Whitman-Williams mode of the 60's had survived not only intact but triumphant.

The same impression emerges from this rich new volume of poems selected from every phase of Galway Kinnell's career, including four early poems in the stiff, formal mode of the postwar period and then 25 to 30 pages from each of five major volumes published between 1960 and 1980. The book includes his famous shamanistic set pieces "The Bear" and "The Porcupine" (from "Body Rags," 1968), which epitomize the intensely primitivistic nature poetry be wrote during the 1960's. It also contains about half of "The Book of Nightmares" and 14 of the 32 poems of "Mortal Acts, Mortal Words" (leaving out some of my favorites). On grounds of quality alone, a selection more weighted to the later poems would have been preferable; the inclusion of the earliest poems, with their hollow echoes of Yeats, is especially questionable. By printing immature poems to which he remains attached, Mr. Kinnell seems determined to show us how far from precocious he was and how much he suffered under the prevailing forms and conventions, which did little to inspire him.

Galway Kinnell's breakthrough came in the late 50's with a long poem called "The Avenue Bearing the Initial of Christ into the New World," where he turned away from literary imitation, religious themes and fictional situations to record instead the sights and sounds of his own neighborhood, along Avenue C on the Lower East Side. The formless, documentary quality of this

15-page poetic album makes it only intermittently effective. Moments of forced sublimity add only a slight gloss to the pedestrian material. "The Avenue" is less a poem than a vast poetic notebook that enabled Mr. Kinnell—by a discipline of attention to the world around him—to slough off the artificialities and tired literary devices of the old style. On the wise advice of William Carlos Williams, he began to work more directly from experience.

A more authentic Kinnell voice can be heard in two striking poems from his first two books, "Freedom, New Hampshire," an elegy for his dead brother, and "Spindrift," another young-man's poem about death, which ends with the following lines:

> What does he really love,
> That old man,
> His wrinkled eyes
> Tortured by smoke,
> Walking in the ungodly
> Rasp and cackle of old flesh?
>
> The swan dips her head
> And peers at the mystic
> In-life of the sea,
> The gull drifts up
> And eddies toward heaven,
> The breeze in his arms . . .
>
> Nobody likes to die
> But an old man
> Can know
> A kind of gratefulness
> Toward time that kills him,
> Everything he loved was made of it.

This is not a point of view "that old man" himself is likely to share. Gratitude toward oncoming death, along with a mystic sense that individual lives form part of a larger ebb and flow (the "in-life of the sea"), is the mark of someone still remote from that rude transition. Yet, with many shifts of emphasis, this has remained Galway Kinnell's principal theme for more than two decades. In 1971 he told an interviewer that, as he saw it, "death has two aspects—the extinction, which we fear, and the flowing away into the universe, which we desire." But a few years later, in another interview, he was forced to add with beautiful tact that "our feelings about death change enormously, since time and circumstance are constantly putting us in a new position with respect to it."

The style of "Spindrift" also foreshadows the later Kinnell. As this selection makes clear, his poetry gets better as the lines get shorter: The literary mannerisms diminish, the diction loses its stiffness, and the poems take on a kind of stripped-down purity. Even the choppy look of the poem on the page reflects Galway Kinnell's fascination with the moment, the quantum of time that nevertheless implies all that is past, passing or to come. His theme is not death as a discrete event but death as the indwelling terminus that conditions our being from birth onward. On the beach the poet's "footprints / Slogging for the absolute / Already begin vanishing."

There is a shocking line in "The Book of Nightmares" in which Mr. Kinnell imagines lovers who "whisper to the presence beside them in the dark, *O corpse-to-be* . . ." In "Selected Poems"—in one of many silent improvements that Mr. Kinnell must owe to reading these poems aloud—the same lovers "whisper to the one beside them in the dark, *O you-who-will-no-longer-be* . . ." Both versions epitomize Galway Kinnell's eerie second sight, his insistence on peering at the bones behind the face—death beneath the mask of life, yet also some kind of ecstatic survival beyond the mask of death. In a child's nightmares he sees "the pre-trembling of a house that falls," and in our joys and loves he discerns "The still undanced cadence of vanishing." This Tiresias-like burden of vision, with its curse of prophetic in-sight, leads to what is strongest in the language of the mature Kinnell: a telescopic foreshortening of time into a single descriptive flash. In "There Are Things I Tell to No One," one of his most recent poems about death, he recalls

> how oddly fearless he felt
> at first imagining the dead,
> at first seeing the grandmother or grandfather sitting only yesterday
> on the once cluttered, now sadly tidy porch,
> that little boned body drowsing almost unobserved into the agreement
> to die.

Some of the most stunning poems in "Mortal Acts, Mortal Words," such as "The Rainbow" and "The Apple" (both curiously excluded from this selection), are written in a style so foreshortened yet so chillingly percipient that they have the effect of puzzles or riddles. In "The Rainbow"—in gnomic language that reminds me of some of Blake's most daring lyrics, such as "The Crystal Cabinet" and "The Mental Traveller"—he telescopes birth, copulation and death into a single "misery-arc" that is completed only when "the carcass expels / defeated desire in one final curve / of groaning breath." On the other hand, "The Apple," which begins with Adam and Eve "poisoning themselves / into the joy / that has to watch itself go away," ends triumphantly with the bodies of dead lovers subsumed in the cycle of nature, yet also surmounting nature, transfigured like

> . . . leaves that have rotted back into the apple
> still brightening its bitter knowledge above us
> which only needs to be tasted without fear
> to be the philosophers' stone and the golden fruit of the risen world.

"Selected Poems" is more than a good introduction to Galway Kinnell's work; it is a full-scale dossier for those who consider him, at 55, one of the true master poets of his generation and a writer whose career exemplifies some of what is best in contemporary poetry. He has not been seduced by modernist obfuscation, technical cleverness or earnest, thin-lipped confessional self-display. There are few others writing today in whose work we feel so strongly the full human presence. His language tantalizes us with a foretaste of meaning, an underlying emotional logic that recalls Whitman's "I am the man, I suffer'd, I was there." Like all good poetry, his finest poems attract and mesmerize us before we really understand them.

[Review of *Selected Poems*]

RICHARD TILLINGHAST

Trying to define for myself the particular excellence of Galway Kinnell's poetry, I thought of something Robert Lowell once wrote about Allen Tate, in many ways Kinnell's opposite. Tate's poetry was, Lowell said, "burly" and written in a style that "would take a man's full weight and that would bear his complete intelligence, passion, and subtlety." Kinnell's poetry has that impressive, "burly" masculinity. He has done that most difficult thing for a writer—he has achieved a style that does not restrict his range but rather allows him to write on all sorts of subjects and to speak in many moods and tones of voice.

Kinnell's *Selected Poems* is the year's most important book of poetry, rivaled only by Charles Wright's *Country Music* (Selected Early Poems). There are very few living poets (James Merrill comes to mind) capable of lines whose music can compare to the great poetry of the past, lines such as "seed dazzled over the footbattered blaze of the earth" or "already in heaven, listen, the golden cobblestones have fallen still" or (of his daughter's birth):

> . . . she skids out on her face into light,
> this peck
> of stunned flesh
> clotted with celestial cheesiness, glowing
> with the astral violet
> of the underlife.

Prosiness is the damnation of many contemporary poets—no, *most* contemporary poets. (It is a flaw that Kinnell himself does not always avoid.) A great deal of nonsense is written about poetry these days, such as the claim of "language poets" that "grammar is prosody," but I still hold with Coleridge's assertion that " 'the man that hath not music in his soul' can indeed never be a genuine poet." Kinnell has music in his soul, and he is a genuine poet—one of the best.

Even more important than Kinnell's musical sense is the seriousness and the deep emotion of his work. In the poems to his children from *The Book of*

This review first appeared in the *Boston Review* 8, no. 1 (February 1983): 36.

Nightmares, looking ahead to a time when he will be dead and they will go on .
living, he projects this wish:

> may there come back to you
> a voice,
> spectral, calling you
> *sister!*
> from everything that dies.
>
> And then
> you shall open
> this book, even if it is the book of nightmares.

Poets from Wordsworth to Yeats to Lowell have infused their poetry with an
awareness that, while it addresses itself most directly to that well-known
stranger, the reader, it also functions as the poet's will and testament, the gift
he bequeaths to his flesh and blood across time and death. *The Book of Nightmares,* especially, is Kinnell's gift to his children. I can think of no more moving statement of a parent's heart-breakingly illogical hope of shielding a child
from the death he accepts for himself:

> I would suck the rot from your fingernail,
> I would brush your sprouting hair of the dying light,
> I would scrape the rust off your ivory bones,
> I would help death escape through the little ribs of your body,
> I would alchemize the ashes of your cradle back into wood,
> I would let nothing of you go, ever. . . .

The weight of these emotions is leavened by Kinnell's ability to laugh,
to lighten occasionally the essential gravity of his vision. Here are his words to
his son, projected into the time after his (Galway's) death:

> . . . Don't cry!
>
> Or else, cry.
>
> On the body, when it is
> laid out, see if you can find
> the one flea that is laughing.

There are lighter poems as well, such as "The Correspondence School
Instructor Says Goodbye to His Poetry Students":

> . . . goodbye
> Miami Beach urologist, who enclosed plain
> brown envelopes for the return of your *very*
> "Clinical Sonnets"; goodbye, manufacturer

> of brassieres on the Coast, whose eclogues
> give the fullest treatment in literature yet
> to the sagging-breast motif; goodbye, you in San Quentin,
> who wrote, "Being German my hero is Hitler,"
> instead of "Sincerely yours" . . .

This book is proof that poems can still be written, and written movingly and convincingly, on those subjects that in any age fascinate, quicken, disturb, confound, and sadden the hearts of men and women: eros, the family, mortality, the life of the spirit, war, the life of nations. I mention the last two because Kinnell has a vision of America in the tradition of Whitman, and is a visionary social critic in the tradition of Blake, as he shows in his justly renowned long poem, "The Avenue Bearing the Initial of Christ into the New World," and in the widely anthologized 1960s antiwar poem, "Vapor Trail Reflected in the Frog Pond," which employs, ironically, a phrase from Whitman:

> . . . I hear,
> coming over the hills, America singing,
> her varied carols I hear:
> crack of deputies' rifles practicing their aim on stray dogs at night,
> sput of cattleprod,
> TV groaning at the smells of the human body . . .

One of his finest pieces is his poem to Robert Frost, which captures both the silly and the sublime side of the old poet, beginning "Why do you talk so much / Robert Frost?" characterizing him as a man cursed "Neither with the mystical all-lovingness of Walt Whitman / Nor with Melville's anguish to know and to suffer, / And yet cursed," and ending with this unforgettable image:

> . . . from the same doorway
> At which you lived, between the house and the woods,
> We see your old footprints going away across
> The great Republic, Frost, up memorized slopes,
> Down hills floating by heart on the bulldozed land.

Kinnell has his faults. He lapses into prosiness, as he at one point admits, speaking of "this poem, or chopped prose." His recent poetry, with striking exceptions, lacks the consistent power of his two best collections, *Body Rags* and *The Book of Nightmares*. But he always meets existence head-on, without evasions or wishful thinking. When Kinnell is at the top of his form, there is no better poet writing in America.

That's It

Roger Mitchell

Galway Kinnell may be the first poet in modern times who did not spend his apprentice years writing hard, dry, witty, ironical poems in the High Modernist manner. His early debts, quite audible in the poems, were to Yeats, Hopkins, and Dylan Thomas. These were masters of a fulsome, high rhetoric, but also poets who clung to earnest personal feeling and who are largely responsible for the revival of a Romantic esthetic in our day. Kinnell said once, in fact, about his early years, "if my poems didn't sound like Yeats, I thought they weren't poetry."

Kinnell's work falls between the intellectualism of High Modernism and the campy extravagance of the Beats and the so-called New York school. Ginsberg and O'Hara were certainly writing against the neo-Metaphysical manner and its underlying assumptions, but their way out, oddly enough, was merely witty in a different way. Kinnell and, before him, Olson and the Projectivists, and after him, the Deep Imagists, all sought the high ground of serious, direct feeling, a thing that had come to seem simple and impossible in the twentieth century. After all, Eliot had said we lived in complex times and required complex ways to respond to these times.

Kinnell's masters may have been technical innovators—certainly Hopkins was—but the impulse of powerful feeling, under the pressure of the technique-ridden fifties, made many poets distrust technique altogether. Kinnell has disclaimed any knowledge of craft and style. "I imagine that in the *Duino Elegies*," he said in an interview, "Rilke wanted to write out truthfully all that he understood, and the last thing that concerned him was technical innovation." The first poem in *The Past* says, "Here I forgot how to sing in the old way and listened to frogs at dusk make their more angelic croaking." And so we have had from Kinnell groping, astonished, revelatory poems in which, as he has said many times, he seeks a kind of self-transcendence. "How many nights must it take," he asks in *Body Rags,*

> one such as me to learn
> that we aren't, after all, made
> from that bird which flies out of its ashes,

Reprinted with permission from *The American Book Review* 9, no. 2 (March / April 1987): 23.

> that for a man
> as he goes up in flames, his one work
> is
> to open himself, to *be*
> the flames?

Any review of Kinnell's work has to take *The Book of Nightmares* into consideration. In many ways it is the work toward which his early poems tend, and there seems no way to avoid using it as a measure for the subsequent work. This may be, I suppose, the burden of writing a masterpiece, even of attempting such a thing. It is obvious in *Nightmares* that he, too, wanted to "write out truthfully all that he understood," as well as open himself to and "be" the flames. As much as I admire *The Book of Nightmares*, I've always been puzzled by it. It seems to reach beyond its words, beyond even its thought and feeling. I presume this is one of the things he strives for, one of the things he means by self-transcendence.

I have been glad, almost relieved, to have poems from *Mortal Acts, Mortal Words,* as I am glad now to have poems from *The Past.* They are more human in scale, less committed to being rituals and myths and more to being responses to what—so it feels—is really there in Galway Kinnell's life.

In the last poem of *The Past,* "The Seekonk Woods," Kinnell imagines his friend, Billy Wallace, come back to the woods "to stand in the past and just look at it." No one can do that, of course, but if they could, they would hardly be able just to "look at it." It's the present we look at. The past, if we care for it at all, as Kinnell does, we mourn. Everything in the past is tinged with a roseate gray, and so this book is a book of elegies for lost friends, poets, roads, cabins, childhood, children, love, everything.

This latest book differs from the earlier ones by being more conscious of loss and of the magnitude of his losses. Most of his life is behind him, which means that the future bears down on him with particular intensity. "Another life is upon us," he says. *The Past* is really about facing death. The little poem, "Prayer," tries to be matter-of-fact about it.

> Whatever happens. Whatever
> *what is* is is what
> I want. Only that. But that.

"What is" are the last words of the book, as well.

> . . . Behind,
> the world made of wishes goes dark. Ahead,
> if not tomorrow then never, shines only what is.

Has he given up wishing? No. After all, what is "shines." To accept death in a manner similar to the way he has accepted life becomes the principal hope of these poems. The angel "who mediates between us / and the world underneath us, trots ahead / so cheerfully." That cheerfulness will never be his, but he sees it and follows it. His tone in the opening poem, "The Road Between Here and There," is almost glib: "For here, the moment all the spaces along the road between here and there—which the young know are infinite and all others know are not—get used up, that's it." That "That's it" is fairly astonishing to someone who knows Kinnell's work, and it is so close to cheerfulness we smile.

Galway Kinnell is always out at the end of his branch whistling, alone with the world. If he sometimes loses the tune, if he sometimes gropes a little too openly for words that will do—the tree "went up in continuous ghost-giving-up" and the like—still he sees us and loves us. Four or five of these poems are as good as anything we write these days. One of them, "Last Holy Fragrance," an elegy to James Wright, is better. It is common to compare Kinnell with Whitman, but I feel he has never left the ground of his early training, Romantic poetry in the English tradition. "Last Holy Fragrance" descends directly from the great English elegies, starting with "Lycidas." It's true that it involves an older, shamanic poetry.

> But poetry sings past even the sadness
> that begins it: the drone of poetry readings
> or the mutterings coming from poets' workrooms—
> as oblivious to emotion as the printed page—
> are only seeking that chant of the beginning,
> older than any poem, that the song men
> of Arnhem Land, who jolt their clapsticks
> with a rebuking force like a spank, think
> they summon, or the shaman in Point Barrow,
> Alaska, having trance-learned it, translates.

But, as with the traditional English elegy, the death mourned is that of the poet (Whitman's great elegy was for a president), and the poem becomes both a definition of the poet and a description of his great task. "Adonais," "In Memoriam," "Hugh Selwyn Mauberly" (an ironic elegy), and "In Memory of W. B. Yeats" are no different.

> It will be a long time before anyone comes
> who can lull the words he will not now ever use
> —words which, now he has left, turn this way and that—
> hum and coax them to press up against,
> shape themselves by, know, true-love, and idolize.

I'm not so sure. Great elegists always manage to pass the baton on to themselves.

From Four Dark Volumes That Manage to Shine

L. M. ROSENBERG

What dark books I have been reading! Despite glimmerings of beauty, glimmerings of humor, or acceptance of the mortal condition, Helen Vendler seems to be right after all, and there is no transcendent poetry—even our mightiest poet of transcendence, Galway Kinnell, has turned to a new word: *evanescence,* in his newest and lovely book.

Kinnell's "The Past" might better have been called "Time" since that is its subject and obsession. Kinnell may be the only poet in America whose poems reliably grapple with the largest ideas. He elbows roughly and sometimes lunkishly past all pettiness, and, like Hercules, wrestles with Death itself—and with immortality, human nature, love, violence. His greatness goes beyond technique, though for sheer beauty and musicality, he is our grandest magician:

> *Moonlight sprinkles stars on the water.*
> *A boat lights up its light.*
> *Out of blue mist comes music of breaking waves.*
> *A breeze blows an accompaniment through the trees.*
> *The moon is almost round, like a ball the angels have been kicking.*

But more than this he is, as all great poets must be, a philosophical poet. This is not to suggest he is heavy-handed or always even serious ("So Kenny Hardman and George Sykes / called 'Gaw-way-ay!' at the back / of the house. If I didn't come out / they would call until nightfall, / like summer insects"), or that his seriousness is always successful, as it's not, I think, in some of the smaller koan-like poems, which I imagine to have been included on bad advice, poems like "Conception," "Some Song," and "Prayer."

This is in many ways a darker book that one would expect—I think perhaps darker than Kinnell himself expected, with all things plunging sorrowfully and lovingly toward death:

This review first appeared in *The Chicago Tribune,* 2 February 1986, 40. Reprinted by permission of the author.

For here, the moment all the spaces along the road between here
and there—which the young know are infinite and all the
others know are not—get used up, that's it.

Beneath this is an undercurrent, an electrical charge of a greater optimism and spirituality, reflected, for instance, in the remarkable fluidity of the syntax, as above, in the Whitman-esque roll and thunder of this opening poem, but Kinnell's conclusions don't yet—except intermittently—reveal the change. The poetry often flags in courage or commitment at the last instant, and there is a curious damped-down effect, as if the heart were too loaded with guilt and grieving to sail forward freely. In this, more than in any superficial or thematic way, the book seems to me truly ballasted in the past.

None of this keeps the book from being a glorious one, certainly the strongest since "The Book of Nightmares." Nor does it suggest a faltering of genius, but, if anything, the adolescent surgings and back-steppings of new powers. "The Fundamental Project of Technology" is far and away the best poem we have on the bombings at Nagasaki and the dangers of the nuclear age—it is utterly without sentimentality or chic. And the last poem. "The Seekonk Woods" (I think I am not imagining the play on the word "seeking"), is the best and deepest exploration here; perhaps the best imaginable for this moment in human time, the most daring—"I have always intended to live forever"—the most magnificent, "So what if we groan? / That's our noise. Laughter is our stuttering / in a language we can't speak yet." "The Past" is Kinnell's first attempt to learn that language, and through his poetry, to teach it to us. . . .

[Review of *When One Has Lived a Long Time Alone*]

Stephen Yenser

If it makes some kind of sense to think of Henri Coulette—cool, witty, calculating, acute—as the poet who has written a syllabic poem that consists of numbers, it is fitting to consider Galway Kinnell a poet who will write in pure onomatopoeia, as in " 'thrump thrump thrump thrump-thrump- / thrump-thrump-rup-rup-rup-rup-rup-r-r-r-r-r-r.' " That is a ruffed grouse drumming, in the seventh section of the title sequence in *When One Has Lived a Long Time Alone*. This section avows that "consciousness consummates" and that "as the conscious one among these others / . . . deep in the woods, all of them in time's unfolding / trying to cry themselves into self-knowing— / one knows one is here to hear them into shining." The passage is characteristic, both in its own music (here the different repetitions, including the long *i* and the homonyms) and in its attention to the world's. To Kinnell's good ear all creation is a heterogeneous orchestra, from which we hear now the "slub clump slub clump" ostinato of the bricklayer's work with mortar and brick, now the ragman's blare which is itself "the noise inside things that have turned into old rags, 'AWWWWRAGHHH!,' " and now the resonant ground note of yearning in the name "Brahms ('Brahms,' nearly the sound dwelling on you forms in my mouth)."

Kinnell has always been a hungry lover of language at its basic level, where sound curls into meaning. Leave it to him to specify "that place . . . where lovers speak, / on lips blowsy from kissing, that language / the same in each mouth." One sometimes has the feeling that he is *making* words out of sound as a potter shapes a pot from clay. Indeed, he often coins words, especially quasi-Anglo-Saxon compounds: "sleep-rags" for bedclothes, "brain-bags" for chickens' heads, "flame-chunks" for firewood. "Kilauea" begins with a volcano and concludes with a furnace that is also the poet's father:

> The father, already in the cellar, yanks
> the great iron lever, the iron teeth
> gnash, ashes dotted with fire

This review first appeared in *Poetry* 158 (July 1991): 217–21. Reprinted by permission of the author.

crash into the ash pit; and shovels in
a new utopia of coal, in a black field,
which lies quiet, then jets up all over
in flickerings like little senseless bluets.
The pipes and radiators of the house
knock and bang in free un-unison.
In the bathroom he strops the razor,
hoots out last night's portion of disgust,
and shaves, a fleshy, rhythmic rasping, like a katydid's.

If "utopia" is a wonderful surprise as a point of departure for the "black fields" and the "bluets" of flame (which term owes something to the influence of "jets"), "un-unison" defines as no other word could the haphazard simultaneity of the pipes' sounds. At the same time that he is a neologist, Kinnell is a scholar, a lover of language at its most *recherché*. In this new collection we find such inkhorn terms as "ramp" (as a verb) and "dulse," "leucoma" and "salep." Some lines in the first section of "The Tragedy of Bricks," with their combination of nonce terms and special terms, concrete images and abstract concepts, are unmistakably his:

The used-up lace-worker bicycling past,
who is about a hundred, suctions together mouth-matter,
tongue-hurls it at the gate of the mill, rattles away.
A spot of gold rowels its trajectory
of contempt across a boy's memory.

Just as Kinnell combines different dictions, so he blurs metaphysical categories. In the last poem here, his lovers "like birds at daybreak / blether the song that is both earth's and heaven's"—and then in the rising sun these two "stand / in a halo of being made one." Like many of his poems, this title sequence is rooted in a sense of fragmentation and solitariness, which is one kind of "oneness," and yet blossoms in a vision of unity, which is another kind altogether. It is important that each of the eleven thirteen-line sections in "When One Has Lived a Long Time Alone" comes full circle by opening and closing with the refrain set out in the title—and that each of these sections is one sentence long. Beginning with the conditions that prevail in the "kingdom of strangers," it moves toward a "halo of being made one: kingdom come," a circle of wholeness, a "halo of being" itself. Singularity and completeness, earth and heaven, lover and lover come together at crucial points in this poetry that is increasingly attentive to a fundamental unity that seems as impossible as it is inescapable.

The title sequence and the book itself aspire to an understanding of unicity that recalls Whitman and Rilke. It is the *Duino Elegies* one thinks of when Kinnell, in his moving elegy for Paul Zweig, gives to his dead friend the following advice (to be given back to him): " 'Let the limits of knowing stretch and diaphanise, / so that life includes more and more death.' " It is *Song of Myself* one hears in the catenation of similes at the middle of "Kilauea," where the poet finds himself nearly encircled by a rainbow:

> . . . Could it be that *I*
> am the pot of gold? Both pots,
> one inside the other,
> like the fire leaping inside the steel drum the night workers
>   hold out their hands to, in the icy air before morning,
> or the pitch-black of speech about to be born through scarlet lips,
> or the child getting off her bicycle inside the old woman
>   the priest has told to get ready to die,
> or the father of Edinburgh rising early inside the son of
>   Pawtucket—to whom on Sundays after church he read
>   the funnies, Scripture in the father-tongue?

The many little connections—gold with fire, pot with drum, night with pitch-black speech, birth of speech with the girl-child, the girl with the boy, the priest with the father who reads "Scripture"—hint at a certain coherence of being. This passage weaves together origins and ends, as in the image of the dying woman's memory of getting off her bicycle and in the corresponding image of the father rising implicitly like the sun inside his son—who is thus his father. (No accident that Kinnell calls "Sunday"—and even "Pawtucket"—into play here.) Whitman's catalogues, themselves rarely put together with more devotion to detail, point to a similar insight. It is as though Kinnell were intimating a kinship with the nineteenth century poet himself.

To be sure, this glimmer of unity is not always suffered without sadness. In another splendid poem about his father, Kinnell concludes with the clear acknowledgment that "the absent will not be present, / ever again." This admission and the pain it involves are one with his cutting of bonds with his dead parent and the dissolution of the other self into existence:

> . . . Then the lost one
> can fling itself outward, its million
> moments of presence can scatter
> through consciousness freely, like snow
> collected overnight on a spruce bough
> that in midmorning bursts
> into glittering dust in the sunshine.

In the snow's "glittering" in the sunshine one sees again the son's "tears" (mentioned earlier in the poem), and the "dust" is partly that from which we come and to which we must return. At the same time, however, that explosion of snow is virtually sexual (in the preceding poem the poet refers to his "balls, densest concentration of future anywhere in my body . . . with the claustrophobia of a million swimmers terrified they will never get out"), and the spruce is an evergreen, and it is morning. This is an image instantly classic, emblematic of transience and creativity, grief and celebration, less complex in language and somewhat lighter in tone but no less touching, to my mind, than that of the skydiver in the last of *The Book of Nightmares*.

Kinnell epitomizes the feelings in such a passage in a fable folded into "Last Gods," which is about a man and a woman who make love on a rock in a lake and who in the course of things "cry / in the tongue of the last gods, / who refused to go, / chose death, and shuddered / in joy and shattered in pieces, / bequeathing their cries / into the human mouth." Those lines have a Yeatsian force, but much of this poem is a cut below Kinnell's best work. When the woman "opens / her legs showing him her great beauty" and then when he "kneels, opens" her "dark, vertical smile / linking heaven with the underearth," the two descriptions seem equally periphrastic, instances both of beating poetically around the bush. In "The Perch," when the poet and his lover "had drained [her lips] with hundreds / and thousands of kisses," and in "Divinity," when "the man touches through / to the exact center of the woman" and "his loving friend becomes his divinity," Kinnell works perilously close to banality—or so it seems, when one compares these passages with, say, such strange, strong poems as "The Cat" (which radiates the uncanny quality of a nightmare) and "Street of Gold" (which interlaces five or six subjects in an unpredictable and fascinating manner), which are small, eccentric, indelible masterpieces.

A Hundred Verses Of Solitude

SARAH CAHILL

Even though he was born in Rhode Island, Galway Kinnell has always seemed like a displaced Irish poet, and it's not just because of his name ("Galway Canal?" my father repeats when I ask if he's read him. "Is that actually in Ireland?"). Kinnell's verse has always echoed the compressed melodic lines of Irish writers; his words, like theirs, ache to be read out loud (he, like they, is also a mesmerising reader) and even read on the page you feel the vowels and diphthongs tumbling in your mouth, each word more potent by its juxtaposition with others. The pleasures of reading become not only intellectual, but deeply physical as well. Many of Kinnell's lines could easily have been written by Irish poets like Paul Muldoon or Seamus Heaney or John Montague or Michael Longley:

> In this bed spooled out of rock maple plucked
> from the slopes above the farm, saints
> have lain side by side. . . .
>
> ("The Auction")

This [*When One Has Lived a Long Time Alone*] is Kinnell's tenth book of poems, and his voice has become progressively surer and more confident over the years. His recent work is structurally taut, pared down to its essence, more economical than the poems in books like *The Avenue Bearing the Initial of Christ into the New World* which burst with expansive exuberance about nature, ideas, books, and, of course, love. In the author's note to that book, referring to the hundreds of poems he wrote in his teens and early twenties, Kinnell admonished himself: "It might have turned out better for me if, during that period of my life, I had written less and given myself more to silence and waiting." In his latest book he seems to have taken his own advice, especially in the long title poem which is composed of the small sounds and movements of a solitary, silent life. Like many other poets (and painters, and composers, and novelists) in

This review first appeared in *East Bay Express* 13, no. 16 (February 1991): 6–7. Reprinted by permission of the author.

their later years, he has stripped away all excess to give each line a distilled, precise clarity.

Kinnell has gained such control over his voice that he can work by instinct, trusting that his idiosyncratic manipulations of speech will add to, rather than detract from, the coherence of the poem. Whatever he chooses to do, however superficially awkward, becomes a minor sacrifice for the resulting rhythms and sounds. Sometimes he distorts syntax or conversational word order: "Today on skis I took a friend / to show her the trees"; or he will offer a seemingly mundane exclamation: "Last night / my God, the shooting stars!"; or introduce us to semicomical situations, like an old man getting a massage; "The hands find coagulated rump tissue—delve / spear, grabble, until the buttocks want to jig"; or he will take his line lengths to extremes for emphasis:

> When we drove a spike too weak into wood too hard
> we got, not
> the satisfied grunt of everything organized to go downward,
> but a sudden yodel,
> like a funny bone singing.
>
> ("Memories of My Father")

Kinnell is one of the rare poets who can write fairly traditional narrative poetry and infuse it with extraordinarily musical power. Often when poetry tries to tell a story, plot and content take over, but when Kinnell is at his best you find yourself paying attention to the sounds of words first and their meanings second, as they assume their own hypnotic rhythms. As with Irish poets, you read Kinnell on several levels—for sound, during which you feel the heft of the line, like a collection of polished stones weighing pleasantly in the hand—and then for content, which then seems surprisingly like an extra bonus.

If Kinnell's poems, with their pithy contrasts of assonances and resonances, manage an element of bodily involvement—the mouth, the tongue, the throat—lending them a built-in sensuality, it comes as no surprise that he's especially successful when he turns his attention to erotic suggestion. Kinnell's very first published works were lyrical love poems, and the themes of marriage, unrequited love, courtship, seduction, and romance have stoked his poetic fires throughout his career. In this new book the rhapsodic celebration of love is replaced by tightly controlled detail, which is somehow distanced from emotional conviction. Sex is occasionally acted out in these pieces, but love in any lasting sense makes itself felt mostly through its absence. The most overtly sexual poem in the book actually involves no contact with another person—it is about examining an orchid:

> . . . I turned and saw
> what everyone else maybe sees at once:
> that in each blossom
> the calyx's middle petal curves up
> and flows over the mons veneris and spreads across the belly,
> and the petal on either side rises over the thigh, one edge following the
>   ridge of the pelvic bone, which is prominent, for she lies on her back,
> and the two petals that are set back hold the roundness of her buttocks,
> and at the center, in the little crown,
> the clitoris leans, above
> the vestibule opening into the center of being
>
> ("Flower of Five Blossoms")

Kinnell may be one of the most linguistically virile of contemporary poets—the muscularity of this kind of writing carries with it a kind of undeniable bravado—but one senses in *When One Has Lived a Long Time Alone* that all erotic energy has been absorbed into language; human interaction has practically ceased. The book resonates with a desolate loneliness. Kinnell, now in his sixties, speaks in a voice which is worn and tired, although still highly libidinous; he weathers rejection and symptoms of aging; his thoughts are increasingly occupied with death. The massage scene turns out to be at a hospital:

> . . . The cadaver
> two beds away spits out the scatological verbs,
> as though he fears they will frisk his heart
> in the next world.
>
> ("The Massage")

These poems might come as a shock to Kinnell's readers who still imagine him as the boyish bard of the '60s and '70s, handsomely craggy, one stubborn lock of jet-black hair over an eye, reciting intensely romantic lyrics in a passionate pitch. These are poems about warily approaching the inevitability of old age, and Kinnell's characters wear their age uncomfortably, like rumpled, ill-fitting suits. The poems do, on the other hand, continue the theme of his struggle between three equally essential conditions: eternal bonding with a mate, the pleasures of inflammatory obsession, and the solitude that is conventionally considered necessary for a creative artist.

These poems come down for the most part in favor of solitude, but not without a sense of loss and a tinge of self-pity. After the end of a love affair:

> . . . that
> trace of eternity love
> brings down among us
> stays, to give
> dignity to the suffering
> and to intensify it.
> ("The Vow")

Loneliness is everywhere: "He feels around— / no pillow next to his, no depression / in the pillow, no head in the depression. / Love is the religion that bereaves the bereft." Absences abound, not just those of lovers but, most crucially and painfully, of parents: "Those we love from the first / can't be put aside or forgotten, / after they die they still must be cried / out of existence . . . the absent will not be present / ever again."

The long title poem, in which eleven stanzas each begin and end with the line "When one has lived a long time alone," is much like Kinnell's poems of the last few decades, like "Tillamook Journal" or "The Past," in which he undergoes some period of isolation ostensibly to sharpen the acuity of his senses. Those earlier pieces usually conveyed a robust sense of adventure, communion with the elements, an invigorating delight in the roughness of cutting one's own path in the wilderness. This time, however, the self-imposed exile has another purpose: the narrator has no desire to be around people. He has grown misanthropic and "abandons hope / of the sweetness of friendship or love." He pays attention to animals he would otherwise ignore, even the fly and mosquito, and "lifts the toad / from the pit too deep to hop out of / and carries him to the grass." As he records each small life-saving event, he discovers that

> . . . more and more one finds one likes
> any other species better than one's own,
> which has gone amok, making one self-estranged
> when one has lived a long time alone.

There is a tone of tragic heroism in these verses, an implication that the narrator, for all his sorrow, is liberated to loom larger than life for having failed in the human community. The loner, we learn from an early age, casts greater shadows, and takes on a more dramatic sense of immortality than people who live close to others. The way to legendary status is a solo flight. But at the same time isolation does not rest easily with the narrator; the world, as the line goes, is too much with him, and beckons. In the final verse:

> When one has lived a long time alone,
> one wants to live again among men and women,
> to return to that place where one's ties with the human
> broke. . .

While Kinnell's complaints about the loneliness he has inflicted on himself are slightly irritating, in the same way that the marriage/love affair dichotomy that has pervaded his work until now has always seemed a tad overwrought, he redeems this long poem with a final moment of vulnerability, humility, and mortality. And that, as we all know, is what finally elevates all tragic figures.

From Meaning in Place: A Moral Essay

Mary Kinzie

. . . Galway Kinnell is an accomplished navigator of the sensory. Having during his poetic career penetrated the various side-chapels of myth worship and the egocentric surreal, Kinnell now "composes" (in the double sense of writing and striking the attractive pose) with no suggestion of effort. Hence many of the poems are genial tableaux of pleasurable perceptual suspense. Even in satiety his *personae* are marked by a style of reserve, almost of decorum, which only increases the riveting effect of the sexuality. "The Perch," "Last Gods" (with its atmosphere of uncanny tenderness as the man orally stimulates the woman), and the last poem in the sequence "When One Has Lived a Long Time Alone"—all celebrate the fiery swoon of sex against a background of pantheistic approval. Even the indifferent cosmos blesses the unions so pearled with perfection:

> *When one has lived a long time alone,*
> *one wants to live again among men and women,*
> *to return to that place where one's ties with the human*
> *broke, where the disquiet of death and now also*
> *of history glimmers its firelight on faces,*
> *. . . where lovers speak,*
> *on lips blowsy from kissing, that language*
> *the same in each mouth, and like birds at daybreak*
> *blether the song that is both earth's and heaven's,*
> *until the sun has risen, and they stand*
> *in a halo of being made one: kingdom come,*
> *when one has lived a long time alone.*
> ("When One Has Lived a Long Time Alone")

One feels in many of the new poems [in *When One Has Lived a Long Time Alone*] the breath of a troubadour dawn, cold, dewy, erotic, alive with bird-song, in an atmosphere of reverence chastening the alert imagination.

It is equally characteristic that in another poem he should present himself inclined against the mantel, with the almost transcendent domestic

This review first appeared in *The American Poetry Review* 21, no. 1 (January–February 1992): 7–14. Copyright © Mary Kinzie.

sophistication one associates with the narrator of *Six Chapters of a Floating Life*, as he looks into the innocently obscene bloom of an orchid, and that then, almost unwittingly, he should put on the player a Romantic sonata. More even than with the field of unmediated sense perception (although cognate with it), Kinnell is significantly at home with music, its history and interpretation, just as (one senses) he is at home in the habit of listening to music in many moods. So when after attending a performance of Haydn's Symphony in F-sharp Minor he imagines the departure of the musicians into an earlier age after the last adagio, we believe in the symbolic truth of the details, even if realistically they are somewhat fanciful in their rusticity:

> *Before leaving each player blows*
> *the glimmer off the music-stand candle,*
> *where fireweed, dense blazing star, flame azalea stored it summers ago,*
> *puffing that quantity of darkness into the hall*
> *and the same portion of light*
> *into the elsewhere where the players reassemble and wait . . .*

What the musicians await is an oboist in the woods who will tune their instruments to a perfect A so as to encourage the creatures and elements in their diurnal cycle, awakening the birds, but also helping the musicians to "play / the phrases inside flames wobbling on top of stalks in the field . . . and in gnats whining past in a spectral bunch." Even in daylight the knowledge of death eclipses the spirit. So, almost immediately, the dawn slides over into night again, and the elegy for the poet Paul Zweig, who died in 1984 nearing 50, takes shape in the duet of the violinists who "scathe the final phrases":

> *In the darkness above the stage I imagine*
> *the face of my old friend Paul Zweig*
> *—who went away, his powers intact, into Eternity's Woods alone, under a*
> *double singing of birds—*
>
> . . . .
>
> *The bow-hairs still cast dust on the bruised wood.*
> *Everything on earth, born*
> *only moments ago, abruptly tips over*
> *and is dragged by mistake into the chaotic inevitable.*
> *Goodbye, dear friend.*
> ("Farewell")

These moments are gripping in their coherence of response. In this poem, as almost everywhere in this book, we never look blurredly through the ambiguousness of perception—the half-glimpsed, the out-of-articulate-reach. Instead, feeling is exact and immediate, apprehended forcefully by the sensibilities and directly spoken by the poetic instrument. Indeed, one can scarcely avoid the metaphor of musical skill when admiring the highly organized array of verbal responses in these poems to the physical responses implied by their themes. Kinnell is very much the adept summoning up and re-deploying his experience of audition throughout the altered context of emotional reawakening. The technique of fine recoil from the obvious (including the subtle reference to his own past work) provides frequent pleasure:

> *The audience straggles from the hall and at once disappears.*
> *For myself I go on foot on Seventh Avenue*
> *down to the little, bent streets of the West Village.*
> *From ahead of me comes the* hic *of somebody drunk*
> *and then the* nunc *of his head bumping against the telephone pole.*
> ("Farewell")

Accompanied by an almost comforting rue, the bereaved friend and fellow poet reenters the world of the exigent and drunkenly broken and yet undeniably benevolent here and now. . . .

"C'mon back" Poems:
Galway Kinnell's *Imperfect Thirst*

FRED MORAMARCO

The title of Galway Kinnell's *Imperfect Thirst* (1994) comes from this dense and somewhat cryptic quotation from the twelfth-century Islamic mystic Sohrawardi:

> If your eyes are not deceived by the mirage,
> Do not be proud of the sharpness of your understanding;
> It may be your freedom from this optical illusion
> Is due to the imperfectness of your thirst.

The quotation can be interpreted to be about pride, clarity of vision, arrogance, and humility all at once. On the one hand a human being can take pride in separating the illusory from the real in the world, but if his thirst were "perfected" the mirage would indeed seem real. To have a perfect thirst means to desire something so much that one creates it. For Kinnell this often seems an emblem of the poet's condition: trying to describe the reality of a world that may be completely illusory. Life may be a dream, but it is the poet's work to chronicle that dream and make it appear as real as possible. Language is the material he uses to make this happen.

In "The Pen," which serves as a "proem" to *Imperfect Thirst* and its first long poem, Kinnell writes, "Much of what pens write stand for 'blah blah.' " This is a candid admission for any writer, and particularly candid for a poet who lives by the precision of words. The burden of writing, Kinnell seems to be asserting in this introductory poem, is that one never does get things exactly right, or even nearly right for that matter. Words often obfuscate rather than clarify; sometimes they move us further from the emotional context of actual experience rather than closer to it. Even when we devote our lives to using them as tools to express our particular view of the world (as poets do), they fall short, leaving us with that Keatsian notion of mystery and uncertainty that he felt was essential for poets to possess. Ironically, a life of

This essay was written especially for this collection and is printed by permission of the author.

writing poetry underscores the irrefutable fact that the most important things in life are often ineffable.

This irony, of course, does not stop poets from writing poems; in Kinnell's case it is in fact a reason for writing poetry, as if to challenge the unfathomable and discover correspondences in a world that defies logical analysis. When we review the events of our lives and try to find words that capture the emotional landscape of our past, we give those lives shape and meaning. If they have no shape and meaning, it may be that our thirst to find that meaning is imperfect, and so we need to try harder, look more intently at the mirage.

In "The Pen," Kinnell finds a wonderful analogy to describe this process:

> In the Roman system, the pen moves to the right, and at the margin
> swerves backwards and downward—perhaps dangerous
> directions, but necessary for re-entering the past.
> The pen is then like the person who gets out of the truck, goes
> around to the rear, signals to the driver, and calls, "C'mon back."

(An earlier version of the manuscript rendered the call to the driver as "momback," a distinctly American coinage, derived by someone who listens to the sounds of language with care and exactitude, recognizing that the discrete English words in the expression "Come on back" become truncated in some kinds of American English as "'momback." It seems a loss that the final version has the more immediately recognizable, but less colorful, "C'mon back.")

Kinnell has always been alert to the way language sounds. He is particularly attentive to unusual sounds that humans conjure to represent the sounds of the actual world we experience. A small sampling of his exotically expressive diction from his earlier books would include words like *clack, tic, ai wuh, mugwumps, croal, haish, yaw, cigit cigit, squinched, rasp, cackle, yap, screech, pelf, fenks, gurry, scritch scritch scritch, wee wee wee, cawhjoosh,* and *dee dee dees. Imperfect Thirst* adds *lacka wanna lacka* (a child mimicking the sound of a train passing), *sheisses* ("a fountain pen sheisses into a shirt pocket"), *skheided* (excrement dumped on grass), *whenua* ("which in Maori means both placenta and land"), *tok-tok-tok-toking* (a bird pecking at a tree trunk) and *zzzing* ("her tongue, zzzing like a blowtorch"). These descriptive approximations of sounds that emanate from humans, animals, insects, and machines are not an end in themselves for Kinnell, but rather an entrance into the idea of correspondences. They demonstrate the connections between all life in the biosphere and even between the animate and inanimate worlds.

A poem called "The Music of Poetry" both examines these links and parodies Kinnell's obsession with sound when taken to academic extremes. The narrator in the poem is giving a lecture on English poetics. He makes analogies between free and formal verse, between a gopher frog's chant and the rumblings of an empty stomach, between the cries of the humpback whale

and the wolf's howl, between an Eskimo shaman chanting and the poetry of
Pablo Neruda, William Butler Yeats, Dylan Thomas, and Muriel Rukeyser
"to let the audience hear for themselves that our poems / are of the same
order as those of the other animals." But all of this seems beside the point and
merely academic as the narrator, bringing his talk to a close, leans on a
podium in St. Paul, Minnesota, and thinks about his beloved "on Bleecker
Street in New York" pulling an eiderdown quilt around herself and turning
out the light. This interior vision creates the "real" poetry of this poem as the
narrator reveals the contrast between the inner world of love and desire and
the external world of verbal exactitude:

> . . . only minutes ago my beloved may have
> put down her book and drawn up her eiderdown
> around herself and turned out the light—
> now, causing me to garble a few words
> and tangle my syntax, I imagine I hear
> her say my name into the slow waves
> of the night and, faintly, being alone, sing.

These aural correspondences and connections are further epitomized by
"The Cellist," which traces the genesis of a particular sound made by a particular musical instrument during a concert. Kinnell seems particularly interested in the way the conjunction of the living and nonliving worlds produces
music. The cellist in this poem coaxes vitality from an inanimate object by
giving it some of her own in order to awaken its former animation:

> Now she raises the bow—its flat bundle of hair
> harvested from the rear ends of horses—like a whetted
> scimitar she is about to draw across a throat,
> and attacks. In a back alley a cat opens
> its pink-ceilinged mouth, gets netted
> in full yowl, clubbed, bagged, bicycled off, haggled open,
> gutted, the gut squeezed down to its highest pitch,
> washed, then sliced into the cello strings that bring
> a screaming into this duet of hair and gut.

This Ovidian metamorphosis of horsehair and catgut creates a magical and
exotic music that

> . . . seems to rise from the crater left
> when heaven was torn up and taken off the earth;
> more likely it comes up through her priest's dress
> up from that clump of hair which by now
> may be so wet with its waters, miraculous as the waters
> the fishes multiplied in at Galilee, that
> each hair wicks a portion all the way out

to its tip and fattens a droplet on the bush
of half notes now glittering in the dark.

So the music of the cello created by this marriage of catgut and horsehair is transformed by a woman's sexuality into a wondrous sound that approximates a religious miracle. When the cellist finishes her performance,

Her face shines with the unselfconsciousness of a cat
screaming at night and the teary radiance of one
who gives everything no matter what has been given.

The human being here has taken on catlike attributes, and the cat has entered the civilized world of humanity. All of this is orchestrated by sexuality, which runs through the poem—and many of Kinnell's other poems—like an electric current charging the words with a primal force beyond their literal and connotative meanings.

Each of the five sections of *Imperfect Thirst* has five longish poems clustered around a single theme or motif. The first contains poems about Kinnell's primary family and his New England upbringing. Four of the five are specifically about his father: "Showing My Father Through Freedom," "Hitchhiker," "The Man in the Chair," and "Picnic." The second section is a group of loosely connected poems, all of which are primarily observations of the contemporary physical world. Unlike the remainder of the book, most of the poems in this section are grounded in the present rather than the past. The exception is "Trees," a beautiful poem about a childhood experience that really seems to belong in Section I but was probably put here for symmetry. Section III is a series of "Sheffield Ghazals"—short but long-lined wry and witty philosophical meditations, each of which mentions the name "Galway" in the final line. The fourth and fifth sections, the strongest poems in the book, are love poems and poems about aging and mortality. Despite these divisions, most of the poems are either "C'mon back" poems—ruminations on past events, movements back into the spaces of memory to search out the meaning of those events—or meditations on particular things like "Flies," "Rapture," and perhaps the ultimate philosophical meditation, "Holy Shit."

The latter is a 78-line contemplation on excrement, human and otherwise, preceded by nine substantial quotations from Plato, Valentinus, Pope Innocent III, St. Bernard, Richard Rolle of Hampole, Chaucer, Buddhaghosa, the *Shacharit,* Martin Luther, and Walt Whitman. It is shit, Kinnell proposes in the opening lines of the poem, that ties us "to some hole in the ground" and prevents us from feeling like the gods. We, of course, don't like this *memento mori* and reminder of our connection to all other animals, so we insist it is an ugly word, an obscenity. In this poem it is merely the "holy metamorphosis" of the earth as it passes through us. That society regards it as an obscene word is the real obscenity, which furthers the illusion that

> . . . we are a people who don't die,
> who come out of the sky like gods and drop
> not shit but bombs on people who shit.

The political implications of those lines clearly have an affinity with Kinnell's earlier work, particularly "The Fundamental Project of Technology," a stronger, more ambitious statement of how technology works toward eliminating death by eliminating life.

The most interesting quality of Kinnell's work in *Imperfect Thirst* is that the poems seem to have a "spiraling" effect. They often begin as meditations or social commentary but whirl outward and wrap around themselves following a kind of whirlwind of associations. "The Road Across Skye," for example, begins with an observation of the Scottish landscape but quickly turns into a childhood reminiscence, which loops into a critique of evangelistic cant, which segues into the last words of the Zen Master Daibei, who composed a parable about a weasel, then returns to more observations of the world in front of the narrator. All of this is threaded with a brief exchange between the narrator and his beloved. She asks if he wants some tea, and he says yes, "With a little honey. And your company." This little conversation allows him to pull the strands of the poem together in the final seven lines and the poems turns into a love poem:

> . . . I think I might yet
> get conscripted into the choir of the coal tit,
> the cow, the ewe, the lambs, the weasel, Daibei,
> the *taisches**, even the Reverend Billy, and especially
> she who just cried to me from a treetop,
> if I could sing all this to her without ceasing
> so that it will not turn into all that.

These lines create a sense of the simultaneity of experience. The "internal" world of the psyche and the "external" worlds that impinge upon it merge in a continuum that includes rather than excludes, that brings together past and present, child and adult, animal and human, the lover and his beloved.

Kinnell's love poems constantly risk sentimentality, and that is their strength. They are unapologetic in their sense of love's distractions and, particularly, of its grounding in physical attraction. "Rapture," one of the strongest poems in this collection, conveys an almost palpable sense of male

---

*Taisches, spirits of people about to die, are referred to elsewhere in the poem.

desire by finding words for its speechlessness. Two lovers have just awakened; the woman is out of bed rummaging in a dresser drawer for her underwear. The man lies in bed watching her.

> . . . She bends
> so low
> her back runs parallel to the earth,
> but there is no sway in it, there is little burden, the day has hardly
> begun.
> The two mounds of muscles for fast walking, leaping, lovemaking,
> lift toward the east—what can I say?
> Simile is useless; there is nothing like them on earth.

It seems anomalous that the failure of language to capture our most memorable experiences should be a prominent poetic theme, but like Wallace Stevens, Kinnell believes in the intense physicality of the world that words can only begin to approximate. Yet the world of words is a world with a palpability of its own, and there is a poetry in the nobility of their failure. The poet goes back again and again to life experiences trying to get them exactly on the page, but offers only words in place of flesh and blood, or, as is the case in these final lines from "The Pen," in place of tears and mascara:

> Then I had a visit from a poet a few years widowed, who talked about
> her husband and how she felt thwarted in her writing and
> had lost her way—though in the rhythmical tumbling forth of
> her words she seemed to be finding it.
> I wished I had collected some of the mascara-blackened fluid on her
> cheeks to mix into my ink.
> But when I started writing about Wendy again, the ink had
> replenished its vocabulary, and from the street came the bleats
> of a truck in reverse gear and a cry, "C'mon back, c'mon back."

Kinnell's work in *Imperfect Thirst* comes back again and again to the life events that generated the poems and recreates them, imperfectly to be sure, but moves as close as ink and paper can to the reality of tears and mascara.

ESSAYS

Galway Kinnell: Moments of Transcendence

SHERMAN HAWKINS

Galway Kinnell was born in 1927 in Providence, Rhode Island, and raised in Pawtucket. He came to Princeton in the summer of 1944 and after only one semester joined the Navy. Six months later he returned to Princeton in the V–12 program and graduated at midyears in 1948. He then took an M.A. at the University of Rochester. His life since then has followed an alternating pattern common among American poets of his generation: teaching and travel, academic appointments and foreign fellowships. For two years he taught at Alfred University, and for three more he was Director of the Liberal Arts Programs at University College in the University of Chicago. Then in 1955 a Fulbright Fellowship took him to Paris to translate the poetry of Villon, and he stayed for another year as a lecturer at the University of Grenoble. In 1957 he came back to America and to New York University, first as a research associate and then as a teacher in the adult education program. In 1960 he was appointed Fulbright Professor at the University of Teheran, and the journey there and back took him around the world. The same year, Houghton Mifflin brought out his first volume of verse, *What a Kingdom It Was.*[1] In 1961 he was again in France, working on his translation of Villon, which will be published by The New American Library (Mentor Books). Since the spring of 1962, he has been living in New York and Vermont, giving poetry readings at various colleges and working on his second volume of poems, *Flower Herding on Mount Monadnock,* which will appear next year. This summer he worked for CORE, registering Negro voters in Louisiana. He has received a fellowship from the Guggenheim Foundation for his poetry and also an award from the National Institute of Arts and Letters.

In a review of the poetry of Charles Bell, Kinnell wrote: "It is good to see bold and rational verse appearing after years of experiment on the verbal level. . . . It is as though what we used to call the 'avant-garde' has scoured the Victorian decay and narrowing, making it possible for poets now to re-attach themselves, with purity of language and greatly broadened subject matter, to the continuing tradition of Western poetry." Such "re-attachment," he declared, is "not a reversion but a fruitful and needed going forward." This

Reprinted from *The Princeton University Library Chronicle* 25, no. 1 (Autumn 1963): 56–70.

statement suggests Kinnell's own practice and intention. The tradition to which his best poetry "re-attaches" is that of transcendental and religious meditation—what Kinnell might call "sacred poetry." But if his work may be considered "rational" in its attachment to tradition, it is "bold" in its continuing development towards a more radical insight and a freer style. Today, indeed, Kinnell considers himself "a kind of unknown avant-garde."[2] His poetry is thus a "going forward": to understand its progress we need to consider the changes in his poetic models and theories as well as in the poetry itself.

The most important influences in his verse are those of Frost, Yeats, and Whitman. All three poets share a surface simplicity and a preference for the idiomatic and colloquial, the grace and toughness of actual speech—what Kinnell calls purity of language. But each is also felt as an individual presence: Frost in Kinnell's recourse to nature as norm and enigma, the special locus of revelation; Yeats in the structural deployment of image and symbol; Whitman in an intense social consciousness and a "oneness with all things." New England landscapes, recurrent imagery of birds, the free flowing line and the deliberately unpoetic catalogue—these stylistic trademarks are as reminiscent as the manner of individual poems: that of Frost in "First Song," of Yeats in "Descent," of Whitman in "The Avenue Bearing the Initial of Christ into the New World." Frost is an early and Whitman a more recent model, but the influence of Yeats has been continuous.

It was at Princeton that Kinnell read Yeats for the first time, with overwhelming effect. "I tried to make them all sound like Yeats. No one else could have told I was imitating Yeats, but if they didn't sound like Yeats to me, I didn't think they were poems. It took a long time to get over that." But in Kinnell's earliest published lyrics, the influence of Frost is even more evident in the natural settings, the deftly rhyming stanzas, the personal and retrospective mode. It was Whitman who changed his notion of what a poem is, showing that the lines laid down by Frost are not the only ones "or that it is perhaps wrong to have lines at all." Frost has compared free verse to tennis without a net; Kinnell admits that meter and rhyme are the best way to play the game, "but what if it is not a game but a war?" For Kinnell, every poem is now part of the poet's life, and his rhymes and rhythms have become increasingly free as he seeks to achieve a more authentic utterance, "to throw the responsibility for the poem wholly on speech itself." Today he considers Whitman the significant influence in his writing. "They speak of Gertrude Stein and Ezra Pound as having purified the language, but Whitman's language—smack in the nineteenth century—seems to me more alive than Pound's. I can't read nineteenth-century English poetry now: every word has been dipped in nostalgia. But in Whitman ordinary and average things are seen in a sacred light. He was the really democratic poet, who standing among the streets, finds the sacred exists there."

This shift from Frost to Whitman marks a shift in attitude to poetry itself. Kinnell explained his earlier theories in the preface to a selection of his work in *The Beloit Poetry Journal*. His main thesis was stated in the title: "Only meaning is truly interesting. . . ." Kinnell argued that in much modern poetry, the emphasis on brilliant verbal effects of individual lines and images detracts from the meaning of the poem and the sense of the whole. Such poetry is an imitation of language rather than of nature. Style should be transparent like a window, so that the effect derives from the action or idea described, not from the language of description. He praised Charles Bell for verse stripped of the obvious devices of poetry, nearly as bare as prose. His own "Spring Oak," a straightforward description, was deliberately written in "a style that is almost the absence of style."

A change is evident in Kinnell's review of Larry Eigner. He admires Eigner's poetry "for its closeness to things, its sense of their mystery and real-ness. . . . At his best he writes in a state of grace with respect to the real, an openness and trust between himself and the world, by which the two blur and real objects keep dissolving towards a deeper, stranger reality. His best lines are less invented descriptions than the acts themselves of this contact." It is a rare gift: "Many poets, of course, write of common, despised objects, but Eigner comes close to making these things the personages of a sacred poetry." This is the kind of poetry Kinnell is trying to write today. Narrative and description (in the usual sense) have almost disappeared. The words no longer form a transparent window; they seem to be "pressed very close to the thing, as if to a mould": each line is an act of contact. Things cease to be objects and take on a life of their own, become personages; there is "explicit consideration of the mystery of being."

No doubt Kinnell still believes that only meaning is truly interesting, but there has been a shift in the meaning of "meaning." In his preface he wrote that the meaning of a poem "though it may be dimly predicted, emerges only in the creative act. The organizing principle comes into full being simultaneously with its embodying detail. In the successful process there is a unifying light, a single vision of meaning, what might be called its tragic illumination." Such moments of enlightenment occur in "the mysteries of life as well as of poetry": Kinnell set out to recreate them "directly, simply, even reverently." Now if a poem re-enacts a moment of enlightenment in the poet's life, then it is a recreation; it is mimetic. But if the meaning is only dimly perceived beforehand and the "unifying light" evolves in the creative act, then the poem itself becomes the moment of enlightenment: it is vision-ary. Of course these concepts of meaning are not mutually exclusive. In the attempt to recreate a moment of enlightenment, its meaning may change and grow, so that the finished poem becomes the fulfillment of the moment of experience. Many of Kinnell's poems seem to result from this double process of recreation and creation. It will not do to divide his poetry into two chronological periods or generic types, the mimetic and the visionary. Nevertheless, the distinction of vision and mimesis is useful: the tension between these impulses and their constantly shifting relationship seems to affect the form and style of individual poems, the line of Kinnell's development, even his deepest intuitions of meaning.

This interplay is obvious in the poems themselves. "The Avenue Bearing the Initial of Christ" is crowded with objects accurately sensed: the propane-gassed bus making its way through the streets with "big, airy sighs," a red kite wriggling like a tadpole, a pushcart market with its icicle-shaped carrots and "alligator-skinned / Cucumbers, that float pickled / In the wooden tubs of green skim milk." This kind of vivid sensory precision has become a minimum requirement in recent poetry. But in Kinnell's poems, these real objects are transfigured by intimations of deeper, stranger, reality: the tadpole kite, as it "crosses / The sun, lays bare its own crossed skeleton." Kinnell's poetry is grounded in reality, but it works constantly towards such moments of illumination, often in climaxes marked by rhetorical device and heightened diction. Mimesis becomes vision as we read.

In many poems this transfiguration takes the form of an ascent from the real to the ideal. The pattern is consciously Platonic. Kinnell's more ambitious poems, with their deliberate repetition of imagery, their frequent division into contrasting sections, their progression towards a synthesizing moment of vision, recall the strategy of certain poems by Yeats. But they are also modelled on the Platonic dialogue, which—considered as a work of art—Kinnell believes to be one of the great poetic forms. "It proceeds as a poem proceeds, using dialectic, images, characters. By the end the whole thing has been raised to a new level: every statement is transformed, has a meaning beyond itself, like the phrases at the end of a great poem." Platonism thus provides a typical structure and a tacit metaphysic for a poetry which is always moving from the reality into the mystery of things.

If the poem ends in the heavens, however, it must begin with things of earth. A poetry like that of Bell which seeks "redemptive beauty in experience" implies an ugliness that needs to be redeemed. The conjunction of the poetic and the unpoetic is a commonplace of modern verse, and this juxtaposition is already a poetic habit in Kinnell's "First Song," with its contrasts of dung and music, its cornstalks metamorphosed into violins, its paradoxical affirmation of the "sadness of joy." In these early poems, Kinnell felt a need to make claims for the beauty of life, and the dung and cornstalks are necessary to save these claims from sentimentality. With the growing recognition that "life is uglier and more beautiful, both, than at that time I understood," the antitheses grow more extreme. The intuition of the sacred involves its opposite; the visionary imagination hungers for that which challenges its transfiguring power—objects not merely common but despised. Thus in "Easter"—itself an early poem—death confers an unresurrecting grace upon a nurse who has been almost ritually defiled: "Raped, robbed, weighted, drowned."

"Where the Track Vanishes" enacts the myth of ascent from earth to heaven, but the goatherd who toils up the mountainside is Pierre le Boiteux, yellow-toothed, hamstrung, hideous in every way. Yet with this increasing stress on the unclean and deformed goes an increasing range of metamorphosis. Pierre becomes Boötes, the heavenly Herdsman; the fields into which he wades are constellations; the track to the churchyard leads out among the stars:

> Where the track vanishes the first land begins.
> It goes out everywhere obliterating the horizons.
> We must have been walking through it all our lives.

So by the tragic principle, negation evokes the vision which affirms. Perhaps this is one reason—artistic rather than biographical—why the recurring subject of these poems is death, for death is the final obstacle, the last enemy to be overcome by the imagination. It is a measure of Kinnell's achievement—and his honesty—that his elegiac poems end with the transcendence and reconciliation proper to the form while actually affirming the personal finality of death.

Kinnell's double commitment to the naturalistic and the visionary shapes and informs his first volume of collected verse. It is divided into four sections, corresponding in sequence to the kinds of poem which have interested him at different times. Each section is arranged chronologically, with the first poems of section II antedating the earliest of section I, and the last of section II postdating the first of section III. But the shape of the book is not quite that of Kinnell's poetic evolution. Many of his early lyrics—including "Spring Oak," his exemplar of the transparent style, and "Indian Bread," a poem he contributed to a collection honoring Robert Frost—do not appear in *What a Kingdom It Was*. This early verse tends to the mimetic: descriptive or narrative in form, firmly controlled in structure, realistic and clear in style. A number of poems, like those which form the first section of *What a Kingdom*, deal with an imagined boyhood and young manhood in the Middle West.[3] The six poems are arranged symmetrically: an introduction, two contrasted pairs of poems, and a conclusion. The unifying action is initiation. "First Song" tells how at dusk in Illinois—a halfway point in space and time—a boy's first song of happiness "woke / His heart to darkness and into the sadness of joy." In the central poems this ambivalent awareness becomes a growing recognition of the divine and the daemonic in nature and in man. "Westport," a conclusion which is also a beginning, sets the static oppositions of "First Song" in motion, heading from east to west, from dark afternoon to a bright evening, and out of evening into night. But this is more than a metaphor of growing up, for here the action of initiation, with all its threat and promise, is extended to the youth of a society, the expansion of the American frontier. This shift from the individual to the community is repeated in the volume as a whole.

The second section, despite an occasional fine poem or significant pairing ("Easter," or "Alewives Pool" and "Leaping Falls"), is the most heterogeneous and least impressive in the book. It is a collection of short lyrics, very different in subject, tone, and quality. The third section is more unified, consisting of six longer poems divided into parts, predominantly elegiac in mood and mode. The next to last, "Freedom, New Hampshire," is a formal elegy for the poet's brother: personal, nostalgic, touching in its restraint of feeling and its refusal of any supernatural solution. In complement and contrast, the final poem in this section, "The Supper After the Last," treats death impersonally, as a problem in metaphysics. The poem enacts the transition from the mimetic to the visionary: it is centrally concerned with margins and horizons, and here real objects actually do blur and resolve towards deeper, stranger realities. A whitewashed house in sunlight, a jug of water and a chair, the blind cat and "red-backed passionate dog" are rendered with the precision of an Andrew Wyeth, only to be transmuted into a vista out of Dali:

> The witnesses back off; the scene begins to float in water;
> Far out in that mirage the Saviour sits whispering to the world,
> Becoming a mirage. The dog turns into a smear on the sand.
> The cat grows taller and taller as it flees into space.

When Kinnell had to select a poem for an anthology called *Poet's Choice,* he chose "Supper After the Last." It makes a fresh start: "I mean towards a poem without scaffolding or occasion, that progresses through images to a point where it can make a statement on a major subject." Such a poem must evolve its moment of insight in the act of its making: it is purely creative. Here, then, the shift from mimesis to vision is complete. If the book ended here, we could perhaps trace the Platonic structure which Kinnell observes in Bell's volume of poems, progressing from physical details to symbolic meanings, from concrete to abstract. But there remains a fourth section, which consists of a single poem, "The Avenue Bearing the Initial of Christ into the New World." And this poem too makes a fresh start. Kinnell acknowledges a debt to *The Waste Land* and to Baudelaire, but the most striking influence is that of Whitman. Here at last the real and ideal are not juxtaposed in contrast or set in transcendent sequence: they blend and mingle; they become one.

The import of this change is clear only on the level of meaning. But poetic meaning is elusive, and our statements about it must be tentative. Kinnell seems to be a religious poet without religion. That is, his intuitions of the sacred do not seem based on any credal affirmation or institutional faith. He was brought up a Congregationalist, but today he finds churches irrelevant. His notions of transcendence, he asserts, derive from Plato and the Transcendentalists, especially Thoreau. Christianity, like Yeats's *Vision,* serves as a source of imaginatively potent words and images, grounded in a total and consistent myth. It has two advantages over Yeats's system: Christianity is a public mythology; and in current literary usage, exploitation need not imply belief. But the matter is not all that simple. Kinnell's deep instinct for the suffering and rejected does not derive from Plato or Thoreau. The figure of Jesus haunts these poems. A short story called "The Permanence of Love" dramatizes this ambivalence in the encounter of the unbelieving protagonist and a nun—significantly a *petite soeur de Jésus*.

The same attraction and withdrawal are expressed in "First Communion" and "To Christ Our Lord," poems juxtaposed in the first section of *What a Kingdom It Was*. In "First Communion" a boy is repelled by the inadequacy of institutional religion and its rituals, the conjuration of Jesus into grape juice and "inferior bread." He tells Christ

> I would speak of injustice. . . .
> I would not go again into that place.

The world of nature, burning in late summer and late afternoon, offers a truer "parable" of death and continuity. "To Christ Our Lord" also contrasts dogma with natural parable. The "Christmas grace" is merely "long-winded," but in slaying and devouring a living creature, the boy experiences what he missed in his first communion. Love stirs within him even as he kills, but "There had been nothing to do but surrender, / To kill and eat; he ate as he had killed, with wonder."

> At night on snowshoes on the drifting field
> He wondered again, for whom had love stirred?
> The stars glittered on the snow and nothing answered.
> Then the Swan spread her wings, cross of the cold north,
> The pattern and mirror of the acts of earth.

Here Christianity and Platonism, "cross" and "pattern," seem to merge: the killing and eating is a sacrament, a finite repetition of the ideal, eternal act of sacrifice. Kinnell's title is the subtitle of "The Windhover," and his wild turkey, like Hopkins' falcon, is emblematic of "Christ Our Lord." But Hopkins' bird is most dangerous and beautiful in stooping, the descent into flesh. The boy in Kinnell's poem looks to the heavenly pattern, the disincarnate Swan. It is more than the difference between the heavenly Logos and the incarnate Christ: it is the difference between Christian incarnation and Platonic transcendence—the point at which Augustine found Platonism, the most Christian of pagan philosophies, to be unchristian.

In much of Kinnell's poetry, then, the intuition of the sacred sets matter against spirit, concrete against abstract. But working against this instinctive dualism is an equally instinctive kinship with all suffering, an impulse which finds expression in his short story as the wish to serve. Countering the upward spiral of transcendence, of the "flesh made word," his poetry also moves outward, horizontally, in sympathy with the commonest forms of life. This is the expanding consciousness of Whitman, who found the sacred not among the stars but in the streets. So in "The Avenue Bearing the Initial of Christ," the kingdom is realized among the perishing humanity of Avenue C. It is a vision of desolating ugliness. Kinnell has ceased to make claims for the beauty of life: "It seems to me now that to become one with a person, or thing, or event and to set it down in its fullness is itself sufficient, or transcends the need for making claims." So in this poem the poet has disappeared; the observer has become one with his subject; there is only the Avenue and the fullness and movement of its life. The tragic illumination of the poem does not come in any cumulative revelation but in "moments of transcendence" drifting in "oceans of loathing and fear," traffic lights blinking through darkness and rain. The representation of reality is uncompromising: walking up Avenue C today, one finds many of the signs Kinnell quotes—Blozstein's Cutrate Bakery, Little Rose Restaurant, Kugler's Chicken Store, Natural Bloom Cigars. But the holy is incarnate in the real. The fourteen divisions of the poem are the fourteen stations of the cross, down the fourteen intersections of Avenue C to the Power Station and East River at the end. So the word is made flesh: at the point where Christ meets Mary his mother, there appears a senile crone dispensing newspapers. Veronica's handkerchief is a stained grocery wrapper; the deposition is accomplished by a garbage truck. This is not symbolism but immanence: fish are simultaneously the traditional figure for Christ and actual gaping carp, crucified upon a wooden counter. An old rabbi is Jacob with his sons; even the vegetables in market carts are omens and images of our condition. The action of the poem is ordeal: as the devotee follows the stations of the cross, sharing in imagination the passion of Christ, so the observer—poet or reader—follows Avenue C. A day passes; the Avenue stretches "From the blind gut Pitt to the East River of Fishes"; and these motions in time and space become the archetype of all human movement. It is the life of man from darkness into dark, from the blind gut to the deep river. It is Israel in exile—the Jews, Negroes, Puerto Ricans who have become God's chosen people because they are despised and rejected of men—bearing, like the Avenue itself, the initial of the suffering man. "From the fourteenth station," writes Kinnell, "one looks back down the whole street and sees it transfigured, but also entirely real." In this transfiguration of reality, death and suffering are not transcended or denied. But against them is set the untiring laughter of the blood, the song of the Jews as they went out of their ghettos to destruction:

> In the nighttime
> Of the blood they are laughing and saying,
> Our little lane, what a kingdom it was!

Notes

    1.   Two significant misprints occur in this edition. In the next to last line of "The Supper After the Last" on p. 64, "Steps" should be "Step" (an imperative). In "The Avenue Bearing the Initial of Christ into the New World," the order of the fourth and fifth lines from the top of p. 83 has been reversed.

    2.   Quotations not from Mr. Kinnell's poems or essays are from conversation or correspondence with the author.

    3.   For all their realism, these poems should not be read as autobiographical. James R. Hurt has shown that the best known of them, "First Song," is based on a passage in *Wayfaring Stranger* by Burl Ives. See *The Explicator,* XX, No. 3 (November 1961), 23, and the references given there to previous discussions of the poem.

Galway Kinnell:
"Everything That May Abide the Fire Was Made to Go Through the Fire."

RICHARD HOWARD

When we speak, as in criticism we are bound and determined to do, of a man's *poetry*, we do a certain fond injustice to his *poems*. As readers, as men ourselves, it is our duty to acknowledge the supremacy of the poem not only over the poet*—our literary experience has taught us to suspect biography, to scorn the equation of soul with sonnet that would enable an Albert Schweitzer to write good ones and even *oblige* a Swinburne to have written bad ones—but over poetry itself. For the language speaks misleadingly of *poetry in general;* the word "poetry" refers poetic works to a form—ideal or abstract—which transcends in order to explain them, in order to judge them. This is not the case; the poem does not look to Poetry as to a power which is anterior to it and from which it must await its justification or even its existence. The poem is not the glow reflected from a constant star, it is not even the momentary manifestation of a power always superior to its works. To understand that the poem is the creative instrument, the primary force of discovery, is to understand that what is general depends on what is unique. A man's poetry, then, comes after the fact—the fact of his poems—and there is always something a little painful, a little patronizing in our collections of evidence, from a man's victories over the silence (or over speech, as the case may be, and was for Swinburne himself), toward that serene and uncontested unity: the poetry of, say, Galway Kinnell. If a poem, as Char once said, detaches itself convulsively from the world's body, then it is our task to account for the withdrawal symptoms.

Yet the reader, even the critical reader, is faced with the paradox of coming only *after* the poem that comes *before* the Poetry. He cannot help seeing

---

*"Perhaps a certain contempt for poetry," Galway Kinnell remarks of Villon's status as the prototype of the *poète maudit*, "is behind a preoccupation with a poet's life."

Reprinted with the permission of Atheneum Publishers, an imprint of Macmillan Publishing Company, from *Alone with America: Essays on the Art of Poetry in the United States since 1950*, enlarged edition, by Richard Howard 304–19. Original edition copyright © 1965, 1966, 1967, 1968, 1969 by Richard Howard. This enlarged edition copyright © 1980 by Richard Howard.

chiefly its engagements with the past—the past of the poet, and the past of all poetry. Of course it is because there is the poem that, for the poet, the future is possible—the poem is that movement toward what does not yet exist and, still more, the ecstasy of what is not granted, the appropriation of a mere possibility. But it is because there is Poetry, on the other hand, that the past is available to us as readers, as critics; and if I indulge a certain guilt upon instancing what the poetry of Galway Kinnell amounts to, if I admit that I am neglecting a little the travail of his poems in order to account for the triumph of his poetry, the culpability of my admission is relieved though not excused because, as a critic, I am committed to the past, the past which accommodates the existence of all of a man's poems taken together—as his poetry—rather than to the present which accommodates the existence of one poem, the poem I am reading (the domain, too, of the teacher), and rather than to the future which is enabled by the writing of the new poem (the domain of the poet alone).

The poetry of Galway Kinnell, then, is an Ordeal by Fire. It is fire which he invokes to set forth his plight, to enact his ordeal, and to restore himself to reality. It is fire—in its constant transformations, its endless resurrection—which *is* reality, for Kinnell as for Heraclitus: "The world is an ever-living fire, with measures of it kindling and measures of it going out." As the American poet translates this, it becomes:

> *And in the sky there burns this shifty jellyfish*
> *That degenerates and flashes and re-forms.*

And just as the pre-Socratic had affirmed that "all things are an exchange for fire, and fire for all things," so Kinnell muses, in his broken, aphoristic way that has so many analogies with the Greek's:

> *The invisible life of the thing*
> *Goes up in flames that are invisible*
> *Like cellophane burning in the sunlight.*
>
> *It burns up. Its drift is to be nothing.*
>
> *In its covertness it has a way*
> *Of uttering itself in place of itself . . .*

Yet there is a terrible and tremendous inflection in Galway Kinnell's pyromania, which we shall trace out in a moment, that altogether transforms his impulse from the orphic pitilessness of Heraclitus. When the Greek says, "Fire in its advance will judge and convict all things," there is awe but no tragedy in it, for there is no belief in incarnation. But when Kinnell evokes mortality as a commitment to the fire, there is an unappeasable grief in his "heart's hell": it is the grief of history, the pain of things happening once and once only, irreversibly,* that is the burden of Christianity, of the Incarnation:

> . . . It is true
> That only flesh dies, and spirit flowers without stop
> For men, cows, dung, for all dead things; and it is good, yes—
>
> But an incarnation is in particular flesh
> And the dust that is swirled into a shape
> And crumbles and is swirled again had but one shape
> That was this man. When he is dead the grass
> Heals what he suffered, but he remains dead,
> And the few who loved him know this until they die.

Between Heraclitus, then, and Kinnell the agonized Believer who remarks, in *Black Light,* of his abject hero: "It was as if his virtue, his very devotion to God, were succeeding where vice had failed, in making an atheist out of him"—the proper mediator, the exegetical figure that will set us coursing over Kinnell's burning landscape in search of clues to the resurrection is, of course, Hopkins, the Hopkins who in his sonnet "That Nature is a Heraclitean Fire and of the comfort of the Resurrection" watched while "Million-fueled nature's bonfire burns on" and declared that the "world's wildfire leaves but ash / in a flash, at a trumpet's crash."** The agony of that knowledge—the knowledge or at least the conviction that all must be consumed in order to be reborn, must be reduced to ash in order to be redeemed—gives Galway Kinnell's poetry its astonishing resonance, the accents of a conflict beyond wisdom as it is beyond piety: "I don't know what you died of," one of the characters in his novel says, "whatever it was, that is what will bring you alive again."

Before collecting our evidences of arson, it might be well to account for the use of quotations from *all* of Kinnell's works indifferently: the three volumes of poetry, *What a Kingdom It Was* (1960), *Flower Herding on Mount Monadnock* (1964), and *Body Rags* (1968), the translation of the poems of François Villon, with an Introduction (1965), and the short novel or *récit, Black Light* (1966). Kinnell is one of those writers insistently present in all his forms, and therefore unlikely to discriminate powerfully among them: his poetry has, as

---

*Kinnell dramatizes this situation, the suffering brought about by Nature's irreversibility, in his novel *Black Light:* "He looked at the leaves again. How would it be, he thought, if one of them, even an unimportant one, should wither of its own free will and creep back into the limb?"

**One of the opening poems in Kinnell's first book takes for its title the dedication of Hopkins' "Windhover": "To Christ Our Lord," and the poem ends with a characteristic Hopkins vision of "inscape":

> Then the Swan spread her wings, cross of the cold north,
> The pattern and mirror of the acts of earth.

noted, a jagged aphoristic thrust without much patience for rhythmic consecution or, after the first poems, for regularity of rhyme. The prose, on the other hand, is heavy with hypnotic cadences, and likely to be the vehicle for a more evidently "poetic" manner than Kinnell will permit himself in his verse: "that is the way with poetry," he remarks in the novel: "when it is incomprehensible it seems profound, and when you do understand it, it is only ridiculous." I take my license to look beyond any formal enclosure for the revealing utterance from Kinnell himself, then, who in presenting his plain version of Villon, without rhyme or regular meters, observes: "It may be that in our day these formal devices have become a dead hand, which it is just as well not to lay on any poetry." Upon such suspicion may be based a highly various practice, as is the case with Kinnell's work—it is not a body of work susceptible of too intent a formal scrutiny. Let us recall merely that, as in his efforts with Villon, Kinnell is concerned "to keep the poetry factual, harsh and active."

The fire opens Kinnell's first book, where it is seen benevolently enough as the vital energy of earthly things:

> Cold wind stirs, and the last green
> Climbs to all the tips of the season, like
> The last flame brightening on a wick.
> Embers drop and break in sparks . . .

The sense of the self-consuming candle as the characteristic avatar of flame is one that will remain with Kinnell to the end—as in *Black Light,* where he speaks, about to blow out the candle, of "the point of the flame, that shifting instant where the flame was turning into pure spirit." Even in this early poem, "First Communion," the fire is seen not only as vital impulse, but as the agent of transmutation, the "last flame" moving up the wick of the trees until they are burnt away to "pure spirit." Then comes the poem called "Burning," the anecdote of a man of the woods who kills the dog that has saved him from drowning, buries it, and goes back into his shack to sleep, leaving the speaker to watch:

> I saw him sleepless in the pane of glass
> Looking wild-eyed at sunset, then the glare
> Blinded the glass—only a red square
> Burning a house burning in the wilderness.

Here the notion of the universal conflagration is more subtly diffused, not only in the sunset that gives all things fire's color ("a red square burning a house burning"), but in the particulars of aberrant human conduct ("a house burning in the wilderness")—it is the man inside, his conscience and his craziness, that are given the appropriate outer emblem by the setting sun reflected on the glass. Between this poem and the next to rehearse Kinnell's fiery theme, intervene a pair of studies in primitivism, "The Wolves" and "West-port," where life's cautery is only obliquely touched on—shooting buffalo in the days of the great herds ("I fired . . . He looked, trotted off, and became dead"), and the look of the land after a storm ("a red streak in the west lit all the raindrops . . . and the shining grasses were bowed towards the west as if one craving had killed them"). It is of course the craving of fire, as murderous as any gunpowder, that Kinnell sees in the west; in a further poem, "Lilacs," he sees that craving not only in the sun's red decline, but in the day's very warmth:

> . . . Down the south slope
> A bitch stretched, and swaths of fierce lilacs
> Opened astonishing furnaces of scent . . .

> . . . The blossoms climbed
> And blazed in the air . . .

The nuance of sexuality is added to the mere growth of animals and plants, and in this poem the woman subject to the "burning" lilacs, "her dry legs crackling in darkness," is drawn into the universal fire, "the hot scent of her-self beating herself out of closets in the well-governed flesh." The recognition of sensual riot, "the nestfire of roses," is another emblem of destruction for Kinnell, one that will obsess him in later work. But at this point in his first book, he is concerned to come, still, to terms with his given faith: in "Easter," one of Kinnell's most successful poems in his earlier, "formal" manner, the death of a nurse, "raped, robbed, weighted, drowned," is conjugated with the Easter service, "the extensive sermon, the outcry of the inaudible prayer"; speculating on the rotting body, "trapped or working loose," and on the mys-tery of Christ's rising, the poet promises to crown the victim with an "Easter Fire" as the "brown water shoves [her] senselessly on past smoking cities, works of disaster"; he urges her to turn her "unwavering gaze" on "the dream you lived through":

> It is as you thought. The living burn.
> In the floating days may you discover grace.

Life is just that continuous conflagration ("the smoking cities") which it is Christianity's effort to transcend by a final "Easter Fire." The beautiful, tenta-tive last line ("In the floating days . . .") of this carefully joined poem sug-gests, though, that no such glory waits for us, victims rather than victors of death this Easter. The living burn, and the dead, if they are lucky, merely dis-solve.

That vision of burning and drowning together is extended in "Alewives Pool," which begins:

> *We lay on the grass and gazed down and heard*
> *The world burning on the pulse of April . . .*

and which ends with an eloquent vision of the possibilities of transfiguration, once the mortal flesh has been consumed away by the processes of life itself:

> *In the trees even the birds are astonished*
> *By the fierce passion of their song. The mind*
> *Can only know what love has accomplished*
> *When love has consumed it in the burning pond.*
>
> *Now on the trembling pulse let death and birth*
> *Beat in the self as in the April grass—*
> *The sudden summer that the air flames forth*
> *Makes us again into its blossomers—*
> *Stand on the pulse and love the burning earth.*

The ecstasy of knowing oneself a part of the world's *physis,* of knowing that within oneself there is the same pulse on which "the world burns," the radiant interchange between mind and love, between body and earth, between water and fire, is here registered in Kinnell's happiest key, when Being is so wrought up in its oneness of possibilities—"the air flames forth"—that a man's "days to come flood on his heart as if they were his past."

It is an easier thing, I suppose, merely to report the world in conflagration without insisting on an engagement of identity, without being rigorously *in question.* Easier or not—and in any case, the act of *seeing* the world as on fire, consuming itself away to a transfigured life, is certainly an involvement of a heroic order—some of the "nature poems" of this book have allowed Kinnell a delicacy in his art that he shrinks from when his persona is committed. "Leaping Falls," an account of a frozen cascade, reveals the diction of a poet who can, when he chooses, enact by the movement of language on the lips and in the mind the very transaction—distinct yet expanding, icy yet intense—he would rehearse in vision:

> *. . . A topmost icicle came loose*
> *And fell, and struck another*
> *With a bell-like sound, and*
> *Another, and the falls*
> *Leapt at their ledges, ringing*
> *Down the rocks and on each other*
>
> *Like an outbreak of bells*
> *That rings and ceases.*
> *The silence turned around*

> *And became silence again.*
> *Under the falls on the snow*
> *A twigfire of icicles burned pale blue.*

There is a wonderful play of contraries here, sound and silence, liquid and solid, heat and freezing, ice and flame—but they are resolved in a place beyond contraries, at a moment of vision, and at that moment the "fire of icicles burned pale blue." It is the ecstatic moment the surrealists were always trying for, when the conventional notions of opposites no longer stood opposed, but worked toward a transcendence where up and down, hot and cold, stillness and motion ceased to gainsay each other, and a man's existence glowed into a kind of godhead—this is what Kinnell means, or it is one of the things he means, by "burning."

Of course he is easier about it than that, sometimes; sometimes it is merely a notation of intensity he wishes to record, existence not transfigured, but merely heightened:

> *. . . the duck took off,*
> *Skimmed the swells as it ascended,*
> *Brown wings burning and flashing*
> *In the sun as the sea it rose over*
> *Burned and flashed beneath it.*

Yet if this is not a major instance of Kinnell's igneous reading of the world, it is significant that the conjugation of water and fire is here enlarged from the alewives pool and the frozen falls to the sea itself that is said to burn. It is as though the poet were reaching for Heraclitus' great truth, as he enlarged his focus like a burning glass: "The transformations of Fire are, first of all, the sea . . ." reads one of the Heraclitean fragments, and in Kinnell's second book, one of his most arresting poems—a kind of nature-log, "Tilamook Journal," in which the poet stares at "the Burn as it went out in the twilight, its crags broken, its valleys soaked in night"—comes to its triumphant conclusion: "It is only steps to the unburnable sea." Unburnable because it is the one thing that cannot be transformed, being already all transformation. Unburnable because it is always burning.

But to continue with *What a Kingdom It Was,* and Kinnell's fire sermon as he develops it, poem by poem: one of the most ambitious poems in the collection, "Seven Streams of Nevis," memorializes seven ruined lives the poet invokes as he climbs Ben Nevis. Speaking of one of these friends, Sir Henry, Kinnell observes that he

> *Decided fire brings out the best*
> *In things, and that anyone who*
> *Has cooked his eyes at the sunrise*
> *Of beauty, and thumbed himself blind, is wise.*

Though merely a characterization, we have had enough clues from the poet to take such wisdom to heart. Especially when, on the top of the mountain, in one of those moments where contraries are resolved,

> *Where merely to be still was temperate,*
> *Where to move was brave, where justice was a glide,*
> *Knowledge the dissolving of the head-hung eyes;*
> *There my faith lay burning, there my hope*
> *Lay burning on the water, there charity*
> *Burned like a sun.*

So even the theological virtues are seen enkindled, sun and water united in the same drastic combustion: "In the heart's hell you have it; call it God's Love." And in the last and longest poem in the book, "The Avenue Bearing the Initial of Christ into the New World," where Kinnell turns on New York's Lower East Side the incandescent scrutiny of a visionary, the religious tenor of the burning is given its most explicit, almost ritual voice. After a few decorative notes, like describing the pushcart vegetables in terms of his old antinomies: "Icicle-shaped carrots that through black soil wove away like flames in the sun"—Kinnell warms to his theme:

> *Children set fires in ashbarrels,*
> *Cats prowl the fires, scraps of fishes burn.*
>
> *A child lay in the flames.*
> *It was not the plan. Abraham*
> *Stood in terror at the duplicity.*
> *Isaac whom he loved lay in the flames . . .*
>
> *The children laugh.*
> *Isaac means* he laughs.
> *Maybe the last instant*
> *The dying itself,* is easier . . .

Only the pain of such sacrifice, here in "the living streets, where instants of transcendence drift in oceans of loathing and fear," can redeem the Fallen City,

> *Burning in the night, flames opening out like*
> *Eyelashes from the windows . . .*
> *   But this evening*
> *The neighborhood comes out again, everything*
> *That may abide the fire was made to go through the fire*
> *And it was made clean.*

From there, the poem goes on in an ecstasy of accountability, for whatever Kinnell sees—and he sees everything:

The garbage disposal truck
Like a huge hunched animal
That sucks in garbage in the place
Where other animals evacuate it
Whines, as the cylinder in the rear
Threshes up the trash and garbage,
Where two men in rubber suits
(It must be raining outside)
Heap it in. The groaning motor
Rises in a whine as it grinds in
The garbage, and between-times
Groans. It whines and groans again . . .
If it is raining outside
You can tell only by looking
In puddles, under the lifted streetlamps.
It would be the spring rain.

—has gone through that refining fire, has been *made clean.* By his ransacked, purified, literally inflamed imagination, Kinnell is able to ransom his world, having reached in his most sustained effort that place where everything which is is blessed.

It is no easy thing to write a sequel to the apocalypse, and one feels, often, about Kinnell's second book, *Flower Herding on Mount Monadnock,* something of the strain, the broken impulse that commands the versification as well as the patchy moments of pyrophany. The moments come, though; after a pair of grim poems on the port of New York, "The River That Is East" and "The Homecoming of Emma Lazarus," Kinnell turns to the Statue of Liberty itself:

The Lady stands by herself
Her electrical hand on fire . . .
. . . her hand, burning,
Hair, flesh, blood, bone.

Facing the Old World, the statue burns, an emblem of the Redeemed City, though only an emblem—"it fades, and the wounds of all we had accepted open." The theme returns, each time "the sun's swath of reality" falls "on the objects of faith, buildings, rocks, birds, oranges"—returns, for example, in Kinnell's tribute to Robert Frost, which begins with the natural world, "a farm, a countryside, a woodpile in its slow smokeless burning," as the poet of "Fire and Ice" had put it, and moves to a vision of Frost himself

Who dwelt in access to that which other men
Have burnt all their lives to get near . . .

acknowledging that there is a point of the flame to which we aspire, a point where all that is "vain" is refined away, and the flame "turns into pure spirit":

> *. . . And from the same doorway*
> *At which you lived, between the house and the woods,*
> *We see your old footprints going away across*
> *The great Republic, Frost, up memorized slopes,*
> *Down hills floating by heart on the bulldozed land.*

There follow, as if like Frost this poet would "set up in the wilderness of his country," a considerable number of poems of the woods, where the "junco flames up from the junkpile" and life consumes itself. As in his more violent vision of the transfigured city, Kinnell sees the natural world redeemed ("the song of the whippoorwill stops and the dimension of depth seizes everything"), and of course it is redeemed by fire, though a slower fire, not one that must be kindled in pain and sacrifice, but consented to as a natural process:

> *I wake in the night,*
> *An old ache in the shoulder blades.*
> *I lie amazed under the trees*
> *That creak a little in the dark,*
> *The giant trees of the world.*
>
> *I lie on earth the way*
> *Flames lie in the woodpile . . .*

Holding up a shell, "fan of gold light," to the sun, the poet sees "as it blazes, the lost life within, alive again in the fate-shine." These are the moments of sanctity, a kind of Godless stigmatization as the poet looks and listens:

> *Turning and craning in the vines*
> *I can make out through the leaves*
> *The old, shimmering nothingness, the sky.*

By the time he gets to the title poem at the end of this short book, Kinnell has earned for himself what he says of Villon in the introduction to his "factual, harsh, and active" version: "He writes in a passion for reality and a deep anguish at its going . . . it is a cry not only over the brevity of existence and the coming of dark, but also over this dying life, this life so horrified by death and so deeply in need of it." In the final section of "Flower Herding," a ten-part journal of natural devotions, Galway Kinnell makes his penultimate accommodation of the life that is being consumed in the fire—it is an accommodation so transfigured that it can be expressed, finally, in a few simple declarative sentences, the ecstatic constatation of the death that is in being, the being that is in death:

> *In the forest I discover a flower.*
>
> *The invisible life of the thing*
> *Goes up in flames that are invisible*
> *Like cellophane burning in the sunlight.*
>
> *It burns up. Its drift is to be nothing.*
>
> *In its covertness it has a way*
> *Of uttering itself in place of itself,*
> *Its blossoms claim to float in the Empyrian,*
>
> *A wrathful presence on the blur of the ground.*
>
> *The appeal to heaven breaks off.*
> *The petals begin to fall, in self-forgiveness.*
> *It is a flower. On this mountainside it is dying.*

After the fire, then, a still small voice. Humbled, reduced, but reduced in the sense of *intensified,* concentrated rather than diminished, life, having passed through what Arnold called "the gradual furnace of the world," life for Galway Kinnell becomes a matter of sacred vestiges, remnants, husks—as he says in his third book of poems published in 1968, *Body Rags.* Consider, from the titles alone, the emblematic leavings, survivals of the initiating arson: "Another Night in the Ruins," "Lost Loves," "The Fossils," "The Correspondence School Instructor Says Goodbye to His Poetry Students," "Last Songs," "Testament of the Thief," "One Who Used to Beat His Way." In all of these, whether testifying as in "The Last River" to the destructive glory of human society ("the air brightens as though ashes / of lightning bolts had been scattered through it"), or observing as in "The Burn" the merest dissolving appearances of the elements ("on these beaches / the sea throws itself down, in flames"), the poet has kept faith with his own fires:

> *On ashes of old volcanoes*
> *I lie dreaming,*
> *baking*
> *the deathward flesh in the sun . . .*
>
> *And yet I can rejoice*
> *that everything changes, that*
> *we go from life*
> *into life,*

and enter ourselves
quaking
like the tadpole, his time come, tumbling toward the slime.

In these poems of astonishing metamorphosis, Kinnell has been concerned to enact, by his "dance of solitude" as he calls the shaman's performance in "The Bear," to articulate the truth of Goethe's great dictum: One learns nothing, but one becomes something. Ever larger in these late poems bulks or—for bulk is not what we get, but rather a flickering ballet around the circumference of what is guessed at in the darkness—breaks in upon us the awareness that in order to achieve transformation the ritual imagination of burning must in our time be abjured for a natural process, with all its attendant waste and weariness: "our faces smudged with light from the fingertips of the ages." It is a sacred flame Kinnell tends:

> *I can hear*
> *a mountain brook*
> *and somewhere blood winding*
> *down its ancient labyrinths. And*
> *a few feet away*
> *charred stick-ends surround*
> *a bit of ashes, where burnt-out vanished flames*
> *absently*
> *waver, absently leap*

—but not, or no longer, a magical one, no longer a pure transfiguring blaze but, like his "smudged" poems, a tragic flare, "a palimpsest, streaked / with erasures, smelling / of departure and burnt stone"—as is revealed by the poet's renunciation of the myth of the phoenix:

> *How many nights must it take*
> *one such as me to learn*
> *that we aren't, after all, made*
> *of the bits of that bird*
> *which creates itself again*
> *in its ashes,*
> *that for a man*
> *as he goes up in flames, his one work*
> *is to open himself, to be the flames?*

It is interesting to see that in his final version of these last lines, Kinnell literally opens himself, breaking apart the language until it illustrates the aperient nature of all such poetry:

> *that for a man*
> *as he goes up in flames, his one work*

> *is*
> *to open himself, to* be
> *the flames?*

These further poems, then, in their licking rhythms, their ragged edges that "break in gold, frankincense and myrrh" like Kinnell's rooster that

> *thrashes in the snow*
> *for a grain. Finds*
> *it. Rips*
> *it into*
> *flames. Flaps. Crows.*
> *Flames*
> *bursting out of his brow—*

these fiery fragments "breathing the burnt odor / of old rocks" quite literally hand on the torch Kinnell has been carrying for a life redeemed:

> *the drifting sun that gives us our lives,*
> *seed dazzled over the footbattered blaze of the earth,*

and for a death transfigured:

> *that sticky infusion, that rank flavor of blood, that*
> *poetry, by which I lived.*

The formal attentions bestowed upon such utterances are by now no more than the bandages for first-degree burns. In "this poem, or chopped prose" of his, what Kinnell wants is not the emollient hands of the nurse, but the fierce dedication of the Vestal:

> *flowers brightening about you,*
> *the skills of fire, of fanning*
> *the blossoms until they die . . .*

The lines are as unique and therefore as perishable, in the strong sense, as flames: not enduring but *changing*, treating reality transitively, and expressly kindled for the fiery impulse they enact:

> *On some hill of despair*
> *the bonfire*
> *you kindle can light the great sky—*
> *though it's true, of course, to make it burn*
> *you have to throw yourself in.*

The Poetry of Galway Kinnell

JANE TAYLOR [McDONNELL]

A speaking voice—genial, reflective, generous—is very much evident in the poems of Galway Kinnell. He neither strives for the objectivity which presents "things" unrelated by rhetorical and narrative connectives, nor does he speak through assumed masks or personae. Perhaps the most pleasing thing about Mr. Kinnell is his simple confidence in the power and sufficiency of his perceptions: in his whole–hearted commitment to what he is saying, one never finds a labored casting about for meaning and significance, nor the kind of evasive and deprecating self-scrutiny which ends in contempt for self and others. Kinnell's poems are expressive, outspoken, exuberant, informal. His language is almost entirely one of praise; few poems are exercises in anger, invective, sarcasm, or scorn. In this poems he continually shows a complex and thoughtful appreciation for the diversity of life, and repeatedly asserts his capacity for wonder.

Many of Kinnell's poems are about exploration, discovery, and vision. Most often they concern the poet's exploration of the natural world, of "primitive" nature (mountains, unsettled plains, sea coasts, deserts, fields and woods in snow). Frequently the challenge of exploring and living in a kind of wilderness incites the poet to thought and feeling, to an inner "voyage of discovery." A number of his poems are travel poems—about setting forth, arrival, return. Often the poet's reflections are those of a man on a promontory or high place, or of a man who has just arrived somewhere or found something.

A sense of place almost always provides the occasion for and defines the nature of Kinnell's perceptions. These are poems of places much more than of people and events. The titles of his two books—*What a Kingdom It Was* and *Flower Herding on Mount Monadnock*—indicate the importance of location, and most of his poems are carefully "placed" in the first lines: "I find it now, the schoolhouse by the tree"; "And so it was I sheered, / Eccentric into outer space"; "We came to visit the cow / Dying of fever"; "All day under acrobat / Swallows I have sat." There is a large descriptive and narrative element in these poems, which are seldom devoted to an exploration of a static

This essay first appeared in *Perspective: A Quarterly of Literature* 15 (1968): 189–200. Reprinted by permission of the author.

situation or a single perception, but usually trace the poet's progress of understanding—often through several parts or sections. These "part" poems are divided into as many as ten sections (usually numbered and more separable than stanzas). In them Kinnell can explore a complex attitude toward a given situation, can approach the meaning of the poem through several avenues of address, points of view, or stages of understanding.

In his best poems this method provides for a rich and complex understanding of his subject—an understanding which is possible only through dramatic development. These poems aren't just the "results" of an experience, but give the several responses (simultaneous or successive, sometimes even contradictory), which constitute the experience. In the less successful poems, however, the "part" method accounts for a certain fragmentariness, irresolution and thinness. Kinnell is occasionally content to set side by side unresolved, briefly seen moments, assuming, perhaps too easily, that one explains another or carries its meaning further. Taken together, the sections hardly make up for their separate thinness (see, for instance, "On Frozen Fields," "A Bird Comes Back," and "Nightfall of the Real" in *Flower Herding*).

Kinnell almost always creates within the bounds of the natural order; a natural setting easily becomes a mental landscape:

> The trees in clouds of November mist
> Standing empty and the massive earth bare
> I bent my head and leaned myself against
> Interior gales and blizzards of unrest
> Bucking the squalor of November air
> ("Earth-Sparrow")

> We lay on the grass and gazed down and heard
> The world burning on the pulse of April,
> And were so shaken and stirred, so cut, we wondered
> Which things may we forget and which recall?
> ("Alewives Pool")

> And so it was I sheered,
> Eccentric, into outer space,
> And tracked with lost paces
> The forgotten journey of a child
> ("Leaping Falls")

In many poems the dominant myth is that of the land itself. Often the poet deliberately "submits" himself to the natural world: he sets forth into unsettled land, land which both invites and frustrates attempts at exploration and discovery. In these poems the poet approaches his meaning gradually, characteristically through passages of description, association and memory. Usually only the conclusions to the poems are highly metaphoric, using the materials of the landscape and interpreting them as analogies to the discovered meaning in the poet's own inner voyage:

> I know that I love the day,
> The sun on the mountain, the Pacific
> Shiny and accomplishing itself in breakers,
> But I know I live half alive in the world,
> I know half my life belongs to the wild darkness.
> ("Middle of the Way")

> Fields into which the limping Herdsman wades
> Leading his flock up the trackless night, towards
> A writhing of lights. Are they Notre Dame des Neiges
> Where men ask their God for the daily bread—
> Or the March-climbing Virgin carrying wheat?
> Where the track vanishes the first land begins.
> It goes out everywhere obliterating the horizons.
> We must have been walking through it all our lives.
> ("Where the Track Vanishes")

> No, it is the River that is East, known once
> From a high window in Brooklyn, in agony—river
> On which a door locked to the water floats,
> A window sash paned with brown water, a whiskey crate,
> Barrel staves, sun spokes, feathers of the birds,
> A breadcrust, a rat, spittle, butts, and peals,
> The immaculate stream, heavy, and swinging home again.
> ("The River That is East")

In one poem this love of exploration and longing for the wilderness takes the form of a search for the lost and difficult land of bondage. In "Towards the Wilderness" a man treks the desert:

> His plan is to look over the far side
> Of the hill on which Moses died looking this way,
> And to see the bitter land, and to die of desire.

The traveler, unregenerate, unsaved, unchosen, "uncivilized," dies of desire for the lost land of bondage—for the wilderness.

In "Westport" it is the very difficulty of a journey across a prairie which commends it to the speaker: "the hardness is the thing you thank." The speaker and his companions put behind them "the forest that half a continent away . . . met our fathers on the Atlantic shore," but the prairie is like the ocean which was crossed with such difficulty by the early settlers of this country: it shifts like an ocean "swell upon swell"; wolves are like porpoises or flying fish, breaching and falling; the travelers are like small craft; the rain falls in a squall. In this poem the speaker and his companions merely "overlook the changes on the world"; they do not "cling" to the land and the land doesn't make them a part of itself. The speaker addresses the wild prairie flowers:

> We toss ahead
> Of you in the wild rain, and we barely touch
> The sad ambages compassed for yourselves.

The poem's resolution (as with so many of Kinnell's poems) is that of a thing well seen, experienced and understood: from a "dark" afternoon comes a "bright evening" and "out of evening we discover night." Kinnell has great confidence in the power of careful description—as the way of understanding the significant aspects of a scene or occasion, as the means toward composed self-understanding and control over the evoked experience. He relies on language both in its suggestive and connotative aspects, and as simple naming and defining. To name something is close to evoking it in prayer, as Kinnell notes in the playful conclusion to "On Hardscrabble Mountain":

> On the way down, passing
> The little graveyard in the woods,
> I gave a thought to the old skulls and bones lying there,
>
> And I started praying to a bear just shutting his eyes
> To a skunk dozing off,
> To a marmot with yellow belly,
> To a dog-faced hedgehog,
> To a dormouse with a paunch and large ears like leaves of wings.

A corollary of this confidence in language carefully and honestly used is the poet's reluctance to see too much significance, to claim too much meaning for a scene or event. Sometimes the most truthful statements one can make are also the simplest. To Kinnell a balanced understanding of something is often one which does not treat that thing as an emblem, interpreting it in terms of some "higher" reality exclusively. A thing is itself, no matter how it may be seen, and Kinnell is perhaps most concerned to see the individual and essential character, the *quidditas* of a thing—as in the beautifully balanced conclusion to "Flower Herding on Mount Monadnock":

> In the forest I discover a flower.
>
> The invisible life of the thing
> Goes up in flames that are invisible
> Like cellophane burning in the sunlight.
>
> It burns up. Its drift is to be nothing.

In its covertness it has a way
Of uttering itself in place of itself,
Its blossoms claim to float in the Empyrean,

A wrathful presence on the blur of the ground.

The appeal to heaven breaks off.
The petals begin to fall, in self-forgiveness.
It is a flower. On this mountainside it is dying.

Many of the poems in which vision, seeing a thing carefully and well, is the dominant motive and subject, take place on a promontory, on the side of a mountain or hill, where the poet can overlook the "changes on the world." "Alewives Pool," "Where the Track Vanishes," "Westport," "On Hardscrabble Mountain," and "Tillamook Journal" are such poems. "Tillamook Journal" (which is like many poems not titled "journal," but which have the structure of notebook or diary entries—separate notations which are rather subtly associated through the presence of the writer) is fairly typical of these poems. The speaker, having explored a mined, stripped and eroded wasteland where "Gigantic tree trunks / Barricade all the directions," climbs to the top of Cedar Butte. The poem ends with his vision of the plundered land and the indestructable sea:

Its crags broken,
Its valleys soaked in night,
Just one more of the
Plundered breasts of the world—
And hearing my heart
Beat in the air
I come over the last summit
Into a dark wind
Blasting out of the darkness,
Where before me the tempestuous ocean
Falls with long triple crashes on the shore
And where behind the snow is putting down
A last, saprophytic blossoming.
It is only steps to the unburnable sea.

In "The Descent" the search for meaning is again associated with mountain-climbing, but here (as the title indicates) the search ends in frustration and disillusionment. In this poem the death of a mountain climbing friend (ironically facing the setting moon at sunrise) and the wanton killing of a crow are two unappeased deaths which the poet must question and investigate within their natural setting:

And had I faced Jan to the sun
Might not the sun have held him here?
Or did he know the day came on
Behind, not glancing back for fear
The moon already was dragging from his bones
The blood as dear to them, and as alien,

As the suit of clothes to a scarecrow
Or the flesh to a cross?

The place (Indian Hill) where the poet as a boy killed, ceremonially washed, and buried a crow, is returned to later. But it offers merely further mysteries of the flesh (in ironic incarnation, crucifixion and atonement images):

I looked for Indian Hill at Easter.
It was bulldozed. A TV cross
Gleamed from the rooftop of a house
Like sticks of a scarecrow. Once more
I turned and ran for spring: I stumbled on
Fields lying dark and savage and the sun

Reaping its own fire from the trees,
Whirling the faint panic of birds
Up turbulent light. Two white-haired
Crows cried under the wheeling rays;
And loosed as by a scythe, into the sky
A flight of jackdaws rose, earth-birds suddenly

Seized by some thaumaturgic thirst,
Shrill wings flung up the crow-clawed, burned,
Unappeasable air. And one turned,
Dodged through the flock again and burst
Eastward alone, sinking across the wood
On the world-curve of its wings. Nor do we know why,

Mirrored in duskfloods, the fisherbird
Seems to stand in a desolate sky
Feeding at its own heart. In the cry
Eloi! Eloi! flesh made word:

We hear it in wind catching in the trees,
In lost blood breaking a night through the bones.

These ironic images of the resurrection—the cross like a scarecrow or TV aerial, the jackdaws which remain "earth-birds" even though "Seized by some thaumaturgic thirst," the fisherbird (or Kingfisher, an "emblem" of Christ) which stands in a desolate sky "feeding at its own heart" (not nourishing others from its pierced breast)—refuse to yield consolation to the poet.

Here and in a number of other poems, Kinnell attempts to establish the possibility of the holy in an unholy world. The secular wonder which informs so many of his poems sometimes takes the form of a religious inquiry—in which religious images can only be used ironically. Other poems ("The Avenue Bearing the Initial of Christ into the New World," "First Communion," "To Christ our Lord," "Easter," "The Supper After the Last"—all poems from Kinnell's first volume of verse) explore the religious or sacramental attitude ironically. "Easter," which takes as its occasion the rape and drowning of a virgin nurse the night before Easter, examines the way this "morning news" is received on Easter morning by churchgoers who "regret they rose at all" to "die" on "the hard wood of the pews" listening to the "disinfected voice" of the minister. Although the poem begins with an ironic parallel between reality and religious vision, it ends by trying to establish a sacramental mood—but in human terms. The poet addresses the girl:

> Do not, moved by goodbyes, be altogether sorry
>
> That the dream has ended. Turn
> On the dream you lived through the unwavering gaze.
> It is as you thought. The living burn.
> In the floating days may you discover grace.

The conclusion of the poem is an unconvincing attempt to find consolation through Christian language used ironically in an un-Christian context. The experience of Easter is lost for the churchgoers and the poet's response remains just a response to a stranger's story in a newspaper: it does not help to try to create pity, sorrow and compassion through ironically in-applicable Christian imagery. The realism and irony of the rest of the poem do not permit the wishfulness of the conclusion: "In the floating days may you discover grace."

This poem is fairly representative of the failing of a number of Kinnell's "Christian" poems. The experience of Christianity cannot be re-invoked or its loss lamented by punning on Christian imagery (as in the congregation regrets "they rose at all" to "die" on the "hard wood of the pews"). In a more recent poem called "The Poem" Kinnell includes this passage:

> On a branch
> in the morning light
> lying on its back at the tip of an icicle,
> the letter C
> comes into being—trembles,
> to drop? or to cling?

> A roman carapace glitters all over it:
> "icicle" hails
> itself the fourth stroke in.

These "visual puns" and puns on words are, of course, accidental: it takes strong conviction on the part of the poet to hold the comparison together. The puns are often just attempts to give an air of consequence, to endow with interest or meaning, an occasion which has lost (or never had) a religious dimension.

Although Kinnell has written a number of short poems giving a single perception or observation, his more usual method is to give a series of notes or small observations on a particular scene, to examine a scene for its several implications which are given in separate sections. In "The Descent," for example, the experience of one death is understood in light of another and both gain significance when re-considered in the quest which ends the poem. "The River That is East" is fairly typical of this method: here the poet examines the scene for its implications for two opposed comprehending personalities—the dreaming boy and the disillusioned older man who still responds simply—and he then resolves this dialectic in his own vision of the river. The river is in part the river of memory, once known "in agony," now the "River that is East" moving into the future, the "immaculate stream, heavy, and swinging home again."

Kinnell begins this poem typically with a passage of description. Buoys, tugs, a carfloat, the Navy Yard, the Williamsburg Bridge, and the Jamaica Local are described. The whole is at first a "chaos of illusions" through which gulls "sideslip" "dangling limp red hands, and screaming as they touch." Concentrating on the gulls, the poet "wakes" to the "reality" of the scene; they are the detail which arrests his attention and leads him into the scene. The second section describes the boy who is like other boys by a river dreaming "of the Huck Finns of themselves." The poet evokes the American dreamers—Citizen Kane, Jay Gatsby, Nick Adams, Eugene Gant—those who went "baying after the immaterial." The third section is devoted to the man on the pier who "has long since stopped wishing his heart were full / Or his life dear to him," but who can still wish he were a gull to "fly out over the water, explode, and / Be beautiful snow hitting the dirty water." The poet concludes this youth / age, dreamer / cynic dialectic with a paeon addressed to the river which, in spite of the debris it carries, is immaculate:

> And thou, River of Tomorrow, flowing . . .
> We stand on the shore, which is mist beneath us,
> And regard the onflowing river. Sometimes
> It seems the river stops and shore
> Flows into the past. Nevertheless, its leaked promises
> Hopping in the bloodstream, we strain for the future,

Sometimes even glimpse it, a vague, scummed thing
We dare not recognize, and peer again
At the cabled shroud out of which it came,
We who have no roots but the shift of our pain,
No flowering but our own strange lives.

What is this river but the one
Which drags the things we love,
Processions of debris like floating lamps,
Towards the radiance in which they go out?

No, it is the River that is East, known once
From a high window in Brooklyn, in agony—river
On which a door locked to the water floats,
A window sash paned with brown water, a whiskey crate,
Barrel staves, sun spokes, feathers of the birds,
A breadcrust, a rat, spittle, butts, and peels,
The immaculate stream, heavy, and swinging home again.

Kinnell concludes this "part" poem with an imaginative resolution: he has come to terms with the scene, achieved a composed state of mind, an affectionate understanding of the external and internal materials of the experience.

This affectionate understanding of an experience is the purpose of most of Kinnell's poems. He frequently writes meditative exercises, examining a scene for its implications, following the ebb and flow of thought, approaching his meaning gradually through deliberate scene-construction and reflection. His poems are meditative as some of Wallace Stevens' are: poems "of the act of the mind," "of the mind in the act of finding / What will suffice."

In writing such meditative poems, the poet must first create a place where he may enact the process of his discovery, he must find a scene within which the thoughts and feelings can take place. His audience is not simply the reader, but also the larger, total mind of the poet himself. Finally, actor and audience (projected self and larger self) come together in a moment of emotional resolution. Thus in "The River That is East" the boy dreaming by the river and the disillusioned older man are in one sense projections of the poet's personality (at least the poet can participate in their points of view). They are past and future selves of the poet and the experience of the scene is controlled by the larger self of the poet—his whole self. The conclusion is an affectionate understanding of "what will suffice."

"Spindrift" is another meditative poem in this special sense. In the first part the poet "composes the place," creates a setting which calls forth and gives dimension to the meditation that follows:

On this tree thrown up
From the sea, its tangle of roots

> Letting the wind go through, I sit
> Looking down the beach

In the second stanza he calls attention to important features of the scene and asks an imagined reader, or an imagined projection of himself, to sit down by the sea, to pluck "sacred shells from the icy surf," to lift one to the sun:

> And as it blazes
> See the lost life within
> Alive again in the fate-shine

Here he makes a deliberate effort to observe, to find significance, addressing a projection of himself in his attempt to do this.

In the third stanza he again examines something in the scene—the tree which has lost hold but "at least keeps the wild / Shape of what it held" and remains "one of the earth's / Wandering icons of 'to have.' " In the fourth stanza he again describes the sea, recalling himself to the scene from his reflections upon it (the poem weaves between the observed scene and the mind's reflections upon it): "I sit listening / To the surf as it falls," "It is the most we know of time." In the fifth section, his mind wanders to another scene, another occasion:

> I think of how I
> Sat by a dying woman
> Her shell of a hand,
> Wet and cold in both of mine

And in the sixth part he again returns to the scene:

> Under the high wind
> That moans in the grass
> And whistles through crabs' claws
> I sit holding this little lamp,
> This icy fan of the sun.

In the end he observes an old man: "What does he really love?" Like everyone else the old man does not like to die, but "can know / A kind of gratefulness / Towards time that kills him, / Everything he loved was made of it." His life is a pilgrimage through time, he himself is a "scallop shell"—fragile, but luminous with meaning to the poet. The conclusion recalls Raleigh's "The Passionate Man's Pilgrimage:"

> In the end
> What is he but the scallop shell
> Shining with time like any pilgrim?

Kinnell has written a long descriptive piece on New York City, an expanded and elaborated version of the "part poem" technique which he prefers. "The Avenue Bearing the Initial of Christ into the New World" invites comparison with other long poems written in the Twentieth Century—Pound's "Mauberly" or Eliot's "Waste Land." But Kinnell's poem, although it too reflects the "plight of the contemporary world," is quite different from these poems. It depends upon associations and contrasts, on a series of discrete pictures, on repeated images in different contexts (the mirror, fire, water, fishes), on a dialectic of sterility and vitality, of struggle and acquiescence, as organizational principles, but it has more obvious and explicit form and direction than do "Mauberly" or "The Waste Land." Kinnell simply gives us more guidance, includes more of the discursive element, in this poem. Although his voice is occasionally a collective one ("We scattered over the lonely seaways") or that of a projected personality ("A crying: you imagine / Some baby in its crib"), a personal voice, a controlling mind and imagination are always apparent in this poem. He avoids the "fallacy of imitative form" in that he doesn't attempt to reflect the disorder of contemporary society in the disorder of the poem. He constructs his poem, as Eliot does, out of "moments of intensity," but they are more closely related and associated through the presence of the poet.

This poem contrasts the present with the past—through the Judeo-Christian ideas of covenants and promises (America as a promised land) and of visionary quests (the old Jew "wading toward his last hour" is a good example of this). But, although there is talk of promises which were broken and promises which broke by themselves, the poet's attitude is finally one of acceptance—even appreciation—for the complexity of life today, for its diversity and richness, which exist in spite of death, violence, poverty, and frustration:

> In the nighttime
> Of the blood they are laughing and saying,
> Our little lane, what a kingdom it was!

Although the distinctive features of Kinnell's poetry (the easy expansiveness of the poet's speaking voice, the slow accumulation of meaning, and the laxness of metrical and verse patterns) can sometimes become a poem's liabilities rather than its virtues (occasionally the poet indulges in casual reminiscence in his willingness to include everything about an experience and the reader sometimes misses the tightness of structure and exactness of vision found in other poems), nevertheless, the two collections of poems Kinnell has published make up an impressive body of work. The poet projects a rich and interesting personality in these poems; it is one we enjoy knowing.

"One and Zero Walk Off Together": Dualism in Galway Kinnell's *The Book of Nightmares*

Andrew Hudgins

In *The Book of Nightmares* Galway Kinnell explores from a contemporary perspective one of the great themes of romantic poetry: What is the proper human response to death? For Kinnell the answer to that question is complicated by his being possessed of a deep spiritual longing while living in an existential world. And death, that ultimate existential fact, is the stumbling block to spiritual aspirations because it implies utter nullity. But even with life ending in the apparent finality of death, people often intuit a harmony beyond death, a unity in the universe. Kinnell, in an interview, has stated the dichotomy succinctly: "death has two aspects—the extinction, which we fear, and the flowing away into the universe, which we desire—there is a conflict within us that I want to deal with."[1] Or to state the proposition in explicitly Freudian terms, people are torn between a drive toward life and a drive toward death. Behind this dualism, however, lies a deeper one; the rational mind looks at the world and sees that life, to all evidence, ends with death, while the irrational mind intuits a mystical oneness in death.

Throughout *The Book of Nightmares* Kinnell struggles with the separation of the conscious and unconscious aspects of the mind, trying to develop a coherent view of life and death, and his examination of his own ambivalences leads him to unravel a string of connected dualities—conscious and unconscious, rational and irrational, mind and body, and ultimately life and death. Like Carl Jung, Kinnell feels that in the modern world the logical mind has grown too powerful at the expense of the unconscious. He therefore exalts the wisdom of the body, which taps into the unconscious, but finds the mind often blocks his access to it. All through the volume the poet honestly confronts both sides of the dichotomy, and never slides off into glib lyricism or the intellectual fuzziness of fashionable mysticism.

This essay first appeared in *American Poetry* 3, no. 1 (Fall 1985): 56–71. © 1985 Lee Bartlett and Peter White, McFarland & Company, Inc., Publishers, Jefferson, NC 28640.

The book begins with Kinnell, after the birth of his daughter Maud, going out into the woods, where "by this wet site / of old fires," he starts a fire for his daughter:

> . . . for her,
> whose face
> I held in my hands
> a few hours, whom I gave back
> only to keep holding the space where she was,
>
> I light
> a small fire in the rain.[2]

While the fire built on the ashes of an earlier fire hints at immortality through one's offspring, the speaker's main concern is about having brought a life, represented by the fire, into a world hostile to it. In spite of the rain, as an act of affirmation, he is able to start the fire. As the wood burns, the deathwatch beetles inside it "begin running out of time" (p. 3). Relishing the wordplay of *deathwatch,* Kinnell introduces a theme he will return to frequently: In the hour of our birth is the hour of our death. But why? The answer, which he will expand on later, is implicit in his description of what happens when the rain falls on the fire. The fire changes the rain as people's attitude to their suffering can change it into a means of attaining wisdom:

> The raindrops trying
> to put the fire out
> fall into it and are
> changed: the oath broken,
> the oath sworn between earth and water, flesh and spirit,
>   broken,
> to be sworn again,
> over and over, in the clouds, and to be broken again,
> over and over, on earth. (p. 4)

In transcending earthly suffering and rising into the clouds, flesh and spirit join, but on earth, which is imperfect and subject to mortality, the joining breaks down, resulting in the uneasy division of the human psyche between mind and body. At death, however, one returns to the universe, unity is restored, and the oath is sworn anew.

The harmony to be found in death can also be seen, though it fades rapidly, in newborn children. The poet's thoughts return to his daughter, who was born just hours ago. Before birth she was whole, "somersaulting alone in the oneness" of the womb (p. 5). Kinnell's description of the child as she is separated from oneness by birth is powerful and moving:

> . . . she skids out on her face into light,
> this peck
> of stunned flesh
> clotted with celestial cheesiness, glowing
> with the astral violet
> of the underlife. And as they cut
>
> her tie to the darkness
> she dies
> a moment, turns blue as a coal,
> the limbs shaking
> as the memories rush out of them. (p. 6)

The memories of the collective unconscious are lost or made sub-servient to the rational mind, and the child dies for a moment, suspended between the life of the unconscious mind and the life of the conscious mind. Once she is born, she is inevitably thrust into the emptiness that follows the loss of the oneness she enjoyed in the womb. While the doctors hold her up by the feet, she draws her first breath, "the slow, / beating, featherless arms / already clutching at the emptiness" (p. 7). Forced out of the har-mony and fullness of the womb, she instinctively embraces the emptiness of the existential world.

Later, the poet hears Maud crying in her crib and attributes her crying to "a sadness / stranger than ours, all of it / flowing from the other world" (p. 7). Behind this description and the description of Maud at birth—"clot-ted with celestial cheesiness, glowing / with the astral violet / of the under-life"—I hear the voice of Wordsworth, another poet who felt intimations of immortality when recollecting early childhood and who described children as born "trailing clouds of glory" that diminish as the conscious mind grows.[3] The longer Maud lives, the more she loses of the dark knowledge of the unconscious from which she came and to which she may, perhaps, return. To provide for Maud when she needs that knowledge and finds her-self cut off from it by the blindness of her own rational mind, Kinnell sings to her so, when the time comes,

> . . . you will remember,
> in the silent zones
> of the brain, a specter, descendant
> of the ghostly forefathers, singing
> to you in the nighttime—(p. 7)

The song she will hear is not the bright song of the unconscious mind but the dark song of the unconscious, which speaks through dream and nightmare, telling us the often frightening truths that we have forgotten. The songs that come back to Maud will be

> not the songs
> of light said to wave
> through the bright hair of angels,
> but a blacker
> rasping flowering on that tongue. (p. 7)

Kinnell is really giving himself the advice he addresses to his infant daughter: Trust the voice of the unconscious as it sings to you in the night.

In "The Hen Flower," the second of ten sections of *The Book of Nightmares*, the poet meditates on death and the human inability to embrace death's inevitability. In the dead hen—the hen flower—that he holds in his hand, the poet sees a parallel to the human situation. When asked in an interview why he is so fond of bird imagery, Kinnell responded that "like everyone" he experiences "the contest between wanting to transcend and wanting to belong."[4] The hen's situation is more complicated, even, than that, and oddly comic too because, though winged and built for flight, it cannot fly. Similarly, humans, though they long to transcend their own earthbound nature, are held to earth by the weight of their bodies.

At the same time that he wants to transcend, the poet longs to live the purely animal life of the hen and not worry about death until it is immediately at hand.[5] "If only / we could let go," he exclaims, and "throw ourselves / on the mercy of darkness, like the hen" (p. 11). But letting go is easy for the hen; it has no rational mind to keep it from being a good animal. In another image, though, the poet merges the two aspects of the psyche when he uses the rational mind to see the world through the body of an animal. Looking through the thin, lucent part of a ram's spealbone—the shoulderblade, a bone sometimes used by primitives as a means of divination—he has a vision of nature and natural processes unchanged by death:

> I thought suddenly
> I could read the cosmos spelling itself, . . .
>
> and in a moment,
> in the twinkling of an eye, it came to me
> the mockingbird would sing all her nights the cry of the rifle,
> the tree would hold the bones of the sniper who chose not to
>   climb down,
> the rose would bloom no one would see it,
> the chameleon longing to be changed would remain the
>   color of blood. (p. 13)

He has his moment of existential insight, but he cannot let go, cannot accept what he sees. In despair at his vision, the poet takes the body of a chicken killed by weasels and flings it into the air in a grotesque simulation of flying, as if to assure himself that death will provide the gift of flight that the

chicken—and he—was denied in life. The effect, of course, is just the opposite. Again he tells himself to "let go" and accept death, even though he is
afraid of it; after all, everyone and everything is afraid of dying, of nonexis-
tence: "even these feathers freed from their wings forever / are afraid" (p. 15).

Deciding to put his fear behind him, the poet, in "The Shoes of Wandering," begins his existential quest. Where is he going? He knows only that he
must first lose his way. What is he looking for? He knows only that he will
not find it. His quest is not his alone but the quest everyone makes in trying
to come to terms with life. In what seems to be a reference to the archetypal
nature of his search, the poet goes to a Salvation Army store and, after sampling "these shoes strangers have died from" (p. 19), he buys shoes for his
journey:

> . . . I discover
> the eldershoes of my feet,
> that take my feet
> as their first feet, clinging
> down to the least knuckle and corn. (p. 19)

As he wears the used shoes, walking "on the steppingstones / of someone
else's wandering" (p. 19), he trusts the instinctive wisdom of the body.
When he becomes frightened that he may have lost the way, he remembers
the Crone who said *"the first step . . . / shall be / to lose the way"* (p. 19). To find
what he is seeking, he will have to forsake the established paths of the rational mind and pick his way across the "swampland" (p. 21) of the unconscious.

On the journey, every step is

> . . . a shock,
> a shattering underfoot of mirrors sick of the itch
> of our face-bones under their skins,
> as memory reaches out
> and lays bloody hands on the future, the haunted
> shoes rising and falling
> through the dust, wings of dust
> lifting around them, as they flap
> down the brainwaves of the temporal road. (p. 21)

As he walks down the road, the "wings of dust" around his feet hint at the
possibility of a limited transcendence rising from the fear of death. The poet
expounds on the connection between wings and feet when he goes on to ask:

> Is it the foot,
> which rubs the cobblestones
> and snakestones all its days, this lowliest

> of tongues, whose lick-tracks tell
> our history of errors to the dust behind,
> which is the last trace in us
> of wings? (pp. 21–22)

The urge to transcend has been, in many ways, deflected into an earthbound restlessness. But the quest is both internal and external; it is not solipsistic. If it were, the poet would have a much easier time deluding himself about his ability to transcend himself. The poet's sense of the outside world is too sharp for any such self-deception. Also, he is clearly aware of the dangers of solipsism and is prepared to avoid them. Though he "longs for the mantle / of the great wanderers" (p. 22) of myth and legend who always, whatever mistakes they made, found the way, he knows the Crone—the outside voice—is right when she tells him, *"you will feel all your bones / break / over the holy waters you will never drink"* (p. 23).

The problem of delusion is examined in more detail in section IV, "Dear Stranger Extant in Memory by the Blue Juniata." In this section, Kinnell reacts to the claims of mystics with irony and some mockery, but it is irony that is sympathetic and even partially self-directed because he would like to believe in these shortcuts to the infinite. Kinnell quotes, in the poem, from letters he has received from Virginia, a mystic. Explaining who Virginia is, Kinnell says in an interview:

> Virginia is an actual person I've had a long correspondence with. She is a mystic, a seer. She is one of those born without the protective filtering device that allows the rest of us to see this humanized, familiar world as if it were all there is. She sees past the world and lives in the cosmos.[6]

This statement may at first sound like approval of Virginia, but, though Kinnell does no doubt admire her, it is worth pointing out that their first and only meeting was unsuccessful. Through letters, Virginia and Kinnell had to "reestablish an intimacy, though we now knew it was in part illusory, being purely platonic."[7] The same criticism applies to Virginia's mysticism, which leads her to reject the world she actually lives in. While Kinnell is compelled by courtesy to be polite in his statements about the actual Virginia, the stance of the poem, as I read it, is that Virginia, with her single-minded commitment to the cosmos, is as wrong as those who can only see the world "as if it were all there is."

Two letters from Virginia are quoted in the fourth section of *The Book of Nightmares*. In the first of them she describes a session of automatic writing and her reaction to it. As her hand grows numb, she finds herself drawing, without conscious control, circles, figure-eights, and mandalas. She drops the pencil, tries to relax, and then:

. . . I felt my mouth open. My tongue moved, my breath wasn't my own. The whisper which forced itself through my teeth said, *Virginia, your eyes shine back to me from my own world.* O God, I thought. My breath came short, my heart opened. O God, I thought, now I have a demon lover.

Yours, faithless to this life,
Virginia (p. 28)

The sentence about the demon lover is wonderfully comic. That is not to imply, however, that Kinnell does not sympathize very deeply with Virginia's desire to be one with the universe; indeed, he shares it. But he realizes that that desire comes at the expense of the body. Virginia herself admits as much in her second letter when she says,

. . . God is my enemy. He gave me lust and joy and cut off my hands. My brain is smothered with his blood. I asked why should I love this body I fear. He said, *It is so lordly, it can never be shaped again—dear, shining casket.* . . . Forgive my blindness.

Yours, in the darkness,
Virginia (pp. 30–31)

Virginia seems to be apologizing for her earlier excesses in response to Kinnell's yearning but cautious question: "Can it ever be true— / all bodies, one body, one light / made of everyone's darkness together?" (p. 30).

As if to reemphasize that his journey is inward, section V, "In the Hotel of Lost Light," opens with the speaker still in the bed he was sleeping in when, in section III, he began his journey. Having taken the Crone's advice and lost the way that is illuminated by the light of the intellect, he resides now in the "Hotel of Lost Light." While lying in bed in his room, he sees and identifies himself with a fly

> . . . whining his wings,
> concentrated wholly on
> *time, time,* losing his way worse
> down the downward-winding stairs, his wings
> whining for life as he shrivels
> in the gaze
> from the spider's clasped forebrains, the abstracted stare
> in which even the nightmare spatters out its horrors
> and dies. (p. 35)

The poet lost on his inward quest is represented by the fly lost on its downward spiral, and what makes the fly shrink is the "abstracted stare" that comes from the spider's brain. The proposed analogy is that the conscious mind is to the unconscious mind as a spider is to a fly: the latter is the prey of the former.

But Kinnell also realizes that the conscious mind is indispensable to our understanding of our situation and that the light it provides must be brought to bear, sympathetically, on the nurturing darkness of the unconscious. The rub is that light shone on darkness destroys the darkness. The poet's task—the human task—is to reconcile the irreconcilable.

"The Dead Shall Be Raised Incorruptible," section VI, is a grim consideration of what happens when the healthy impulses of the unconscious are repressed by adherence to a conscious creed. The result is "Christian man," who revels in violence and death. The Biblical quotation that Kinnell takes for the title of this section pinpoints the false reasoning that has led to the Christian susceptibility to violence. Saying that "the dead shall be raised incorruptible" implies that people in their human, embodied form are corrupt—that mortality and moral failing are intrinsically linked. Kinnell maintains, in other words, that Christianity is based on contempt for the body. This section also seeks to establish a Freudian connection between anality and "Christian man," who is afflicted by, as Kinnell speaks for him, "my iron will, my fear of love, my itch for money, and my madness" (p. 44). The madness derives from Christian man's development being arrested in the anal phase, something that is made clear in the beginning of the section, where the speaker sees a corpse smoking in a field and reacts with a list of words that make explicit the connections between death, dirt, food, and money:

> carrion,
> caput mortuum,
> orts,
> pelf,
> fenks,
> sordes,
> gurry dumped from hospital trashcans. (p. 41)

At the center of this emphasis on decay and its scenes of warfare is a savage attack on the mentality that has produced these abominations. Using a form derived from Villon's *Testament*, which he has translated into English, Kinnell speaks as Christian man in "the Twentieth Century of my trespass on earth" (p. 42). He recounts the people whom he has killed, including "a whole continent of red men for living in unnatural community / and at the same time having relations with the land" (p. 42). Later in his testament, in one of the sharpest stabs of the volume, he leaves "my flesh to the advertising man, / the anti-prostitute, who loathes human flesh for money" (p. 43).

There is something, though, some living essence, that resists death. An unidentified voice, apparently that of a wounded GI, says:

> *my neck broken I ran*
> *hold my head up with both hands I ran*
> *thinking the flames*
> *the flames may burn the oboe*
> *but listen buddy boy they can't touch the notes!* (p. 44)

The same point is made, even more dramatically, by an image that frames this section of the book; the section begins and ends with the image of a burning corpse, perhaps a victim of napalm: *"Lieutenant! / This corpse will not stop burning!"* (pp. 41 and 45).

After the nightmare of section VI, the poet turns to his daughter, and his love for her, as Robert Langbaum points out,[8] restores him: "my broken arms heal themselves around you" (p. 49). Section VII primarily consists of the poet's meditations on his daughter and his advice to her. Remembering when he heard her tell a flower not to die, he says he would, if he could, keep her from dying. But, by calling her with odd and compelling tenderness *"O corpse-to-be"* (p. 50), he acknowledges that she—like everyone—will die:

> . . . perhaps this is the reason you cry,
> this the nightmare you wake screaming from:
> being forever
> in the pre-trembling of a house that falls. (p. 50)

Already she seems to grasp and be disturbed by the existential realization that life has no intrinsic meaning.

As Maud grows, the poet sees her entering the Freudian anal phase, in which the mind strives to dominate, even exclude, nature; he sees that she might become estranged from nature and the body, might even become as dangerously divorced from nature as to be like "Christian man." He remembers a time when, in a restaurant, Maud climbed into his lap and cried at the food, *"caca! caca! caca!"* (p. 50). The child reacts so enthusiastically to the restraints of the anal phase that Kinnell fears she might, like Christian man, get stuck there, confusing nourishment and excrement. The connection is made much clearer when Kinnell describes the reaction of the other diners to his daughter's cry: "each spoonful / stopped, a moment, in midair, in its withering / steam" (p. 50). The image evokes the opening lines of the previous section, lines that are followed by the list of archaic or unusual words that have associations with anality: "A piece of flesh gives off / smoke in the field" (p. 41).

Kinnell can foresee a time when these natural maturing processes will cut Maud off from nature. He imagines her standing in a field,

> . . . the raindrops
> hitting you on the fontanel
> over and over, and you standing there
> unable to let them in. (p. 51)

When and if this alienation occurs, he advises her to let her knowledge of death and "the sorrows / to come" cause her to embrace the present. In short, his advice is *carpe diem:*

> learn to reach deeper
> into the sorrows
> to come—to touch
> the almost imaginary bones
> under the face, to hear under the laughter
> the wind crying across the black stones. Kiss
> the mouth
> which tells you, *here,*
> *here is the world.* This mouth. This laughter. These temple bones.
>
> The still undanced cadence of vanishing. (p. 52)

The insight implicit in this passage is stated explicitly as the section ends. Out of the pain and suffering caused by death there arises one compensation: "*the wages / of dying is love*" (p. 53).

From this crucial insight, the poet progresses to "The Call Across the Valley of Not-Knowing," a title that brings to mind Kierkegaard's "leap to faith." Though Kinnell does not leap across his valley, he calls across it and receives in reply intimations that harmony is possible in the world beyond. Occasionally he experiences something that lets him sense the possibility of wholeness, as he did once while in love with a woman whom he thinks of as the other half that completes his divided nature. The allusion, of course, is to Plato's speculation that the two sexes were once united beings whose union made them powerful enough to challenge the gods. Kinnell found, briefly, the half that made him whole but had to leave her because of "cowardice / loyalties, all which goes by the name of 'necessity'" (p. 58)—reasons in which mind dominates instinct.

Expanding on the idea that "the wages of dying is love," he sees that it is death and suffering that gives us the power to reach, temporarily, beyond ourselves and feel flashes of oneness, even though we are not with the exact other half we are looking for and have to settle for our "misfit":

> it must be the wound, the wound itself,
> which lets us know and love,
> which forces us to reach out to our misfit
> and by a kind
> of poetry of the soul, accomplish,
> for a moment, the wholeness the drunk Greek
> extrapolated from his high
> or flagellated out of an empty heart,

> that purest,
> most tragic concumbence, strangers
> clasped into one, a moment, of their moment on earth. (p. 58)

The union of two people in love and in sex is the closest people come to experiencing the integration of mind and body, but it is also tragic—it will not last, it hints at a unity that everywhere else eludes those seeking it. But in one such moment of love Kinnell has a vision of total integration. He thinks of a time when he and his wife were young and "not yet / dipped into the acids / of the craving for anything" (p. 58). They lay under a pear tree, "on the grass of the knowledge / of graves" (p. 59), where they felt perfect harmony of mind and body, felt the perfect interpenetration of the two opposing aspects of the self:

> And the brain kept blossoming
> all through the body, until the bones themselves could think,
> and the genitals sent out wave after wave of holy desire
> until even the dead brain cells
> surged and fell in god-like, androgynous fantasies—
> and I understand
> the unicorn's phallus could have risen, after all,
> directly out of thought itself. (p. 59)

As if to emphasize that this vision is a vision and not the normal state of affairs, the poet recounts the story of a Southern sheriff in a civil-rights march, curses and spits. What he remembers most about the sheriff, though, is "the care, the almost loving, / animal gentleness of his hand on my hand" (p. 59) as he was finger-printed. The sheriff's racist beliefs have overwhelmed and perverted his natural kindness, or, to put it another way, his mind has been tainted by pernicious ideas that have squelched the natural goodness that still resides in his body. He has let his mind become so alienated from his body that, in effect, he no longer has a body:

> Better than the rest of us, he knows
> the harshness of that cubicle
> in hell where they put you
> with all your desires undiminished, and with no body to
>   appease them. (pp. 59–60)

Cut off from the body, he is cut off from that which brings people together, that which affirms life even in the face of death. If we listen, even standing in a field "where the flesh / swaddles its skeleton a last time / before the bones go their way without us," we still might hear

> . . . even then,
> the bear call
> from his hillside—a call, like ours, needing

to be answered—and the dam-bear
call back across the darkness
of the valley of not-knowing
the only word tongues shape without intercession,

yes . . . yes . . .? (p. 61)

The only word the body forms without the intercession of the brain is one of affirmation and the instinctive but tentative response of one human being to another.

If section VIII considers the relationship of humans to the beyond, "The Path Among the Stones" explores the relationship of people to the present, inanimate world, and the poet ponders the curious fact that he himself has been inanimate and will be again. At one point he speaks of arrowheads; they are

stones
which shuddered and leapt forth
to give themselves into the broken hearts
of the living,
who gave themselves back, broken, to the stone. (p. 65)

Later, in an image that provides the descent into the underworld of this inner epic, the poet imagines entering the earth—a reversal of the arrowhead entering the human body. Going down into the earth, he encounters an old man who is foolishly using his intellect—the light at his forehead—in an attempt to avoid death. Inevitably he fails:

An old man, a stone
lamp at his forehead, squats
by his hell-flames, stirs into
his pot
chopped head
of crow, strings of white light,
opened tail of peacock, dressed
body of canary, robin breast
dragged through the mud of battlefield, wrung-out
blossom of caput mortuum flower—salts
it all down with sand
stolen from the upper bells of hourglasses . . . (p. 67)

The amused irony of "salts it all down" reveals the poet's response to the old man's efforts. The attempt, by logic, to conjure from their dead bodies the birds' ability to fly, and therefore to transcend the world, is doomed to failure; as is the attempt to extract immortality from the unexpended sand in the top section of the hourglass. All these efforts, the poet says, result in "nothing. / Always nothing." (p. 67). Immediately, however, he sees that something is gained by the striving, even, perhaps especially, if failure is unavoidable. Climbing up from the underground, he realizes the struggle has taken him to the essence of life: "I find myself alive / in the whorled / archway of the finger-print of all things" (p. 68).

At this insight, "the hunger / to be new lifts off" (p. 68) his soul; at long last he seems to have reconciled himself to mortality. He sees in the sacrifice of his life, a sacrifice every human has to make, the chance for a greater real-ization of self than would otherwise be possible:

> . . . Somewhere
> in the legends of blood sacrifice
> the fatted calf
> takes the bonfire into his arms, and *he*
> burns *it*. (p. 68)

To understand this enigmatic passage, I find an observation by Jungian scholar Marie Louise von Franz helpful. Speaking of sacrifice, von Franz says, "It is *the* possibility for the ego to experience the superior presence and reality of the self."[9] By suffering, the ego realizes that it is not paramount but is part of a larger whole; and by sacrifice it acknowledges that fact. Therefore, it is through suffering and sacrifice that people move toward the integration of the psyche. This pragmatic insight is what the book has been working toward throughout the first nine sections.

With "Lastness," the tenth and final section, the book comes full cir-cle; but it more closely resembles a Mobius strip than it does a circle. While the setting the poet has returned to is more or less the same—the fire he started in the first section is "somewhere behind me" (p. 71)—and while time has passed, what seems to be the same bear is performing what seem to be the same actions he performed then. This odd wrinkle in time points up the inner nature of the poet's journey. He returns to the same place and events and finds that though they have remained the same, he has changed. He has a more profound and empathetic feeling for the world around him. His mind reaches out and he becomes the bear he is watching. The scene also suggests the ease that the poet has acquired with the natural side of himself:

> . . . He sniffs the sweat
> in the breeze, he understands
> a creature, a death-creature
> watches from the fringe of the trees,
> finally he understands
> I am no longer there, he himself
> from the fringe of trees watches
> a black bear
> get up, eat a few flowers, trudge away, . . . (p. 71–72)

By imagination, he breaks down the subject-object dichotomy and abridges his alienation from the world outside himself. The circular movement of the volume takes the speaker back to where he began, but in his internal odyssey he has come out in a different place. The process of suffering has allowed him the opportunity to acquire knowledge, perhaps wisdom, and to achieve glimpses of himself as a whole person.

But that sense of unity is momentary and far from absolute. About this last section, the poet asserts:

> This is the tenth poem
> and it is the last. It is right
> at the last, that one
> and zero
> walk off together,
> walk off the end of these pages together
> one creature
> walking away side by side with the emptiness. (p. 73)

This stunning and witty image powerfully brings together the ideas of individuation and death, personal oneness and existential emptiness. To some extent, then, the dichotomy that has defined his struggle through the first nine sections of the book is resolved. He has achieved some integration of his own psyche, but then there rises a new dichotomy: The whole man lives in an empty world. The human condition is to be suspended between the two extremes, but in the end the poet has a stronger sense of his oneness than he has ever had before.

How, then, does this knowledge reflect itself in an attitude toward life? How does a sense of oneness exist "side by side with the emptiness"? The answer is embodied in the image of a skydiver who is both one and divided as he plummets through the air toward the ground, as we—all of us—plummet through life toward death. His life is a

> . . . concert of one
> divided among himself,
> this earthward gesture
> of the sky-diver, the worms
> on his back still spinning forth
> and already gnawing away
> the silks of his loves, who could have saved him,
> this free floating of one
> opening his arms into the attitude
> of flight, as he obeys necessity and falls . . . (p. 75)

He is compelled to assume the "attitude / of flight" though he knows the transcendence he longs for is impossible. The best he can hope for is that the worms, which represent his fear of death, don't eat away the parachute of "his loves, who could have saved him."

The imagery here becomes a bit ungainly as the poet tries to jam too much information into it, to qualify the image. But the poet's risking awkwardness to be as exact as possible points up a very great strength of the book: its honesty. Kinnell never slides into a facile vision of mystique unity. And what tenuous unity he does attain is matched by the emptiness without. But the zero added to the one raises it to a higher power, forming a new and much higher number than they do separately.

Notes

1. Galway Kinnell, *Walking Down the Stairs: Selections from Interviews* (Ann Arbor: University of Michigan Press, 1978), 23.

2. Galway Kinnell, *The Book of Nightmares* (Boston: Houghton Mifflin, 1971), 3. Page citations of all subsequent quotations from this book will be given parenthetically in the text of the article.

3. Other instances of Wordsworth's influence on Kinnell are mentioned in Robert Langbaum, "Galway Kinnell's *The Book of Nightmares,*" *American Poetry Review* 8 (March–April 1979), 30.

4. Galway Kinnell, "An Interview with Galway Kinnell," conducted by Thomas Gardner, *Contemporary Literature* 20 (1979), 427.

5. Langbaum, 30.

6. *Walking Down the Stairs,* 108.

7. *Walking Down the Stairs,* 109.

8. Langbaum, 31.

9. Marie Louise von Franz, *C. G. Jung: His Myth in Our Time,* trans. William H. Kennedy (New York: Putnam, 1975), 229.

The Music of Galway Kinnell's
Mortal Acts, Mortal Words

JOYCE DYER

Strains of music persistently flow throughout Galway Kinnell's volume *Mortal Acts, Mortal Words* (1980), appearing, disappearing, reappearing. Music haunts all of Kinnell's volumes: the music made by frogs and boys in "First Song" from *What a Kingdom It Was;*[1] the songs of "the last birds / coasting down the twilight" from "Last Songs" in *Body Rags;*[2] the Bach concert in *The Book of Nightmares.*[3] But in no single volume does Kinnell turn to music as frequently or mysteriously as he does in *Mortal Acts, Mortal Words.* Chords of beauty and grace-notes of hope urge us to accept our mortal state.

In "The Choir" Kinnell admires the awkward songs and sounds of children, "their mouths gaping, saying / 'Ah!' for God, / 'O!' for an alphabet of O's."[4] Like the children, we all must learn to sing a song that does not come easily to us, a song that admits kinship with both life and death: "[E] yes, nostrils, mouth strain together in quintal harmony / to sing Joy and Death well" (p. 10). Singing in Kinnell is always initially uncomfortable and difficult. For music can only be formed when mortality is admitted and adored. ". . . [M]ortal beauty, acts, and words have put all their burden on my soul" reads Kinnell's epigraph from Petrarch.

The courage song demands, receives Kinnell's continual praise. In "Brother of My Heart," the poet's tribute to Etheridge Knight, Kinnell sees in the "cried-out face" of "this bravest knight" a song. "Therefore," he writes, "as you are, this once, / sing, even if you cry: the bravery / of the crying turns it into the true song" (p. 12). Only such a sad but courageous song can help Kinnell—and the world—recover. Although his optimism is qualified, it is the best we can hope for: "in this emptiness only the singing sometimes almost fills" (p. 12).

Love often mixes mysteriously with courage to make music in Kinnell's verse. In "Flying Home" the poet thinks, "love is very much like courage, / perhaps it *is* courage, and even / perhaps / *only* courage" (p. 72). We hear, then, the "aftersinging" (p. 21) of Kinnell's nights of love in "In the Bamboo Hut," the songs of "the sea-birds and breeze" (p. 13) in "Fisherman," which remind a soli-

Reprinted by permission from *Notes on Contemporary Literature* 16, no. 3 (May 1986): 5–8.

tary man of his dead wife, and the weird music of tree stumps and spruce needles in "The Last Hiding Places of Snow" that poignantly helps the poet
remember his mother's love, her "goodness of being, of permanence" (p. 42).

Two poems, "Wait" and "There Are Things I Tell to No One," are
symphonies of sound, combining the various strains and melodic lines heard
faintly in the background of other poems. "Wait" urges our trust in the
world, in both its happiness and sorrow. Kinnell believes that if we try to
survive agony—and express gratitude for the chance—we will be less
empty.

> Only wait a little and listen:
> music of hair,
> music of pain,
> music of looms weaving all our loves again. (p. 15)

Our mortality, our pain, our capacity for love and sacred; they are the true
music of our life and the only music we will ever hear. Kinnell's closing
metaphor assures us that existence is song: "Be there to hear it, it will be the
only time, / most of all to hear / the flute of your whole existence, / rehearsed
by the sorrows, play itself into total exhaustion" (p. 15).

"There Are Things I Tell to No One" works its message through elaborate metaphors of sound. Section 1 introduces the subject, the musical
theme, in a simple, straightforward manner: "There are things I tell to no
one" (p. 59). The next four sections offer musical variations and extensions of
the musical subject, the secrets of existence too great to utter except in song.
Section 2 presents the image we saw earlier, "the music of grace / that we
hear, sometimes, playing to us / from the other side of happiness" (p. 59).
The music, again, is physical, made out of our own flesh: "it speaks in notes
struck / or caressed or blown or plucked / off our own bodies" (p. 59). Section 3 explores specific sounds of the mortal symphony, recording strange
similarities. All music has both "Joy and Death," as the children in Kinnell's
choir have begun to know. All music, too, bridges time and "spent existence[s]."

> Just as the supreme cry
> of joy, the cry of orgasm, also has a ghastliness to it,
> as though it touched forward
> into the chaos where we break apart, so the death-groan
> sounding into us from another direction carries us back
> to our first world . . . (p. 60)

In section 4 Kinnell presents to us the most "ardent note"—the note of
gratefulness for all existence that is so intense it has no choice but to "[disap-
pear] into . . . music" (p. 61). And finally, in section 5 a grand crescendo of
mortal sounds moves all of us to listen:

> Yes, I want to live forever,
> I am like everyone. But when I hear
> that breath coming through the walls,
> grace-notes blown
> out of the wormed-out bones,
> music that their memory of blood
> plucks from the straitened arteries,
> that the hard cock and soaked cunt
> caressed from each other
> in the holy days of their vanity,
> that the two hearts drummed
> out of their ribs together,
> the hearts that know everything (and even
> the little knowledge they can leave
> stays, to be the light of this house),
>
> then it is not so difficult
> to go out, to turn and face
> the spaces which gather into one sound, I know now, the singing
> of mortal lives, waves of spent existence
> which flow toward, and toward, and on which we flow
> and grow drowsy and become fearless again. (pp. 61–62)

Mortality shared and endured and remembered, and mortality alone, is what our songs consist of, and what enables us to sing.

Galway Kinnell once spoke about the development of his poetry. "As for the growth, or change, in my poetry from the beginning, it hasn't been radical. There've been no abrupt departures. It has changed a lot, but there aren't any visible seams, nor any holes. It just went along and changed itself without my ever wanting or asking it to. The second section of *The Book of Nightmares,* for example, resembles closely 'The Bear' and 'The Porcupine.' And in *Body Rags,* there are poems exactly like ones in the previous book."[5]

As we look at *Mortal Acts, Mortal Words,* we continue to see essential similarities between the poems in this volume and those in earlier collections. The emphasis on love, for example, is an essential theme of all his works. In his novel set in Iran, *Black Light,* a wise, yellow-faced old man urges Jamshid to listen to the words of Hafez: " 'Time stops not, gather the Rose of Love in your arms.' "[6] As Donald Hall notes, in *The Book of Nightmares* "Eros brings about the birth that ends in the death that pays us with love."[7] Kindness toward all of nature's creatures is urged from volume to volume. The title of the one poem, of all poems, writes Kinnell in *The Book of Nightmares,* must be "Tenderness toward Existence."[8]

Charles Molesworth's remark about several of Kinnell's volumes of the 60's rings true for *Mortal Acts, Mortal Words* as well: "Kinnell's poetry in this period involves itself with a virtual rediscovery of how to view objects intensely, while continuing to avoid any prescribed system."[9] And Ralph J.

Mills' comment about poems from *What a Kingdom It Was* essentially describes all of Kinnell's volumes thereafter: in 1960, Mills contends, Kinnell departed from the "witty, pseudo-mythic verse" of the 50's to engage in a "naked metaphysical confrontation."[10]

But the metaphysical struggle Mills outlines, the struggle "with the universe, the identity of the self, the possibilities of an absent or present God, or the prospect of a vast, overwhelming nothingness,"[11] is not the variety we witness in *Mortal Acts, Mortal Words*. We find in these poems minimal religious concern. Instead, mortality is what the book almost exclusively struggles to accept and does finally celebrate—largely through song. This celebration, full of grace-notes and quintal harmonies, makes "nothingness" an impossibility. Where there is music, there cannot be the terrible silence of a nihilistic universe. Where there is music, there cannot be an empty room—or heart.

Notes

1. *What a Kingdom It Was*, in *Avenue Bearing the Initial of Christ into the New World: Poems 1946–64* (Boston: Houghton Mifflin Co., 1974), p. 41.

2. *Body Rags* (Boston: Houghton Mifflin Co., 1968), p. 23.

3. *The Book of Nightmares* (Boston: Houghton Mifflin Co., 1971), p. 74.

4. *Mortal Acts, Mortal Words* (Boston: Houghton Mifflin Co., 1980), p. 10. Further references to this volume will be cited parenthetically in the text.

5. "The Weight that a Poem Can Carry: An Interview with Galway Kinnell," *Ohio Review*, 14, No. 1, p. 32.

6. *Black Light* (Boston: Houghton Mifflin Co., 1966), p. 66.

7. "A Luminous Receptiveness," *The Nation*, Oct. 18, 1971, p. 377.

8. *The Book of Nightmares*, p. 29.

9. "The Rank and Flavor of Blood: Galway Kinnell and American Poetry in the 1960's," *Western Humanities Review*, 27 (1970), p. 226.

10. "A Reading of Galway Kinnell," *Iowa Review*, 1 (Winter 1970), p. 66.

11. Ibid., pp. 66–67.

Galway Kinnell's Poetry of Transformation

David Kleinbard

AT THE TIME OF ITS PUBLICATION in 1971 Galway Kinnell's *The Book of Nightmares* was praised as an evocation of a national trauma, the Vietnam war and its effects on this country. Now, after more than a decade, it seems more remarkable as an expression of private experience in visionary images. Cumulatively these images develop an epic scope and a timeless range of reference reminiscent of Kinnell's models, "Song of Myself" and *Duino Elegies*. Kinnell has said that *The Book of Nightmares* is an account of a journey whose starting point is dread and that "the book is nothing but an effort to face death and live with it."[1] This does not mean stoic acceptance, but a rediscovery of the child's capacity for living with time, decay, and death "almost as animals do." Recurrently these ten poems suggest that one can "surrender to existence" only by letting go of the dread of extinction.

For Kinnell, as for Whitman and Rilke, dying is a return to the "oneness" with the world which we lose at birth. As he says in an interview, it may be seen as "the flowing away into the universe which we desire . . ." (*Walking*, p. 23). Kinnell's most compelling poem on this theme is "The Last Hiding Places of Snow," an elegy for his mother published in *Mortal Acts, Mortal Words*. Drawing upon the traditional associations between the foetal "underlife" and death as a return within maternal earth or nature,[2] this poem recognizes not only the power but the danger of the longing to be with the mother again, particularly when the mother's desire for reunion, her desire to engulf her child, nurtures that longing in him:

> My mother did not want me to be born;
> afterwards, all her life, she needed me to return.
> When this more-than-love flowed toward me, it brought darkness;
> she wanted me as burial earth wants—to heap itself gently upon but
>   also to annihilate—
> and I knew, whenever I felt longings to go back,
> that is what wanting to die is. That is why
>
> dread lives in me,
>
> dread which comes when what gives life beckons toward death,[3]

This essay first appeared in *The Centennial Review* 30, no. 1 (Winter 1986): 41–56. Reprinted by permission of the author.

This mother's "more-than-love" is all the more fearful because she is dead. Dying is the only way to be reunited with her. In the darkness of the woods Kinnell hears his mother's sorrows and her love sighing and moaning:

> from the darkness of spruce boughs,
> from glimmer-at-night of the white birches,
> from the last hiding places of snow,
>
> a breeze,
> that's all, driving
> across certain obstructions: every stump
> speaks,
> the spruce needles play out of the air
> the sorrows cried into it somewhere else.[4]

In the resonant simplicity with which it lets one hear and feel the living presence of the dead in nature "The Last Hiding Places of Snow" has powers of evocation which bring to mind T. S. Eliot's concept of the "auditory imagination," "the feeling for syllable and rhyme, penetrating far below the conscious levels of thought and feeling, invigorating every word: sinking back to the most primitive and forgotten, returning to the origin and bringing something back," combining "the most ancient and the most civilized mentality."[5]

As the elegy suggests, Kinnell's conception of death and of the longing for the various forms of darkness which his poems define is at least partly a response to the "mother-love" which "every stump / speaks" and "the spruce needles play out of the air." This "more-than-love" exerts such a strong pull towards death because it has such power to protect and redeem.

The memory of his mother's love crying out of the darkness in the woods makes the poet feel "annointed" and "lighted" as if by sunlight in the deserted house of the world from which she is gone, so that he can wander through any "foulnesses" and "contagions" "and find my way back and learn again to be happy."[6]

The dead mother's sorrows cried out of "the last hiding places of snow" recall the strange sadness of the poet's infant daughter in "Under the Maud Moon," the first poem in *The Book of Nightmares*. When she cries, Maud's sadness flows "from the other world," "the darkness" of the foetal life "in the oneness under the hill, under / the old, lonely belly button" (pp. 7 and 5). Here, too, Kinnell draws on traditional associations between the foetus' existence and death, mother and earth.

Thinking of this incomprehensible sadness from "the other world," the poet remembers that he used to sing to his daughter the song that he learned listening to the "long rustle of being and perishing" on riverbanks where the marshy land sent up "the underglimmer / of the beginning" (pp. 7–8). The "underglimmer / of the beginning" recalls "the astral violet / of the underlife" which Maud brings with her at birth. This may be the glimmer of the moon and the stars in the "cold streaks" which the "earth oozes up" (p. 8). But "underglimmer" also brings to mind the glow of marsh gas as these are the marshes along the "riverbanks." The marsh fire rises from the decay of dead things, but it is also "the underglimmer / of the beginning" of life under the soil where the decay nurtures new sprouts and newly hatched creatures. For Kinnell it is a sign of the unity of "being and perishing."

Maud's birth, too, has helped to teach him that the processes of dying, change, growth, ripening, aging, death, and decay, are vital and inextricable elements of life, of living. The song which has begun to glimmer in Kinnell's mind at the time of her birth, his "only song," is a response to this discovery. Rilke, whose influence is pervasive in *The Book of Nightmares*, formulates the same wisdom in terms which offer a clear and precise statement of Kinnell's implicit argument:

> And so you see, it was the same with death. Experienced, and yet in its reality not to be experienced . . . never rightly admitted by us . . . death, which is probably so near us that we cannot at all determine the distance between it and the life-center within us without its becoming something external, daily held further from us. . . . Now this might still have made a kind of sense had we been able to keep God and death at a distance, as mere ideas in the realm of mind; but Nature knew nothing of this removal we had somehow accomplished—if a tree blossoms, death blossoms in it as well as life, and the field is full of death, which from its reclining face sends out a rich expression of life. . . . love too takes no heed of our divisions. . . . Lovers do not live out of the detached here-and-now; as though no division had ever been undertaken, they enter into the enormous possessions of their heart, of them one may say that God becomes real to them and that death does not harm them: *for being full of life, they are full of death* (the italics are the poet's).[7]

Implicitly, like Rilke's *Duino Elegies* and his *Sonnets to Orpheus*, the ten poems of *The Book of Nightmares* are saying that a culture which ignores the closeness of death to "the life-center within us" shuts out a large part of the richness of existence. The "ladies and gentlemen who would never die" in the tenth poem, "Lastness," recall the people in Rilke's tenth Duino Elegy who throng the market of empty diversions and drink a bitter beer called "Deathless," which is sweetened by ever new distractions.

At the end of "Under the Maud Moon" Kinnell imagines his daughter in the future, "orphaned," tasting the "cursed bread" which is the knowledge of death. He expresses the hope that out of the bitterness and emptiness of this experience a voice will come back to her, "spectral, calling you / *sister!* / from everything that dies" (p. 8).

Here the awakening to death is reminiscent of "Out of the Cradle Endlessly Rocking," where Whitman recalls his response as a boy to the song of a mocking bird grieving for its dead mate. The bird's grief in bringing the boy the awareness of death makes him hear "a thousand singers, a thousand songs, clearer, louder and more sorrowful than yours," and hear them with such imaginative empathy that "A thousand warbling echoes have started to life within me, never to die."

At the end of his poem Whitman recalls that it was the consciousness of death which first enabled him to see the bird as his "dusky demon and brother" and to "fuse" his song "With the thousand responsive songs at random, / My own songs awakened from that hour."

The dominant theme of *The Book of Nightmares* might well be defined by the last words of the seventh poem, which is also devoted to Maud: "*the wages of dying is love*" (the italics are the poet's).

II.

Earlier I mentioned Kinnell's statement that *The Book of Nightmares* is an account of a journey whose starting point is the dread of death. The journey, which gets underway in the third poem, "The Shoes of Wandering," takes the protagonist (really the poet, himself) through a series of encounters with death. Like Dante at the beginning of *The Divine Comedy,* he has lost his way. But unlike the voyager in *The Divine Comedy,* he affirms his confusion as the "first step" towards finding a new way of living (p. 19).

The poet makes his journey in a pair of secondhand shoes bought at a Salvation Army store, and these become a metaphor for his desire to leave behind the life he's led. He tells us that the stranger who first wore these shoes "died from" them (p. 19). This leaves one wondering. Did they cause his death? Did *they* wear *him* out? In casting off the shoes, the poem suggests, the stranger shed a part of himself or an earlier existence.

In the last part of "The Shoes of Wandering" a crone gazing into the crystal ball of Kinnell's skull tells him that he lives "under the Sign / of the Bear" (pp. 22–3). His fantasy of wearing shoes that a stranger has "died from" recalls his earlier poem, "The Bear," in which he imagines that by crawling into the dead animal he may find out what it's like to be a bear and absorb some of its nature. The shoes of wandering will take him into another life. This is primitive magic. It's also a metaphor for casting yourself upon the mercy of the darkness, for letting instinct take you on "this path / inventing itself" (p. 22). The poet longs to join the great wanderers, like Whitman, Lawrence, and Rilke, whose "lamp," he believes, was "pure hunger and pure thirst." ". . . [W]hichever way they lurched was the way" (p. 22).

In the fifth poem, "The Hotel of Lost Light," the quester, who has wandered in the shoes of the stranger, lies in the bed where an unknown drunk has died in a freeway motel room. He watches a fly dying in the web of a spider that becomes, as Kinnell describes it, a fearful embodiment of death and destructiveness.

Lying in his bed, the quester seeks to identify himself with the drunk who cast off all the confinements of middle-class life along with its comforts and saving graces before casting off in death even the confinement of the self-conscious ego.

He assures those of us who recoil from this descent into "The Hotel of Lost Light" that "*To Live* / has a poor cousin, / . . . who pronounces the family name / *To Leave* . . ." and changes her body rags each visit, as the poet dies to an earlier existence when he sets off on the freeway of his imaginative life, finding his way to a new birth of poetry (p. 37).

In his journeying Kinnell's protagonist calls to mind Rilke's surrogate in *The Notebooks of Malte Laurids Brigge.* Malte commits himself to a life of desperate poverty after coming to Paris, associating with homeless, uprooted grotesques, husks, the sick, and the dying in the belief that only by going through an experience as fearful and radical as death or madness, no less complete in its destruction of customary logic and meaning and of all the familiar links between words and the things they name, can one come to the new and different ways of perceiving and thinking about oneself and the world which are the primary source of genius.

III.

The last three poems in *The Book of Nightmares* follow Kinnell's acknowledged model, the *Duino Elegies,* more closely than poems I through VII (see *Walking,* pp. 35 & 41). The eighth, "The Call across the Valley of Not-Knowing," takes up Rilke's concept of "the open," the focal theme of the eighth Duino Elegy. The ninth, "The Path among the Stones," is concerned with the idea of transformation, the main subject of Rilke's ninth elegy. The tenth, "Lastness," recalls the tenth Duino Elegy's exploration of a fantastical realm of death and lamentation.

For Rilke, the experience of "the open" obliterates boundaries and barriers which common sense puts between the living and the dead.

In the eighth Duino Elegy Rilke defines this kind of consciousness paradoxically, likening it to the life within the womb. A small insect, such as the gnat, he says, lives as if it never left the womb (*"die immer bleibt im Schosse,"* "which always remains in the womb," line 53). For it the infinitely spacious and timeless world is like a "maternal body" within which, completely secure, "it does nothing but leap for joy."[8]

The eighth elegy contrasts human and animal consciousness. Rilke observes that we take children and turn them away from the timeless existence which animals enjoy, free from the prospect of death. We face them into a world constricted by mental constructs and distinctions, such as time;

oppositions between self and other, subjective and objective, human and natural; moral and social prescriptions; ideas of property and possession.

Haunted by death, we "are always taking leave" (line 75). At home nowhere, we live like tenants subject to eviction at any time. Unlike the small insects in their womb of security, we are "spectators" or "onlookers" always and everywhere, without relief.

Free from our deadening self-consciousness, our superego-burdened lives, the more primitive animals live without any sense of being watched over in *"das Reine, Unüberwachte,"* "the pure, unwatched-over," which Rilke also calls *"Nirgend ohne Nicht,"* "nowhere without not," an existence which is completely free in the absence of spatial limitation, time, and any form of negation (11. 17–18). Being nowhere in particular, one has the feeling of being everywhere, of encompassing and flowing all through the cosmos, as in this description of a mystical experience:

> . . . the cry of a bird . . . did not, so to speak, break upon the barriers of his body, but gathered inner and outer together into one uninterrupted space. . . . That time he had shut his eyes, so as not to be confused in so generous an experience by the contour of his body, and the infinite passed into him so intimately from every side, that he could believe he felt the light reposing of the already appearing stars within his breast.[9]

Though the eighth poem in *The Book of Nightmares* is a variation on Rilke's focal theme in the eighth Duino Elegy, it has none of the weightiness of metaphysical implication which interested Heidegger in Rilke's letters and poems about "the open."[10] In its focus on a close personal relationship Kinnell's approach to this theme is characteristically different from Rilke's.

"The Call across the Valley of Not-Knowing" contrasts Kinnell's marriage with an ideal, largely imagined relationship with a woman he met once in Waterloo, Iowa. The comparison and contrast between the reality of marriage and the ideal of the imagined relationship develop around the Greek myth that our primordial ancestors were hermaphrodites, that these were torn in half, and the longings of men and women for each other arise out of the desire to be reunited with one's lost other half and the craving for psychic wholeness which the primordial hermaphrodites must have enjoyed.

Kinnell's marriage, like so many others, has brought together "two mismatched halfnesses." At the beginning of the poem the poet is lying beside his wife, whose pregnancy both connects and separates them. She "sleeps on / happy, / far away in some other, / newly opened room of the world" (p. 57).

Though he feels excluded from this "newly opened room" and thinks of his wife and himself as "mismatched halfnesses," in her blissful pregnancy she becomes for him a luminous and sensuous image of wholeness and plentitude:

> Her hair glowing in the firelight,
> her breasts full,
> her belly swollen,
> the sunset of firelight
> wavering all down one side, my wife sleeps on. . . . (p. 57).

In part 6 of the poem Kinnell imagines a meeting between himself and the "woman of Waterloo." They meet "in our own country," a phrase which suggests metaphorically that they are at home with each other and consequently also feel at home in the world. They look "into each other's blindness" (p. 60). This inversion, typical of Kinnell, calls to mind D. H. Lawrence's conception of the blind, mindless instinctiveness of passionate lovemaking and Kinnell's remark during an interview that Lawrence's "best love poems move into mystery . . . into acts of cosmic adoration" (*Walking*, p. 54).

If this had been a real meeting, the poet imagines, he might have "moved / from then on like the born blind, / their faces gone into heaven already" (p. 60). In this ultimate vision of psychic wholeness the poem conceives of a life lived entirely by the sure wisdom of instinct in unreflective, unselfconscious bliss like that of the pregnant mother's waking sleep or the foetus in the darkness of his underlife or the gnats leaping for joy in the womb of Rilke's cosmos.

In a deceptively simple passage, which recalls "The Hen Flower," the second poem in *The Book of Nightmares,* the faces of the poet and the woman of Waterloo incline toward each other "as hens / incline their faces / when the heat flows from the warmed egg / back into the whole being" (p. 60). This comparison with the hen and the egg giving back the maternal warmth implicitly links the poet and the woman of Waterloo with the pregnant mother and her foetus in part 1 of the poem, and in particular it links them with the sense of wholeness and fullness which she enjoys.

But "The Call across the Valley of Not-Knowing" does not set up a simple contrast between the marriage and imagined perfection. Paradoxically, the mismatch of marriage so intensifies the pain of the open wound, which is the consciousness of being fragmentary, incomplete and insufficient, that it "forces us to reach out to our misfit / and by a kind of poetry of the soul, accomplish / for a moment the wholeness" defined by the myth of the hermaphrodite (p. 58).

In part 4 of the poem Kinnell recaptures one such moment in which he and his wife experience an ecstatic intimacy with nature and each other:

> we two
> lay out together
> under the tree, on earth, beside our empty clothes,

> our bodies opened to the sky,
> and the blossoms glittering in the sky
> floated down
> and the bees glittered in the blossoms
> and the bodies of our hearts
> opened . . . (p. 59)

"the bodies of our hearts" suggests that the division between sublimated feeling and egocentric desire was healed and that these were fused in this ecstatic experience. The next verse paragraph in part 4 has the brain "blossoming all through the body . . ." (p. 59). This conceit describes the cure of that basic evil, the split between body and mind. With characteristic wit Kinnell imagines that as a result of the brain's blossoming all through the body, "the bones themselves could think."

The healing of the rift between reflective thought and instinctive body and the curing of the sense of alienation from all other human beings and from nature frees sexual desire from the infection of sin, guilt, and shame: "and the genitals sent out wave after wave of holy desire" (p. 59). The line reveals how close Kinnell comes in this poem to the spirit in which Blake radically revised the mythology, the values, and the visionary expectations of traditional religion.

The new sense of self which the experience generates reverses the puritanical myth of the fall of the sexes into hostility through their sexuality. It takes the form of "androgynous fantasies" which are "god-like." With this result the remembered ecstatic communion of the husband and wife brings to a culmination the poem's development of the myth of hermaphroditic wholeness. Kinnell's celebration of their "god-like, androgynous fantasies" calls to mind the traditional conception of poetic genius as hermaphroditic. The most memorable American expression of this idea is the daring image of the poet's narcissism in "Song of Myself":

> I mind how once we lay such a transparent summer morning.
> How you settled your head athwart my hips and gently turn'd over
>   upon me,
> And parted my shirt from my bosom bone, and plunged your tongue
>   to my bare-stript heart,
> And reach'd till you felt my beard, and reach'd till you held my feet.
> Swiftly arose and spread around me the peace and knowledge that
>   pass all the argument of the earth,
>
> And I know that the hand of God is the promise of my own,
> And I know that the spirit of God is the brother of my own . . .

(The "you" in this passage is "my soul").

IV.

Such openness and tenderness toward oneself, other persons, and all things in nature as "The Call across the Valley of Not-Knowing" defines are essential to the poet's gift for transformation. The ninth poem in *The Book of Nightmares,* "The Path among the Stones," manifests this gift with consummate mastery.

Thinking about Whitman, Kinnell conceives of the poet as a kind of shaman who can transform himself into anything, not only another person or an animal, but even a stone (*Walking,* p. 23). Mastering the language to describe what it is to be stone would be among the most difficult tasks of the poet seeking to encompass all existing things.

Accomplishing this task would involve such complete absorption and transmutation of the qualities of stone into one's physical and mental being that, in the words of Rilke, the stone will have "turned to blood within us, to glance and gesture, nameless and no longer to be distinguished from ourselves."[11] If the poet accomplishes this transformation, the language of his poems "truly accords to the stones their own existence" (*Walking,* p. 63). "If a stone could speak your poem would be its words" (*Walking,* p. 23). This is the primary aim of "The Path among the Stones."

In part 3, the poet discovers "great, granite nuclei, / glimmering . . . with ancient inklings of madness and war" (p. 67). Kinnell may be thinking of megaliths such as those at Stonehenge. The giant rocks seem images of irrationality and violence within nature and within himself, irrationality radiating through all human culture and history.

"Ancient inklings of madness and war" also brings to mind "Ancestral voices prophesying war" which Kubla Kahn hears through the tumult of the sacred river in Coleridge's poem about the fearful shaping and destroying power of poetic genius.

These "inklings of madness" and violence prepare for the poet's descent, in part 4, into a place filled with "everything I ever craved and lost," where "hell-flames" burn up out of a brew full of dismembered parts of bodies, reminiscent of the broth made by the witches in Shakespeare's tragedy of insane destructiveness, *Macbeth* (p. 67).

The broth is stirred by an old man with a stone lamp on his brow, who seems to be associated with time as he salts his concoction with sand "stolen from the upper bells of hour glasses." It is time that dismembers and devours all things.

Having descended into this hell of craving and loss, dismemberment and devouring time, having, perhaps, attained to something like the kind of understanding that Dante found in hell, the poet emerges in part 5 surprisingly "alive" and finds himself "in the whorled / archway of the fingerprint of all things, / skeleton groaning, / blood strings wailing the wail of all things" (p. 68).

This is to say that through his journey represented in the eight preceding poems and its microcosm in the four preceding parts of this poem, he has become so closely identified with "everything that dies," that their voices have all become part of his own wailing, part of the "concert of one / divided among himself," as he calls his "music" in the next poem, "Lastness" (p. 75).

"The whorled / archway of the fingerprint of all things" means literally that stone, in its fossils, contains the prints of all forms of life. But the line also alludes to and echoes a passage in the preceding poem, "The Call across the Valley of Not-Knowing," as so many lines in "The Path among the Stones" allude to earlier passages in the book, gathering major themes and motifs and metaphors of the first eight poems into a coherent culmination.

"[T]he whorled archway of the fingerprint of all things" echoes "whorls / and tented archways" of fingerprints, which is one of the images of openness in "The Call across the Valley of Not-Knowing" (p. 59). They open into "the tabooed realm, that underlife / where the canaries of the blood are singing."

Kinnell is remembering being fingerprinted by a southern sheriff, a jailer who seems a projection of himself. He imagines that this jailer knows better than anyone else the hell experienced in a cell "with all your desires undiminished, and with no body to appease them" (p. 60).

But the jailer's sense of the life in the men whose fingerprints he presses into the police-blotter becomes a way out of that hell. The poet's fantasy is that the memory of all those hands the jailer took in his hands with "almost loving, / animal gentleness" to fingerprint them will make him feel the creation touching him all over his body. In this way he will enter, through "the whorled archways of / all those / fingerprints" the "underlife," (his own and theirs), the "darkness" of ordinarily buried consciousness where the "moan of wind / and the gasp of lungs" and the wailings and sighs of all beings "call to each other" in communion (p. 60).

Now that he has stood in that archway and has learned the sounds and other resonances of "all things" in his very bones and "bloodstrings," in the last two parts of "The Path among the Stones" the poet achieves the task of transformation, which gives to all things a new life and at the same time, as he says, "accords to" them "their own existence" in his poem (p. 68).

The image of this transformation is the "eerie blue light" of "the hunger / to be new," which lifts off his soul and "blooms / on all the ridges of the world" (p. 68). In achieving this metamorphosis the passionate imagination consumes the "bonfire" of destructiveness, of "madness and war," in its own fire of creative energy (pp. 68, 67).

Having arrived at this version of the saving power of poetic genius, Kinnell concludes the poem with images which are metaphors for the healing love of all things for one another and metaphors for the resurrection of the dead to life.

In part 3 of "The Path among the Stones" the stones send up "ghost-bloom / into the starlight . . . / . . . seeking to be one / with the unearthly fires," the stars (p. 66). But their reflected light falls back, an image of the poet's sadness at his inability to sing in the register of the glorious and sub-lime and of his need to express the existence of ordinary things, "the glitter of the bruised ground" (p. 66).

In part 7 of the poem the stones attain their yearning, but not because they ascend. Instead, the stars "kneel down in the star-form of the Aquarian age: / a splash . . . on the grass of this earth even the stars love, splashes of the sacred waters . . ." (p. 68). Literally the rain or dew of early morning reflects the light of "the last scattered stars," including the constellation Aquarius, the water-bearer, sign of our eleventh-hour epoch.

Speaking about the ninth Duino Elegy in one of his interviews, Kinnell observed, "Rilke says, in effect, 'Don't try to tell the angels about the glory of your feelings, or how splendid your soul is; they know all about that. Tell them . . . something that you know better than they, tell them about the things of this world' " (*Walking*, p. 35). The stars, "unearthly fires," in "The Path among the Stones," are images of the glory and splendor of the visionary imagination. Their kneeling on the grass expresses the love of the visionary imagination for the ordinary things of this world. The dew or rains which transfigure these things with the reflected fire of the stars are "sacred," heal-ing waters.

As Seamus Heaney says of another poem, these lines "cunningly" make their "cast" and raise "Blake in the pool of the ear."[12] They echo lines from "The Tiger": "When the stars threw down their spears, / And water'd heaven with their tears." This echo reflects the close affinity between the concluding stanzas of this poem and Blake's writings.

For, the concluding stanzas of the "The Path among the Stones" express a visionary conception of the world's redemption which is shaped by feelings and ideas that derive from the Bible and Christian eschatology as well as the religious and visionary literature that has grown out of them.

Despite this heritage (Kinnell's earliest poems are explicit expressions of his Christian background), like Blake's visions of the world's redemption, this one creates a universe without a deity. Implicitly the poet's imagination has taken the place of the Divine Savior who resurrects the dead.

In the last stanza of "The Path among the Stones," the stones, which have been the protean central metaphor developing the argument and jour-ney of the poem through an extraordinarily fertile and coherent variety and range of images and meanings, are grave markers. Here, however, they are not symbolic of death, but have been transformed with delicacy and limpid simplicity into moving images of the miraculous new life which poetic genius can bring to a dead world in a nightmarish time:

So below: in the graveyard
the lamps start lighting up, one for each of us,
in all the windows
of stone (p. 68).

Notes

1. Galway Kinnell, *Walking Down the Stairs* (Ann Arbor: University of Michigan Press, 1978), pp. 46–7. Hereafter this book will be designated *Walking* and the page(s) will be indicated in parentheses in the text.

2. Galway Kinnell, *The Book of Nightmares* (Boston: Houghton Mifflin, 1971), p. 6. Hereafter page numbers will be indicated in parentheses in the text.

3. Galway Kinnell, *Mortal Acts, Mortal Words* (Boston: Houghton Mifflin, 1980). pp. 42–3.

4. *Ibid.*, pp. 41–2.

5. T. S. Eliot, *The Use of Poetry and the Use of Criticism* (Cambridge: Harvard University Press, 1933).

6. *Mortal Acts, Mortal Words,* p. 42.

7. *Letters of Rainer Maria Rilke, 1910–1926,* trans. Jane Bannard Green and M. D. Herter Norton (New York: Norton, 1947, 1948), pp. 148–9.

8. I have consulted Leishman-Spender, MacIntyre, and Garney-Wilson translations of the *Duino Elegies* before translating them for this essay.

9. Rainer Maria Rilke, *Duino Elegies,* trans. J. B. Leishman and Stephen Spender (New York: Norton, 1939), p. 126.

10. See Martin Heidegger, *Poetry, Language, Thought,* trans. and introd. Albert Hofstadter (New York: Harper & Row, 1971), chapter 3, "What Are Poets For?"

11. Rainer Maria Rilke, *The Notebooks of Malte Laurids Brigge,* trans. M. D. Herter Norton (New York: Norton, 1949), p. 27.

12. Seamus Heaney, *Preoccupations: Selected Prose 1968–1978* (New York: Farrar, Straus and Giroux, 1980), p. 157.

To Take Hold of the Song:
The Poetics of Galway Kinnell

SUSAN WESTON

"What is a text, anyway?" was the title of the colloquium, an exchange of ideas among a structuralist, a phenomenologist, a feminist, and a deconstructionist during which no particular text was used. I felt increasingly impatient with the occasion, being the sort of person who tends, when asked "What is a text, anyway?" to wave *the* text that I am reading. I realize the limitations of this gestural response, as well as the limitations behind its premises. I too have enjoyed the heady buzz gained from the intellectual champagne of watching a text recede into strange hieroglyphics on white paper, or of trying to locate the "ontological situs" of the text among thousands of duplicate pages or hundreds of varying responses. But a colloquium on text without any specific text seems to me symptomatic of an ever-widening gulf between literary criticism and the theory of criticism, between the experience of a particular work of literature and the experience of critical theory itself as a form of literature.

Toward the conclusion of this colloquium, I found myself silently reciting lines from Galway Kinnell's *The Book of Nightmares*. The passage comes from "Under the Maud Moon," where Kinnell gives one of the most memorable descriptions of a birth I have ever read, then goes on to talk about the development of this infant who "puts / her hand / into her father's mouth, to take hold of / his song." I did not at the time understand why the lines were occurring to me, so I could not stand up and recite them without appearing daft. Now I realize that they occurred as a comment on our loss of critical innocence: we can no longer take childlike pleasure in the text—put our hands in the poet's mouth—for the song has become not a physical thing but an intellectual formulation.

Galway Kinnell is a poet struggling with the inadequacies of our "pre-Darwinian language" to "speak for mute things" (*Past* 36 and 51). Striving for something beyond an "in-the-tongue language," Kinnell writes to capture the exquisite hinged moments of life when *here* becomes *there, now* becomes *then,* or two individual lovers become an exalted unit, a "shimmering har-

This essay first appeared in *The Literary Review* 31, no. 1 (Fall 1987): 73–85. Reprinted by permission of the author.

monic" (*Past* 49). Called by L. M. Rosenberg "our mightiest poet of transcendence" (40), Kinnell sees poetry as a product of and approach to the body, and the body itself as the vehicle of transcendence.

Although Kinnell is unmistakably an American poet in the post-Romantic tradition, obsessed with death and metamorphosis, a look at his shamanistic poem "The Bear" shows how different Kinnell is in temper, tone, and vision from the Emersonian "poet." If Kinnell is a seer, he sees not with his mind's abstracting eye, but with his body. "The Bear" begins with Kinnell's favorite visual word, "glimpse": "In late winter / I sometimes glimpse bits of steam" (*Body Rags* 60). It is as if Kinnell cannot know a thing merely seen; compare his "glimpse" with Wallace Stevens's favorite "behold," the element of sight turned into an embrace. For Kinnell, by contrast, knowledge comes principally from the senses of taste, smell, touch, and movement. Only when the speaker puts his nose down does he "know / the chilly, enduring odor of bear."

Norman O. Brown has suggested that the tendency toward abstraction, which he regards as a "mode of keeping life at a distance," is accompanied by the dominion of the audiovisual sense over all others (172–73). In his essay "Poetry, Personality, and Death," Kinnell similarly criticizes the analytical gaze:

> The fatal moment was when the human mind learned the knack of detaching itself from what it studied, even when what it studied was itself. The mind became pure will: immaterial, unattached, free of the traumas of birth and death . . . The eye trained to scientific objectivity and glowing with the impersonal spirit of conquest, becomes a deathray. What it kills is the creative relationship between man and thing. (61–62)

About the "creative relationship between man and thing," "The Bear" is written in the language of immersion-in rather than meditation-about. The speaker becomes the bear that he tracks. The process of identification is remarkable, beginning when the hunter rests where the bear has rested and climaxing when the hunter climbs inside the bear's dead body to dream that he is what he has hunted.

The hunter's troubled dream centers on the bear's bloody excrement, the trail left by an internal wound inflicted with the hunter's bait of coiled bone concealed in blubber. By this trail the hunter has both tracked the bear and sustained himself:

> On the third day I begin to starve,
> at nightfall I bend down as I knew I would
> at a turd sopped in blood,
>
> . . . .
>
> and thrust it in my mouth, and gnash it down . . .

Ingested, the bloody excrement transforms the hunter into a creature "stabbed twice from within" by the coiled bone, and, like the bear, splattering a bloody trail. The anguished dream climaxes:

> Until one day I totter and fall—
> fall on this
> stomach that has tried so hard to keep up,
> to digest the blood as it leaked in,
> to break up
> and digest the bone itself: and now the breeze
> blows over me, blows off
> the hideous belches of ill-digested bear blood . . .

In a wonderful distortion of the Romantic metaphor of inspiration—the Aeolian harp—Kinnell has the breeze blow "across / my sore, lolled tongue a song / or screech."

This mysteriously compelling poem that seems to redefine "inspiration" as "in-digestion" concludes with the speaker, who awakens but remains "hairy-soled," asking

> what, anyway,
> was that sticky infusion, that rank flavor of blood, that
> poetry, by which I lived?

The poet John Logan was the first to comment on the implications of this imagery and of similar imagery in "The Porcupine" and "The Testament of the Thief." Logan wrote:

Poetry is a wandering trail of blood and bear shit. It is a pewkworm wound through a hole in the buttocks or cheek of a man. It is the tree-hooked entrails of a porcupine. The images are all repulsive and they are all figures of the slow destruction of the self.

But, Logan qualified:

I would insist that poetry is not a record of self-destructive experience. Rather, it is often a record of recovery from them. It is not the blood-soaked shit of a dying bear. Rather, it is the gold into which that stuff is turned by the magus gift of the poet. (245)

Actually, Kinnell's gift comes from his ability not to alchemize but to digest. Alchemy transmutes; digestion converts. As Kinnell says in "The Path Among the Stones" (a poem in *The Book of Nightmares* describing a descent into the earth in search of the alchemist's wisdom): "Always nothing. Ordinary blood." You cannot turn a base metal into gold; you can, however, simply by accepting it for what it is, convert blood-soaked excrement into something life-sustaining and life-transforming.

In this respect, Kinnell's poetry represents a departure from the tradition established by America's solipsistic seers who have tended to absorb rather fastidiously—usually intellectually and by a process of abstraction. Kinnell imagines biologically and in terms of immersion: sexuality, ingestion, excretion. These are all ways of breaking down the barriers between self and non-self, or seeing the individual as part of a process whereby everything in the world is on its way to becoming something else.

It is not surprising, then, that of all American poets Kinnell most admires Whitman; it is Whitman's ability to "enter many lives" that Kinnell respects (*Walking* 64). But what he calls that "mystical all-lovingness of Walt Whitman" comes in for some telling criticism in "The Last River." This Dantesque long poem depicts the racist hell of a lost America where even Whitman, "my old hero," is not exempt from guilt. Whitman is first shown wiping buffalo- and Indian-blood off a knife, singing at each swipe "mein herz." Whitman explains to the dumbfounded Kinnell that he, Whitman, is also guilty of America's crimes:

> Seeking love . . . love
> without human blood in it,
> that leaps above
> men and women, flesh and erections,
>
> .   .   .   .   .   .
>
> seeking love . . .
> failing to know I only loved
> my purity . . . *mein herz*!

This passage provides another context for "The Bear" and for Kinnell's poetry in general, repudiating as it does the purified notion of a "self" located in the head rather than in the flesh. When the hunter dreams that he is the bear "splattering a trail behind me," it is the excremental path that prevails "no matter which parabola of bear-transcendence / which dance of solitude I attempt." Thus transcendence is associated with solitude and repudiation of the bear-body. The thing syntactically linked to the attempt at transcendence is the excremental trail, both a spatial and a temporal construct suggesting the animal biology of the human creature and its inescapable community with other creatures.

The poetics implicit in this vision are further adumbrated by Kinnell's fine poem, "The Porcupine," in which the association of poetry with visceral activities again occurs. First described as "fatted," "swollen," "puffed up," and "ballooned," the porcupine "drags and bounces his last meal through ice." This porcupine, we learn from a later section, has been shot by a farmer and has fallen from a tree, hooking its gut on a branch:

> . . . On the ground
> it sprang to its feet, and
> paying out gut heaved
> and spartled through a hundred feet of goldenrod
> before
> the abrupt emptiness.

Kinnell again establishes his own identification with the wounded animal; just as the hunter becomes the bear "stabbed from within," so here Kinnell becomes the insatiable porcupine, the "self-stabbing coil / of bristles reversing, blossoming outward." Towards the poem's conclusion, the intestinal image reappears:

> I have come to myself empty, the rope
> strung out behind me
> in the fall sun
> suddenly glorified with all my blood.

The paid-out gut of the intestinal image becomes the equivalent for the speaker's terrified, solitary fall into his own emptiness.

Kinnell gives the porcupine his highest tribute when he calls it an "ultra-Rilkean angel." The allusion is to this section of Rilke's ninth Duino elegy:

> Praise the world to the angel—not the inexpressible realm:
> You can't impress him with the splendor of your feelings;
> you are only a beginner in the cosmos where he feels more feelingly.

Even more important than the angel is the subsequent passage of the elegy, which might stand as an epigraph to most of Kinnell's work:

> . . . The things that live on departure
> are aware of your praising: transitory themselves, they count
> on us to save them, us, the most transient of all.
> They want us to transmute them in our invisible hearts,
> into—oh infinitely—into our selves, whoever we are.
> ("Poetics" 124–25)

Like Rilke, Kinnell praises the things that live on departure; he sees, however, in terms that are simultaneously more geological and more minute. His porcupine is a "Rilkean angel"

> for whom the true
> portion of sweetness of earth
> is one of those bottom-heavy, glittering, saccadic

>bits
>of salt water that splash down
>the haunted ravines of a human face.

With its remarkable conflation of terms, this passage achieves the Rilkean transmutation of "things" into "ourselves." Continuing the ingestion pattern with the gustatory "portion of sweetness," the passage suggests that the porcupine-speaker's eating is one way of achieving the Rilkean task. The geological metaphor for the human face, moreover, makes the human face—"us, the most transient of all"—both world and reference point.

Everything lives on departures—including a poem. Kinnell has said, "The subject of the poem is the thing which dies," and in that opinion he echoes Rilke. He adds his own intense vision of the mortality of all things when he says, "Poetry is the wasted breath" ("Poetics" 125). "The Poem," one of Kinnell's rare poems explicitly about poetry, begins by comparing earth, face, and poem:

>On this hill crossed
>by the last birds, a sprinkling
>of soil covers up the rocks
>with green, as
>the face
>drifts on a skull scratched with glaciers.
>
>The poem too
>is a palimpsest, streaked
>with erasures, smelling
>of departures and burnt stone.

In this landscape that analogizes the vanishing poem and the vanishing earth, the poet hunts for "the wild hummingbird / who once loved nesting in these / pokeweed-sprouting, pismired / ribcages dumped down all over the place." Among the bones of the departed, the ephemeral living—hummingbird, pokeweed, ant, and poet—construct their ephemeral futures.

What is a text? A splattered trail of bloody excrement, intestines strung out in the sun, the surface of geological strata on earth, or face, or paper? Galway Kinnell would have little patience with the linguistic notion that every word is an abstraction and thus removed from the thing that it represents. Preoccupied as he is with other kinds of departures, meditating about the relationship between language and reality plays a small and not very distinguished part in his repertoire. Kinnell's tender comment in "Whitman's Indicative Words" applies equally to Kinnell himself:

Whitman loved words as physical entities, but entities which could only become physical through absolute attachment to reality. For it's curious with words, they can't be loved for themselves alone. Like our human lovers, words attach to a deeper life than their own, and are loved for their own particular qualities, yes, but loved supremely because in them flowers that which we more deeply love. (10)

Kinnell also shares Whitman's text-obliterating notion of the poem: "Your very flesh shall be a great poem." Kinnell, who has perceived Whitman flounder in that very enterprise by trying to rise above the body into "purity," sees a poem as both a product of and a way to the body.

But there is another kind of relationship that Kinnell questions—obliquely at least—and that is the poet's individual relationship to this departing reality. The solitary poet, the "man without impediments," as Emerson called him, when conscious of death as Kinnell is, must question his relationship not so much to death as to life. The *cultural* significance of this question has been suggested by Harold Bloom in *Figures of Capable Imagination,* where Bloom compares the American poet's attitude toward death with the European dialectic of the communal and the solitary. In European culture, Bloom comments, "the consciousness of death's necessity calls into question the purposiveness of all human action that is not somehow communal." But for American poets, Bloom continues, "Dying, whatever else it is for our native strain, for the genius of America, is not a social act" (98).

Insofar as Bloom's generalization is accurate, it points up another source of tension in Kinnell's poetry—a dialectic not so much between the solitary and the communal as between the solitary and the familial. In "The Bear," for example, the speaker awakens to a life of solitary wandering that is juxtaposed and, surely, contrasted to the generative community suggested by the female bear. The speaker remains isolated and preoccupied with the ground (the site of the "trail"), while the dam-bear is "licking / lumps of smeared fur / . . . into shapes / with her tongue." The displacement of the "shaping tongue" onto the reproductive dam-bear hints at a dissatisfaction with the solitary, painful process of the poem itself.

The conclusion of "The Porcupine" raises similar questions:

> And tonight I think I prowl broken
> skulled or vacant as a
> sucked egg in the wintry meadow, softly chuckling, blank
> template of myself, dragging
> a starved belly through the lichflowered acres,
> where
> burdock looses the arks of its seed
> and thistle holds up its lost blooms
> and rosebushes in the wind scrape their dead limbs
> for the forced-fire
> of roses.

"Vacant" and "blank" suggest that this might be a dejection poem about lost or spent creativity, but the vehicles of these figures—"vacant as a sucked egg" and "blank template"—equally suggest isolation from a genetic community. Moreover, the plants that he comes across in the field—burdock, thistle, and rosebush—all of which resemble the prickly porcupine (and thus the speaker)—are all reproducing themselves. Even the rosebushes, dormant during the winter, are rubbing their sticks together to make the "fire" of life, roses.

For a revealing comparison, set Kinnell's passage beside one from Emerson's "The Poet":

> Genius is the activity which repairs the decay of things, whether wholly or partly. . . . Nature, through all her kingdoms, insures herself. Nobody cares for planting the poor fungus; so she shakes down from the gills of one agaric countless spores, any one of which, being preserved, transmits new billions of spores tomorrow or next day. . . . She makes a man; and having brought him to ripe age, she will no longer run the risk of losing this wonder at a blow, but she detaches from him a new self, that the kind may be safe from accidents to which the individual is exposed.

But the poet's work is placed "outside" of nature, and the whole process of reproduction is reduced to analogy when Emerson continues:

> So when the soul of the poet has come to ripeness of thought, she detaches and sends away from it its poems or songs . . . deathless progeny which is not exposed to the accidents of the weary kingdom of time. (330)

But Kinnell, as I have suggested, considers the poem just as mortal as a hummingbird, just as natural a "product" of the human body as excrement. His conviction makes a mockery of the Emersonian poet, the "man without impediments" who must "leave the world" in order to repair it. For Kinnell, the notion of the "immortal poem" outside the "weary kingdom of time" is a kind of obscenity.

Though Kinnell continues to write out of an intensely felt solitude, the sense of isolation and vacancy pervading *Body Rags* changes dramatically in *The Book of Nightmares,* written after the birth of his two children. Kinnell's nightmare vision of a world gone mad with hatred and denial is heightened by a father's hectic love for his children, who make him feel more keenly his own mortality as well as the necessity of accepting it.

The very structure of *The Book of Nightmares* suggests the complexity of the struggle, for the book has two framing devices that create a dialectical effect between the solitary and the familial. One frame is provided by the birth of the two children, and the other by a description of "this wet site / of old fires." About the first framing device, Kinnell has spoken eloquently in *Walking Down the Stairs:*

From one point of view, the book is nothing but an effort to face death and live with death. . . . [Children] live with death almost as animals do. This natural trust in life's rhythms, infantile as it is, provides the model for the trust they may struggle to learn later on. *The Book of Nightmares* is my own effort to find the trust again. I invoke Maud and Fergus not merely to instruct them, but also to get help from them. (45–46)

About the second framing device Kinnell says nothing, though the entire poem is located within this single brief narrative sequence. The book begins with the speaker lighting a "small fire in the rain" and concludes some seventy pages later, "Somewhere behind me / a small fire goes on flaring in the rain."

The tension generated by these two frames makes *The Book of Nightmares* more than a book about accepting death; it makes the book a definition of what Rilke calls life-AND-death, of the life that lets death be a part of its process, and a definition of art as well. A brief look at the second framing device, therefore, must precede an analysis of the effect of the double frame.

The book begins with the futile effort of a man seeking comfort in the rain. It is quickly clear that the cold and hunger are emotional rather than physical, for the small fire is kindled

> . . . for her,
> whose face
> I held in my hands
> a few hours, whom I gave back
> only to keep holding the space where she was.

Describing his emotion in terms of the things around him, Kinnell hears in the burning wet wood "the snap / and re-snap of the same embrace being torn" and in the interaction of the fire and rain that obliterate each other: "the oath sworn between earth and water, flesh and spirit, broken." As he sings "one of the songs I used to croak / for my daughter, in her nightmares," the "love-note" curves off into a "howl." The book ends at the same wet site, but with the victory of peace of mind:

> Somewhere behind me
> a small fire goes on flaring in the rain, in the desolate ashes.
> No matter, now, whom it was built for. . . .

That the first and last poems of *The Book of Nightmares* are integrally connected by the site and its correlative emotion is clear from their original publication in *The New Yorker* in 1971, where the first parts of "Under the Maud Moon" and sections of "Lastness" are treated as a single poem called "The Path Toward the High Valley" (38). The "path" is the equivalent of both the meditative process of the poem and the temporal "road" of life. Looked at in its original integrity, the poem shows the essential themes and images of the entire book: the images of "held nothingness," of birth, of the path; the themes of life, death, and of death assimilated into life. The premise of the entire book is stated in the poem's conclusion: "Living brings you to death, there is no other road," with the emphasis not on the death, but on the living, the road. What *The New Yorker* version does not show is the cost of that affirmation in the heaped details of horror and pain that occur in the book between the first and last moments on that "path."

More important than the structural stability this organization gives the book, however, is its power to *motivate* the entire book: this scene by the fire generates all the other scenes in *The Book of Nightmares* by forcing the speaker to explore the damaging ways that we can travel that temporal road. Of all the ways that we can distract ourselves from our mortality—with notions of transcendence, by distancing ourselves from our dying bodies in a variety of sublimations and abstractions and drugs—the idea of perfect romantic love is for Kinnell the most tempting. It too is a denial of death.

In "The Call Across the Valley of Not-Knowing," the eighth poem, Kinnell explores our reasons for seeking "enduring love." Angrily he rejects the notion of perfect love:

> Aristophanes ran off
> at the mouth—made it all up, nightmared it all up
> on the spur
> of that moment which has stabbed us ever since.

It's not true, then, that "each of us / is a torn half / whose lost other we keep seeking across time / until we die, or give up— / or actually find her." The poet pivots, contradicts himself: "as I myself . . . / . . . / . . . actually found her / held her face a few hours / in my hands." There is the "held face" of "Under the Maud Moon," the "torn" embrace, and the corroboration of the myth of perfect love. "And yet," Kinnell goes on, veering off, struggling to find his balance, his center of belief, "And yet I think / it must be the wound, the wound itself, / which lets us know and love." In the penultimate section of this poem, Kinnell imagines that if he had stayed with this woman, "I might have closed my eyes, and moved / from then on like the born blind, / their faces / gone into heaven already." And that is precisely what Kinnell wants to show is not desirable; the bliss of living is to love what vanishes, to affirm even the sorrows of departure.

Returning now to the two framing devices, we can see their relationship: the children's birth and the failure of love are comparable experiences, but each modifies the other. Thus in "Under the Maud Moon," Kinnell interrupts the development of the one sequence—the howl of personal pain at holding an emptiness—by turning to another, the birth of his daughter and her first song, the scream of the first breath. When Kinnell describes the infant Maud "already clutching at the emptiness," the imagery recalls the first section where he is "holding the space where she was." The juxtaposition of the two experiences and of the two songs of pain suggests a comparison between "holding nothing" and existence itself.

In "Lastness," similarly, Kinnell takes the newborn Fergus in his hands and smells the infant "as empty space / must have bent / over the newborn planet." This startling imagery of emptiness contrasts with the image of one-ness which occurs for both the fetus before existence and for the lover when he finds his "perfect other." Just as Maud flips and leaps in fetal bliss in the "oneness / under the hill," the lovers are imagined "on a hill called Safa," the hill where Adam and Eve will meet when they meet again.

There is something mind- (or heart-) catching in the repetition of the word "necessity" at two crucial points in *The Book of Nightmares.* "Necessity" is the reason he gives himself for leaving the finally found "lost other" (in "The Call Across the Valley"), and "necessity" is the life-and-death he accepts in "Lastness" when Kinnell's free-floating skydiver opens "his arms into the attitude / of flight, as he obeys the necessity and falls . . ." But how different is this, finally, from the confrontation with death in what Harold Bloom calls the American poets' "gorgeous solipsism"? "Dying," Bloom says, "is the ultimate solipsistic adventure, at once Bacchic, erotic and neces-sitarian, and as much an act of solitary fulfillment as the writing of a poem is" (102).

Kinnell certainly falters at the very close—trapped perhaps by the Rilkean structure of the sequence, or perhaps by a failure of vision. The book concludes with Kinnell accepting—"falling" into—his own death, but not with a vision of community. Though the father's last poem of lastness was surely intended as a positive gesture of conferring life to a next generation, the last two sections of the sequence fall far short of merging the self-absorbed self with the communal life.

And yet by the conclusion of *The Book of Nightmares,* Kinnell has rede-fined poetry itself as the resolution of the solitary, individually felt pain. The "howl" that begins the book is transformed into the music of a Bach concert. When "the violinist / puts the irreversible sorrow of his face / into the opened palm / of the wood,"the imagery movingly connects artistic expression to the other images of "held faces" and "held nothingness." The music made by the violin's bow comes, conveniently enough for Kinnell's recurrent image pat-tern, from "the sliced intestine / of cat." Thus the "sexual wail" that he hears even in the Bach music is the essential voice; the nature that simultaneously links us to the biological community and condemns us to decay and death *is* the voice of art.

This is an abiding vision, informing Kinnell's poetry from *Body Rags* to *The Book of Nightmares* to the most recent collection, *The Past.* Early on, poetry is a "map of the innards." That self-absorbed private project yields to the more collective voice of *The Past:*

> . . . So what if we groan?
> That's our noise. Laughter is our stuttering
> in a language we can't speak yet.
>   ("The Seekonk Woods")

Poem and body are inseparable, as Kinnell suggests again and again in his groan-laughing song-screeching poetry of passion and departures, his lyrics to an evanescent "here and now" inescapably hooked into both the past and the future. In "Whitman's Indicative Words," Kinnell expresses the relationship overtly, even outrageously:

> Since words form in the poet's throat muscles, they can be said to come out of his very flesh. And since the reader's throat muscles also have to form the words, the words enter the reader's very flesh. Poetry goes not merely from mind to mind, but from the whole body to the whole body. (9)

But this last comment is by the essayist, struggling to say what the poet expresses better:

> And she who is born,
> she who sings and cries.
> she who begins the passage. . . .
> .   .   .   .
> the mist still clinging about
> her face, puts
> her hand
> into her father's mouth, to take hold of
> his song.

Works Cited

Bloom, Harold, *Figures of Capable Imagination.* The Seabury Press, 1976.

Brown, Norman O. *Life Against Death.* Middletown, Conn.: Wesleyan University Press, 1979.

Emerson, Ralph Waldo. *The Selected Writings of Ralph Waldo Emerson.* New York: Modern Library, Random House, 1950.

Kinnell, Galway. *Body Rags.* Boston: Houghton Mifflin, 1967.

———. *The Book of Nightmares.* Boston: Houghton Mifflin, 1971.

———. *The Past.* Boston: Houghton Mifflin, 1985.

———. "The Path Toward the High Valley." *The New Yorker,* 17 April 1971.

———. "The Poetics of the Physical World." *Iowa Review* II, 3 (Summer 1971).

———. "Poetry, Personality, and Death." *Field* 4 (Spring 1971).

———. *Walking Down the Stairs. Selections from Interviews.* Ann Arbor, Mich.: University of Michigan Press, 1978.

————. "Whitman's Indicative Words." *American Poetry Review,* March–April 1973.

Logan, John. "The Bear in the Poet in the Bear." *The Nation,* 16 September 1968.

Rosenberg, L. M. Review of *The Past. The Chicago Tribune,* 2 February 1986.

From Irony to Lyricism:
Galway Kinnell's True Voice

GRANVILLE TAYLOR

To read the poetry of Galway Kinnell is to witness a poetic evolution. The Kinnell canon includes nine volumes of poetry and offers a paradigm for the present-day romantic struggling to free himself from his Christian inheritance yet to affirm that the world contains order, meaning, and the sacred. Kinnell's poetry begins with an attempt to reconcile Christian theology, particularly the resurrection, with human mortality and suffering. As this effort proves futile, he surrenders explicitly Christian references in favor of a natural theology that views the world as sacramental and emphasizes immanence over transcendence. Natural theology does not define the Absolute as a Being. Instead of Christian theism, Kinnell's notion of God is of Being itself which is embedded in creation. There is no transcendent realm over against creation. We might call Kinnell's sense of the holy a nontheistic sacramentalism, or echo Nathan Scott in calling it "panentheism."[1] Charles Altieri offers perhaps the clearest description:

> For the postmoderns, meaning and significance tend to depend on the immanent qualities manifested in the particular. As Olson put it, meaning is "that which exists through itself," or in Roethke's terms, "intensely seen, image becomes symbol"—a symbol is not a way of raising particulars to higher orders of significance . . . but a particular charged with numinous force. This does not mean there are no universals, only that the universals that matter are not conceptual structures but energies recurring in numinous moments.[2]

In short, Kinnell's poetry develops from Christian to natural theology, from irony to lyricism, and from pessimism to affirmation and joy. The initial poems depict the gulf between the contingencies of existence and the assertions of Christian theism. As he drops theistic references, his vision becomes sacramental and brings the holy into his poems.

Although raised a Congregationalist, Kinnell is most authentic as a romantic, not a Christian poet. The romantic is, more than anything else, alone. The old gods or myths are no more. One is left to discover meaning on

This essay first appeared in *Christianity and Literature* 37, no. 4 (Summer 1988): 45–54.

personal terms. The romantic existence is, therefore, unmediated. No longer does one have the Incarnation or God-man as mediator; no longer are there rituals which recreate sacred time. One faces, as George Steiner says, a "world gone flat."[3] Yet an unmediated world is also a world of possibilities, for it can be made profane or sacred. John S. Dunne points out:

> The modern man ... finds his hell and purgatory on earth in the form of despair, and he seeks accordingly to find his heaven upon earth too, perhaps in some ideal change of circumstances or inwardly in some kind of inner assurance.[4]

The task, therefore, is to create one's own mythos and entails a fundamental redefining of the connectedness of human-world-divine to discover what, if any, sacred realm remains. Whereas the orthodox Christian's relation to the world is a derivative of the relation to the Christ, the romantic seeks to discover a relation to the world that allows or even causes the sacred to be revealed.

In his first two volumes, *First Poems* and *What a Kingdom It Was,* Kinnell essentially fights the wrong battle. He argues against his religious upbringing instead of accepting romanticism. It is as if Kinnell has to kill his parental ghosts before he can speak in his own voice. The protagonists of these poems cling to a mediated existence and, in so doing, confront the inadequacy of the Christian mythos for the complexities of contemporary existence. They continue to look for transcendence in a flat world and to look in vain. The result is a poetry which is ironic, pessimistic, and unromantic. Not surprisingly, an orthodox critic like Donald Davie claims that in these poems Kinnell "should not having turned his back on Christian dispensation, continue to trade surreptitiously in scraps torn arbitrarily from the body of doctrine he has renounced."[5]

The central problem is death. For Kinnell, theology is at best an evasion of human mortality and at worst a delusion:

> Theology and philosophy, with their large words, their abstract formulations, their airtight systems, which until recently they imagined forever, deal with paradigms of eternity. The subject of the poem dies.[6]

Kinnell's point is that to begin with a myth is to begin from the wrong direction. Conceptualization dilutes one's sense of reality; it distorts one's vision. Because existence does not fit a system, the early poems are filled with irony. Kinnell depicts the dilemma in these terms: "The poetics of heaven agree to the denigration of pain and death; in the poetics of the physical world these are the very elements."[7] The poetics of heaven offer explanations; the poetics of the physical world offer one a sense of existence. Elsewhere, Kinnell says, "What do we want more than that oneness, which bestows—which is—life?

We want only to be more alive, not less."[8] For him, to be alive is to relinquish one's preconceptions of existence and to accept the inevitable duality of existence: joy/pain and life/death. These first poems, therefore, demonstrate the inadequacy of the poetics of heaven.

"Easter" is representative. The focus of the poem is death—specifically the death of a "virgin nurse." "Raped, robbed, weighed, drowned," her body drifts below the river's surface. Although the poem's protagonist wishes a resurrection for her—"In the floating days may you discover grace"—the poem offers little hope of its occurrence. In this world, rather:

> Death is everywhere, in the extensive
> Sermon, the outcry of the inaudible
> Prayer, the nickels, the dimes the poor give,
> And outside, at last, in the gusts of April.[9]

Death, therefore, is unalterable and pandemic. Humankind can wait and pray for resurrection, but there is little chance that anyone will emerge from the tomb. The only hint of any afterlife is the sea, the body's final destination. It signifies a return to universal nature. The thrust of the poem, however, is to demonstrate the distance between theology and existence. Death exists in the very sermon that denies its reality. The body does not rise but will forever drift. If grace is to occur, it will not negate death's finality. Grace is possible in Kinnell's world, but to occur it must be translated from Christian to natural theology. The later volumes contain such occurrences because by then the translation is complete.

The style of the poem is also quite different from those that follow. Its formality is uncharacteristic. Kinnell feels that "rhyme and meter, having lost their sacred and natural basis, amount to little more than mechanical aids for writing."[10] These devices made sense if one believed in a "natural harmony" or sought "to call back in poetry, the grace disappearing from everything else."[11] The contemporary poet is not interested in either endeavor. Living an unmediated existence, he cannot go by any models but seeks to create a new voice—a voice that "does not subjugate speech, but conforms to its irregular curves, to the terrain itself."[12] That Kinnell here adopts rhyme indicates both the inauthenticity of this voice and an attempt, modelled on the concept of Easter, to fit a dynamic reality into a static form.

An equally clear example of Kinnell's ironic use of Christian subjects is "The Supper After the Last." Christ returns in the poem, but his message is, surprisingly, that death is final:

> . . . Your
> Lech for transcendence?
> I came to prove you are
> Intricate and simple things
> As you are, created
> In the image of nothing (p. 101).

Here the poet points to future poems. To understand the essence of Christ's message—that one is to become a vehicle for and a receiver of grace—is paradoxically to let go of theology. Humans are miraculous as they exist. Instead of hoping for redemption beyond this world, one is to look for it within this world. In short, grace will be immanent and not transcendent.

To deny death, therefore, is to block grace from occurring. The poem opens with an example of the futility of such a gesture:

> . . . Near shore
> A bather wades through his shadow in the water.
> He tramples and kicks it; it recomposes (p. 100).

At the poem's end, the Christ returns to affirm the permanence of the shadow or death:

> I cut to your measure the creeping piece of darkness
> That haunts you in the dirt. Step into the light—
> I make you over. I breed the shape of your grave in the dirt (p. 102).

The Christ has not come promising resurrection but death and, as a result, the tone of the poem is dark and ironic. Kinnell presents the attempt of translating the language of faith into the actuality of existence as doomed to failure. As the Christ of the poem admits, the distance is too great: "You are the flesh; I am the resurrection" (p. 102). Whatever the nature of the Christ, whatever the claims of theology, humankind's dilemma remains a certain extinction with no promise of an afterlife. As long as one hopes for a heaven above time, one misses the fullness of the present. Eternity is to be found existentially. Kinnell writes elsewhere:

> In the desolation of the universe, the brief, tender acts, the beauty that passes, which belong to life in the world, are the only heaven.[13]

His religious vision, then, is an inversion of orthodoxy. Instead of "The Word was made flesh," his poem "The Descent" claims, "In the cry / *Eloi! Eloi!* flesh was made word" (p. 92). Creation is not an expression of an already existent deity. Rather, in its depth creation gives expression to the sacred. The Christ was not the Word in the beginning, but becomes the word by fully being flesh. In his essay, Kinnell explains, "Zeus on Olympus is a theological being; the swan who desires a woman enters the province of poetry. In *Eloi, Eloi, laura sabacthani,* so does Jesus."[14] The universe is dynamic and demands the "poetics of the physical world" for expression of its sacred dimension. To put this differently, grace can be found if one lives a full existence in the present moment. Like rhyme and meter, theology leads to a false existence and a false poetry. In those moments in the gospels when Jesus was living authenti-cally, he gave expression to wondrous poetry. Christ crucified can be a media-tor but not Christ resurrected.

The poetry of the early Kinnell is, therefore, unsatisfactory because he has yet to find his true voice. He points to a sacramental view of the world and suggests that an attentiveness to the very things and beings of life brings one into a participation of mystery. Existence is to be an ongoing revelation of a natural grace, but his revelation only occurs if one accepts death. These early poems hint at this vision but fail to give it adequate expression because of their concern with showing the inadequacy of a Christian concept of resur-rection and immortality. Irony, after all, is rarely a vehicle for grace. This Kin-nell is actually closer to Robinson Jeffers than to Thoreau, Williams, or Roethke. It is only after he discards all Christian references and relinquishes his attempt at reconciliation that he joins his true literary ancestors.

The poems in *Mortal Acts, Mortal Words* are radically different from the earlier work. Instead of ironic, they are lyrical. Instead of the futile attempt to make the Word flesh, these begin with the flesh and sometimes discover the words of grace. In these poems, however, grace is not expressed in words but in music. The logic of this metaphor is obvious. Music is nonverbal and is, therefore, based on nonrepresentational logic. Since music does not separate subject and object, the poet can more easily express an existent unity of fun-damental connectedness to the universe. Lastly, music exists in time. It begins and ends. One can become part of it while it lives, but there is no delusion that it points to an existence above time.

Kinnell is not, of course, the creator of this metaphor. Since Ptolomaic cosmology music has been associated with divine order. Henry David Thoreau, however, is Kinnell's most immediate precursor. *Walden* describes Emerson's self-reliant person as one who steps "to the music which he hears, however, measured or far away."[15] In his essay "The Service," Thoreau indi-cates the true source of harmony: "To the sensitive soul the universe has her own fixed measure and rhythm, which is its measure also and constitutes the regularity and health of its pulse."[16] To discover the sacred is to align oneself with the rudimentary rhythms that pervade the world. These can only be found by attending to the particulars of nature. For Thoreau, grace enables one to align the inner sense of order with an outer, but for Thoreau there is a greater sense of an external order than with Kinnell. The cost of giving up theism is that meaning increasingly becomes solely existential and private. Thoreau equates the personal harmony with the Universal. The modern or postmodern poet wonders if perhaps music does not come from the heavens but only from the self. Thoreau offers a metaphor for grace, but Kinnell extends the metaphor by making grace more private.

"There Are Things I Tell to No One" offers the most explicit expression of this image:

> I say "God"; I believe,
> rather, in a music of grace
> that we hear, sometimes, playing to us,
> from the other side of happiness.
> When we hear it, when it flows
> through our bodies, it lets us live
> these days lighted by their vanity
> worshipping—as the other animals do,
> who live and die in the spirit
> of the end—that backward-spreading
> brightness. And it speaks in notes struck
> or caressed or blown or plucked
> off our own bodies.[17]

The "music of grace" is Kinnell's "flesh made word." It comes from the body and flows through the body. As the agent of grace, the music affirms the essential connectedness of creation in time. It sounds not from the other side of life but from the other side of happiness. It enables us to worship the life force in "the spirit of the end."

Later in the poem, the music again sounds and reunites the persona with life's rhythms:

> Yes. I want to live forever.
> I am like everyone. But when I hear
> that breath coming through the walls,
> grace-notes blown
> out of the wormed-out bones,
>
> . . . .
>
> then it is not so difficult
> to go out, to turn and face
> the spaces which gather into one sound. . . .[18]

The essential music of existence brings grace. Its rhythm connects the human with that which is essential and, in so doing, shows the sacramental nature of reality. The depth of life is founded on the fact of death; the "grace-notes" are "blown / out of the wormed-out bones." As Kinnell says elsewhere:

> Everyone who truly sings is beautiful.
> Even sad music
> requires absolute happiness:
> eyes, nostrils, mouth strain together in quintal harmony
> to say Joy and Death well.[19]

The music, or poetry, comes from harmonizing death with life.

The stylistic differences between earlier and later poems are obvious as the content. Instead of a tight formal stanza and rhyme, the poems are in free verse and employ a speech rhythm. Most of all the perspective of the persona is subjective. He is looking through existence to discover meaning instead of down on existence from a detached position.

Perhaps Kinnell's most affirmative poem is "The Still Time." The poem opens with a frank expression of faith:

> I know there is still time—
> time for the hands
> to open, for the bones of them
> to be filled
> by those failed harvests of want,
> the bread imagined of the days of not having.[20]

"Still" has its double meaning: "yet" and "not moving." Each sense expresses Kinnell's faith in the powers of creation for renewal. The bread of life is immanental, in time. The hope is not for life after death but a deepening of life before; that is, for *chronos* to change to *kairos*.

The poem ends with a passage that echoes Hopkins' celebration for the sheer mystery and wonder of existence:

> as though a prayer had ended
> and the changed
> air between the palms goes free
> to become the glitter
> on common things that inexplicably shine.
>
> And all the old voices,
> which once made broken off, choked, parrot-incoherences,
> speak again,
> this time on the palatum cordis, all of them
> saying there is time, still time,
> for those who groan
> to sing,
> for those who can sing to heal themselves.[21]

This is a world of participation: human with natural and the living with the dead. The common things shine inexplicably. Again the flesh becomes word. The final result is to sing or to join in the natural rhythm. The world, therefore, is sacramental; it is the vehicle for grace. Grace in this context satisfies "our deepest desire, which is to be one with all creation."[22] Kinnell typically insists upon the mixture of joy and pain. It is "those who groan" who sing. Moreover, in an unmediated world, one must heal oneself—albeit with creation's help. "The Still Time" shows the possibilities for a religious view that remains faithful to human mortality yet affirms the possibility of ecstasy in time.

There are, then, two Galway Kinnells. As long as he seeks to emulate Milton and to "justify the ways of God to man," the poet can only write in a voice that is ironic, pessimistic, and, finally, false. All that he affirms is the fact of death. When he alters his direction and focuses on the flesh itself, the poet's voice is lyrical, affirmative and true. The world becomes sacrament; creation becomes a choir that sings of "Joy and Death."

Kinnell's career demonstrates the difficulty of remaining true to the givens of modern existence while using the Christian myth as a paradigm. Perhaps in a world of Vietnam, Cambodia, and Ethiopia all one can see is Christ crucified. For Kinnell this leads to irony. For others it might lead to apologetics. A few certainly can still see such occurrences and witness the resurrection. Galway Kinnell's poetic development is not paradigmatic for all contemporary poets, nor does it demonstrate that poetry can no longer be orthodox. Rather, Galway Kinnell's poetry shows that the sacred dimension can be found in contexts which are not explicitly Christian and even explicitly non-Christian. His poems call for an expansion of interpretations of grace and sacrament. Dietrich Bonhoeffer once stated that the modern task is discovering how to speak "in a secular fashion of God."[23] In his later poems Galway Kinnell has made such a discovery.

Notes

1.   Nathan Scott, *The Wild Prayer of Longing: Poetry and the Sacred* (New Haven: Yale University Press, 1971), p. 58.

2.   Charles Altieri, *Enlarging the Temple: New Directions in American Poetry during the 1960's* (Lewisburg: Bucknell University Press, 1979), p. 42.

3.   George Steiner, *In Bluebeard's Castle* (New Haven: Yale University Press, 1971), p. 55.

4.   John S. Dunne, *A Search for God in Time and Memory* (Notre Dame: University of Notre Dame Press, 1977), p. 216.

5.   Donald Davie, "Slogging for the Absolute," in *On the Poetry of Galway Kinnell: The Wages of Dying*, ed. Howard Nelson (Ann Arbor: University of Michigan Press, 1987), p. 151.

6.   Galway Kinnell, "The Poetics of the Physical World," *The Iowa Review*, 2 (1971), p. 125.

7.   Kinnell, p. 119.

8.   Galway Kinnell, "Poetry, Personality, and Death," in *Claims for Poetry*, ed. Donald Hall (Ann Arbor: University of Michigan Press, 1982), p. 230.

9.   Galway Kinnell, *The Avenue Bearing the Initial of Christ into the New World* (Boston: Houghton Mifflin, 1974), p. 58. All further references to this work appear in the text.

10.   Kinnell, "Poetics," p. 113.

11.   Kinnell, "Poetics," p. 113.

12.   Kinnell, "Poetics," p. 120.

13.   Kinnell, "Poetics," p. 122.

14.   Kinnell, "Poetics," p. 125.

15.   Henry David Thoreau, *Walden and Other Writings* (New York: The Modern Library, 1981), p. 290.

16.   Henry David Thoreau, "The Service," in *Reform Papers*, ed. Wendell Glick (Princeton: Princeton University Press, 1973), p. 11.

17. Galway Kinnell, *Mortal Acts, Mortal Words* (Boston: Houghton Mifflin, 1980), p. 59.
18. Kinnell, *Mortal,* pp. 61–62.
19. Kinnell, *Mortal,* p. 10.
20. Kinnell, *Mortal,* p. 20.
21. Kinnell, *Mortal,* p. 58.
22. Kinnell, "Poetry," p. 223.
23. Dietrich Bonhoeffer, *Letters and Papers from Prison* (New York: Macmillan, 1966), p. 92.

The Wages of Dying Is Love:
Galway Kinnell's *Book of Nightmares*

THOMAS GARDNER

> It is written in our hearts, the emptiness is all.
> That is how we have learned, the embrace is all.[1]

These lines, appearing in 1980—nine years after Galway Kinnell's deliberate grappling with "Song of Myself" in *The Book of Nightmares*—make explicit what, for Kinnell, were the personal grounds for Whitman's work in that poem. That Whitman's use of the embrace was both limited by and formulated in rich reaction to the fact of "emptiness"—what we love vanishes—seems to Kinnell both inescapable and never directly displayed in the poem. If Whitman "clarified [the] madness" that stemmed from seeing that desired embrace blocked and found in that personal clarification the basis for a new sort of openness—"joyful health"—that struggle was, according to Kinnell's reading, conducted only as an act of "supererogation."[2] What Kinnell challenges himself to do in *The Book of Nightmares*, then, following Whitman's lead, is to meet head on the "curse" of human emptiness.[3] Although he and Berryman identify different personal difficulties preventing the poet's full embrace of his surroundings (an inherited illness, the dread of death), they both point to, and attempt to unpack the rich implications of, what Kinnell calls the single "moment" in Whitman in which the limitations of the embrace are exposed and the device is then reformulated.[4]

One way to begin to understand the deliberateness of Kinnell's unfolding of that moment is to look first at his use of the embrace in two significant early poems, "The Bear" and "The Porcupine." In both poems, Kinnell powerfully imagines himself into a union with an animal. In the first, a hunter trails a bear for seven days, living, in the hunt's final stages, on the animal's blood and droppings. The ritual identification is completed when the hunter

This essay first appeared in *Discovering Ourselves in Whitman: The Contemporary American Long Poem* (Urbana: University of Illinois Press, 1989), pp. 59–77. Reprinted by permission of The University of Illinois Press and the author.

finally encounters the dying animal, cuts it open, and climbs under the skin. In so doing, he gains not only warmth and sustenance but also a new means of expression; as he sleeps, he dreams of himself as the bear, first "lumbering flatfooted / over the tundra," then collapsed and awaiting death, with the wind blowing "across / my sore, lolled tongue a song / or screech, until I think I must rise up / and dance" (BR, 62). Likewise, in the second poem, remembering a porcupine shot from a tree ("On the ground / it sprang to its feet, and / paying out gut heaved / and spartled through a hundred feet of goldenrod / before / the abrupt emptiness") Kinnell dreams of himself as that animal, "pricking the / woman beside me until she cries" (BR, 58). Again, this connection gives him a way to identify and speak of his own feelings of confusion and failure: "I have come to myself empty, the rope / strung out behind me / in the fall sun / suddenly glorified with all my blood" (BR, 59). In both poems, although the step-by-step process of merging poet and medium is carefully worked out and the newly acquired language is explored, little attention is given to the conditions that make the union possible. That is, just as he had observed about "Song of Myself," Kinnell works out the connections between these two worlds without focusing on what prompts that contact in the first place. In these early poems, Kinnell is content simply to suggest that an inner emptiness in the central figure—he is "starved" in one poem, "vacant as a / sucked egg" in the other—is the source of his openness to the dying animals.[5] In *The Book of Nightmares,* in contrast, that initial emptiness becomes a central rather than an incidental concern—so central that one almost overlooks the fact that the poem is also a self-portrait formed out of the series of limited embraces Kinnell initiates in grappling with this problem. In bringing his personal confrontation with the problem of emptiness into the foreground, Kinnell comes close to directing our attention away from the equally important struggle with the mechanics of the embrace also conducted in his poem.

Appropriately, *The Book of Nightmares* begins with Kinnell walking through a black landscape marked by the ashes where tramps "must have squatted down, / gnawing on stream water, / unhouseling themselves on cursed bread" (BN, 3). As the remains of these failed communions demonstrate, the world of this poem, the context within which its meditation unfolds, is, from the beginning, cut off and cursed with aloneness. Kinnell is marked as well, suffering what he later describes as the "irreversible sorrow" (BN, 74) of having lost a lover "whose face / I held in my hands / a few hours, whom I gave back / only to keep holding the space where she was" (BN, 3). Here in its simplest form, the empty space Kinnell cups in his hands is the problem implicit in Whitman with which *The Book of Nightmares* struggles: the embrace is never full because it does not last—in Berryman's terms, "empty grows every bed." Like those abandoned men before him, Kinnell builds a fire which, instead of comfort, offers only echoes of that loss. In the snapping and spitting wood, he hears "the snap / and re-snap of the same *embrace* being torn"; in the hissing rain he senses:

> . . . the oath broken,
> the oath sworn between earth and water, flesh and spirit, broken
> to be sworn again,
> over and over, in the clouds, and to be broken again,
> over and over, on earth.
> (BN, 4)

And worse, as he sings into the fire, what he hears is his voice changing, cherished memory twisting into bitterness: "one / held note / remains—a love-note / twisting under my tongue, like the coyote's bark, / curving off, into a / howl" (BN, 4). *The Book of Nightmares,* fundamentally, is a poem meditating on its own song which, springing from a broken embrace and sung over empty hands, threatens to twist into an account of ashes and bitterness. As with *The Dream Songs,* it asks whether it is possible to move beyond that "self-hugged," abandoned howl back to an embrace of this "broken" world—whether, beginning with a limitation toward which Whitman only gestured, his passionate openness is possible.

The remainder of this first poem—first of ten—concerns Kinnell's daughter Maud, but as he tells the story of her birth and early years, we see that her presence is primarily a means of describing his own self-reflexive desires for his song. At birth, he remembers, Maud was exiled from wholeness ("the flipping / and overleaping, the watery / somersaulting alone in the oneness / under the hill" [BN, 5]) and abandoned into the world. And yet, her first response to this broken connection, as "her tie to the darkness" was cut, was not to mourn the loss of wholeness but rather to open her arms and embrace, in all its limitation, this new emptiness:

> they hang her up
> by the feet, she sucks
> air, screams
> her first song—and turns rose,
> the slow
> beating, featherless arms
> already clutching at the emptiness.
> (BN, 6–7)

Then, imagining Maud grown up and in the same situation in which he now finds himself ("orphaned, / *emptied* / of all wind-singing, of light, / the pieces of *cursed bread* on your tongue" [BN, 8, emphasis mine]), Kinnell prays that in that future time she will remember the songs "of being and perishing" he sang to her as a child: "not the songs / of light said to wave / through the bright hair of angels, / but a blacker / rasping flowering on that tongue" (BN, 7). And, crucially, he prays that those black songs, stored in "the silent zones / of the brain" will return to her richly as songs of comfort and connection: "may there come back to you / a voice, / spectral, calling you / *sister!* / from everything that dies" (BN, 8). He prays, that is, for Maud to regain the open-armed union with the dying world she had as a child—"the light heart / we started with, but made of time and sorrow" (MA, 11), he writes in another poem[6]—for that would be a sign that *his* song of being and perishing, sung then over her cradle and sung now into this fire in the rain, had come to more than a howl of pain. His struggle with the emptiness not yet begun, and his daughter not yet in a position to describe back to him the effect of his song, Kinnell simply stares into his cupped hands, wonders, and "open[s] / this book" (BN, 8).

The five poems following this prologue attempt to nudge that howl of abandonment back into a love song. They do so through a series of partial identifications with dying, with already dead, creatures—a hen, a drunk, a soldier, a seer. As Kinnell studies these subjects, weaving himself in and out of their worlds, constructing different structures to make that union possible, he finds those patterns making visible his own unstated fears about death, extinction, and abandonment. Unlike Berryman, who moves to his songs of identification only *after* working through his various illnesses, Kinnell attempts to do both simultaneously. What he finally discovers thematically— that emptiness empowers the embrace, rather than negates it—is just what these incomplete, although forceful, identifications have demonstrated silently. "Now that the fear / has been rummaged down to its husk," Kinnell writes in another poem, ". . . there is time, still time, / for those who can groan / to sing, / for those who can sing to heal themselves" (MA, 57–58). If the poem begins with the slip from song to groan having already been made, the book as a whole attempts—as Kinnell said about Whitman—to heal itself by finding in that fear a new way of singing.

"The Hen Flower," second poem in sequence, spells out the challenge of this movement.[7] The hen, Kinnell writes, is like an infant, able to "let go" of fear and throw itself "on the mercy of darkness" (BN, 11). Hens, he feels, are drawn to what we dread most—that moment when our conscious attachment to the things of the earth is broken: "head / thrown back / on the chopping block, longing only / to die" (BN, 11). "If only / we could let go / like her," he muses to himself, then begins a series of drifting connections, imagining himself into her position. They are linked physically: he is lying face down on a pillow, "biting down on hen feathers," with "bits of the hen" he had for dinner still stuck in his teeth (BN, 11). They are linked emotionally: he remembers killing a hen and the sensation—part physical, part imaginative—as he dangled it from his hand: "wing / of my wing, / of my bones and veins, / of my flesh / hairs lifting all over me in the first ghostly breeze / after death" (BN, 12). And finally and most explicitly, they are linked conceptually: just as the hen has wings but is "unable / to fly," so he has been "made" to embrace but is "unable to hold another" in his arms. Just as he cups emptiness in his hands, so the opened cadaver of a hen reveals, in "the mass of tiny, / unborn eggs, each getting / tinier and yellower as it reaches back toward / the icy pulp / of what is," what Kinnell calls "the zero" (BN, 13).

This progression drives Kinnell away from an impression of the uniqueness of his position. He is not yet able to let go like the hen—he still dreads death—yet the various connections he has spelled out between himself and that other creature have helped him begin to read his own condition. In fact, he is reminded of an earlier "reading" of the omnipresence of death. All things vanish:

> When the Northern Lights
> were opening across the black sky and vanishing,
> lighting themselves up
> so completely they were vanishing,
> I put to my eye the lucent
> section of the spealbone of a ram—
>
> I thought suddenly
> I could read the cosmos spelling itself,
> the huge broken letters
> shuddering across the black sky and vanishing.
> (BN, 13)

Although the poem ends with Kinnell still in bed and afraid, he has learned that his position is not unique ("even these feathers freed from their wings forever / are afraid" [BN, 15]) and that it should be possible to learn from others how to understand that fear. Having identified the problem ("Listen, Kinnell, / dumped alive / and dying into the old sway bed, / . . . let go"), he has also been led to a new method—reading the "broken letters" of himself and "the cosmos" through the "spealbone" of others.

One of the reasons that it is so difficult to let go of that fear, Kinnell begins to understand in the next poem, "The Shoes of Wandering," is that, without an established system of belief, we must each invent our own way of facing death, step by stumbling step. Unlike the hen or a child, we no longer have an instinctive acceptance of that emptiness on which to rely; nor, by the same token, do we have "the mantle / of the great wanderers, who lighted / their steps by the lamp / of pure hunger and pure thirst" (BN, 22). Instead, Kinnell's struggle, as he *flounders through chaos* without a lamp, will be one of continually losing and finding his way—a condition he rightly dreads.[8] He reads that fear in this poem by literally putting himself in another's shoes, buying the "dead shoes" of a stranger at a Salvation Army store and walking out, painfully, "on the steppingstones / of someone else's wandering" (BN, 19). Returning to his hotel, homeless again, Kinnell collapses in another bed and the drifting sense of identification intensifies:

> And the old
> footsmells in the shoes, touched
> back to life by my footsweats, as by
> a child's kisses, rise,
> drift up where I lie
> self-hugged on the bedclothes, slide
> down the flues
> of dozed, beating hairs, and I can groan
>
> or wheeze, it will be
> the groan or wheeze of another—the elderfoot
> of these shoes . . . (BN, 20)

As the heat of his body brings the old smells back to life, Kinnell is momentarily forced away from his "self-hugged" closeness; his breathing is opened to the drunk's and soon takes on the other's wheeze: "the groan / or wheeze of one / who lays bare his errors by a harsher light" (BN, 21). The point here is that as Kinnell "shudder[s] down to [the drunk's] nightmare," he is able to see his own groaning fears intensified, laid bare under a "harsher light" than he is able to turn on himself. The nightmare, accordingly, is a fevered, heightened account of life as a stumbling journey across "swampland streaked with shined water," through "jungles of burnt flesh, ground of ground / bones," and down the bloody road of time. The journey, he notes, is conducted down the paths of his own "brainwaves." As those waves are intensified, Kinnell sees in surreal colors that what is most to be feared about the nightmare of loss through which he wanders is that there is no alternative to this "temporal road." There is no full union: *"you will feel all your bones / break / over the holy waters you will never drink"* (BN, 23).

The fourth poem picks up at morning in that same desolate hotel. Kinnell hears a bell-tower's chime, then traces out the implications of the suggested pun: "—chyme / of our loves / the peristalsis of the will to love forever / drives down, grain / after grain, into the last, / coldest room, which is memory—" (BN, 27). Although we would love the things and creatures of the world "forever," they are, and we are, soon broken and ground down, reduced to the cold, distant fragments of memory by the forces of time nightmarishly described in the previous poem, and by our own impossible need to handle and hold them forever. This striking label for memory makes possible the introduction of another figure through which Kinnell can read himself: a woman named Virginia, who lives along the Juniata River, a region Kinnell has seen mistakenly described as "now vanished, but extant in memory, / a primal garden lost forever" (BN, 28). Like the drunk and the hen, Virginia can be said, because of the mistake, to speak from the ground-away, vanished land of memory. She is already lost to the poet. As her letters indicate, she is a kind of visionary who, in fact, does sense that she has already left this broken world. She is "an actual person I've had a long correspondence with," Kinnell comments in an interview. "She is a mystic, a seer. . . . She sees past the world and lives in the cosmos" (WDS, 108). What Virginia tells him from her vanished world—she signs her letters "faithless to this life" and "in the darkness"—are, for this poem, the same, increasingly familiar facts, delivered in the impassioned language of mandalas, figure eights, and demon lovers: the body is a *"dear shining casket,"* God's "prey," and does not last.

Perhaps more interesting is the manner in which Kinnell tries to put himself in Virginia's place, a slightly different manner of reading himself than that used in the two previous poems. First, he imagines the destruction of her first world, its "primal garden" being overrun by "root-hunters" who lever-up and pull away the potent mandrake roots:

> On this bank—our bank—
> of the blue, vanished water, you lie,
> crying in your bed, hearing those
> small,
> fearsome thrumps
> of leave-taking trespassing the virginal woods at dusk.
>
> (BN, 29)

Next, he asks himself what a seer would do when confronted with such a loss: perhaps concoct a magic ritual in which the violated roots are ground up (as those we love are broken down by time's "digestion"), then fermented and drunk. What sort of knowledge would such a potion bring? Kinnell invents a speech in which Virginia describes his surprising vision on awakening: not the lost, "virginal" world recovered, but a world composed only of the "scraps / and jettisons of time mortality / could not grind down into his meal of blood and laughter" (BN, 29); not a world made new, but this one where what we love is "drawn / down by the terror and terrible lure / of vacuum." But what she also lets him see is that the continual disappearance of the world brings with it an openness toward the scraps that remain, that although his lost lover will not be returned, a new sort of face will materialize in his empty hands: "a face materializes into your hands, / on the absolute whiteness of pages / a poem writes itself out: its title—the dream / of all poems and the text / of all loves—'Tenderness toward Existence' " (BN, 29). What Virginia has done, then, insofar as the poet has been able to enter her position, is give Kinnell another voice with which to reject the improper dream of transcending this world. From her superior position, already beyond this world, she has allowed him to suggest that the empty hands of a shattered embrace might be filled by a poem, turning itself—like Whitman—tenderly toward existence. Although the poem ends with Kinnell, in his own voice, on his own "dark shore," still holding on to his fear ("I lie without sleeping, remembering / the ripped body / of hen"), an advance has been made (BN, 30).

"In the Hotel of Lost Light" moves that advance a bit farther. It is set in the same hotel, Kinnell stretched out on the bed in which the drunk died and watching a fly:

> . . . I watch, as he
> must have watched, a fly
> tangled in mouth-glue, whining his wings,
> concentrated wholly on
> *time, time,* losing his way worse
> down the downward-winding stairs . . .
>
> (BN, 35)

Now, however, the fly that had been whining and struggling against time, a figure for Kinnell's own stumbling journey down his "temporal road," is seen to transform itself by accepting the inevitability of its death:

> Now the fly
> ceases to struggle, his wings
> flutter out the music blooming with failure
> of one who gets ready to die, as Roland's horn, winding down
> from the Pyrenees, saved its dark, full flourishes
> for last.
>
> (BN, 35)

The fly functions as a kind of summary—as it "lets go" (Poem 2) of its struggle to permanently embrace the world, it blossoms. Maud ("the blue / flower opens"), the hen ("hen flower"), and Kinnell's dark crib song ("a blacker / rasping flowering on that tongue") have been described in similar terms, and now we see why: they bloom with "failure," for in ceasing to hold, self-hugged, onto life, an unfolding or opening occurs. As we have seen in both Whitman and Berryman, giving up the impossible struggle to embrace the world naively, and giving up any resultant bitterness, they flower into the dark, full recovery of "Tenderness toward Existence."[9]

But, it is one thing to see this blooming in a fly, quite another to accomplish it oneself. Again, to begin approaching this knowledge, Kinnell draws on someone outside of himself—a medium. He notes first that he rests in the same lefthand sag of the bed in which the drunk died ("my body slumped out / into the shape of his" [BN, 35]), then—like the hunter in the body of the bear, or his warm feet in the old, dead shoes—he finds himself filling out the other's emptied form and gaining a new voice:

> Flesh
> of his excavated flesh,
> fill of his emptiness,
> after-amanuensis of his after-life,
> I write out
> for him in this languished alphabet
> of worms, these last words
> of himself . . .
>
> (BN, 36)

Taking dictation from the drunk, borrowing his alphabet of concerns, Kinnell begins to describe death in terms that are, if not yet those of "one who gets ready to die," certainly those of one experimenting with a new sense of expectancy. So, in his creation of the drunk's words, death is described as a flowering of sorts ("I blacked out into oblivion by that crack in the curb where the forget-me blooms"), a change of colors ("I painted my footsoles purple for the day when the beautiful color would show"), or simply a shucking-off of flesh ("*To Live* / has a poor cousin, / who calls tonight, who pronounces the family name / *To Leave,* she / changes each visit the flesh-rags on her bones" [BN, 36–37]). In all of these descriptions, we hear the first notes of a healing, a new song, delivered with some hesitancy and, as yet, solely in another's voice, in which the "shards and lumps" of what we love "re-arise / in the pear tree, in spring, to shine down / on two clasping what they dream is another" (BN, 37).

The sixth poem, "The Dead Shall Be Raised Incorruptible," challenges that new song. It argues that rather than the vision of death as a flowering ("Violet bruises come out / all over his flesh, as invisible / fists start beating him a last time; the whine / of omphalos blood starts up again, the puffed / bellybutton explodes" [BN, 37]), we prefer, as a culture, the dream of incorruptibility—death as an extension of life. Rather than those broken fragments "re-arising" in a proper attitude toward what remains, we insist that they "be raised incorruptible"—miraculously untouched by death. And it argues further that the institutions and policies we have created to keep death at bay have the same root as Kinnell's own fears and thus are also, as they will be for Robert Duncan as well, voices he must acknowledge playing within himself. The obvious example, for a poem published in 1971, is Vietnam. Kinnell begins this poem with a three-part structure designed to expose that shared dream. First, he describes a burning "piece of flesh" abandoned on a battlefield, then the remains of other bodies scattered behind a hospital: "carrion, caput mortuum, / orts, / pelf, / fenks, / sordes, / gurry dumped from hospital trashcans" (BN, 41). The tone here—supported by the unfamiliar language—is one of deep disgust, a disgust linked to the presence of death of which these shattered body parts forcibly remind us. The next two scenes offer examples of what we have done to suppress that dread. In one, Kinnell imagines a Vietnam-era tailgunner, confined to a mental ward and obsessively reliving a series of indiscriminate killings. They were killings, we realize as we overhear, made attractive by the sensation of his weapon in action: " 'It was only / that I loved the *sound* / of them, I guess I just loved / the *feel* of them sparkin' off my hands . . .' " (BN, 42). In the other scene, Kinnell chants the familiar, equally obsessive litany of television: "Do you have a body that sweats? / Sweat that has odor? / False teeth clanging into your breakfast? / Case of the dread?" (BN, 42). The connection between these three scenes is the last word quoted—dread. Fear of death is translated into fear of the flowering flesh of the body and then into the search for a means of disguising its nature. That product, whether a gun or deodorant, this poem suggests, replaces the "feel" and "sound" of the broken world with the shine of technology. "Technology," Kinnell explains in an interview, "is the latest of the methods we use to overcome the fear of death. The sense of dominion it gives us allows us to suppress the knowledge of our own mortality" (WDS, 98–99).[10] What the opening poems of *The Book of Nightmares* try to do is just the opposite—make visible again what we have suppressed.

The voice Kinnell takes on in this poem to "read" his position is that of our entire dying race delivering a last will and testament; he calls himself "Christian man," remarking in an interview that it is a term he uses to mean "technological man" (WDS, 98). Acknowledging the various acts of domination that have separated him from the earth, and, through the itemizing suggested by the form of a will, forced to see himself as eventually broken and shattered ("My stomach, which has digested / four hundred treaties giving the Indians / eternal right to their land, I give to the Indians"), Kinnell looks at the life he has lived with "eyes that can't close" then "give[s] the emptiness my hand" and "ask[s] a ride into the emptiness" (BN, 43–44). This marks a turning for the poem; after facing and acknowledging the most extreme results of our fear of death, Kinnell is now able to let that fear go, no longer seeking to suppress his knowledge of the emptiness.[11]

The Book of Nightmares turns outward at this point and begins to examine the expansive embrace prompted by no longer denying death. Two brief scenes at the close of the sixth poem anticipate that second, and new, movement. First, a soldier with his body ruined by war runs from battle (*"my neck broken I ran / holding my head up with both hands"*) but, rather than howling or groaning, clings to his life and the world whose beauty is suddenly clarified for him: *"the flames may burn the oboe / but listen buddy boy they can't touch the notes"* (BN, 44). So, too, when Kinnell imagines a final, postwar world populated only by the scraps of humanity's leavings (as in Poem 4), he discovers that even these fragments ("memories left in mirrors on whorehouse ceilings, / angel's wings / flagged down into the snows of yesteryear") stubbornly cling to existence: *"do not let this last hour pass, / do not remove this last, poison cup from our lips"* (BN, 45). In both scenes, as Kinnell remarks in an interview, there is a "pray[er] for earthly experience to continue no matter

how painful and empty it has become" (WDS, 109). What the first movement of *The Book of Nightmares* has done, then, is rummage the fear of death
down to its husk, arriving at a stubborn celebration of earthly existence.
Once that fear has been made visible through the voices of others, the argument of the poem goes, it can be overcome, and death can be seen to
heighten and empower the embrace. Of that new knowledge, Kinnell comments in an essay, "That we last only for a time, that everyone and everything around us lasts only for a time, that we know this, radiates a thrilling,
tragic light on all our loves, all our relationships."[12] Or, in the soldier's pan-
icky phrase that now reveals unexpected significance: "*This corpse will not stop
burning!*"—it flowers into something new. In fact, one suddenly realizes, it
has been no accident that Kinnell, obsessed with death, has made his way to
this argument by reading himself through other dying creatures; for what
has been acted out by these readings is precisely that fact that such a shared
condition (they are all corpses-to-be) might issue forth in powerful, although
indirect, union.

In the last poems of the sequence, Kinnell concentrates on working out
the tragic radiance of human relationships within his own family and does so
in his own voice. But, although he moves on to embrace the world, each of
these next three poems is also centered on a problem; each struggles with the
temptation to forget what was learned and to give in again to fear. In a sense,
there is a constant stumbling, as Kinnell learns and relearns, finds and loses
his way. With each public misstep, he insists on the struggle involved in seeing and accepting the implications of embracing what dies.

The seventh poem, "Little Sleep's-Head Sprouting Hair in the Moonlight," is addressed to Maud one night when she wakes screaming from a
nightmare. Kinnell lifts her from her crib, embraces her, then interprets—or
rather, misinterprets—the significance of that action. "You cling to
me / hard, / as if clinging could save us," he writes. "I think / you think / I
will never die" (BN, 49). That is, he supposes she clings because of her fear of
the night and of death, clings to be saved. Moved by her apparent need for
his power and "permanence," he attempts to act that role, protectively whispering "I would brush your sprouting hair of the dying light, / I would scrape
the rust off your ivory bones, / I would help death escape through the little
ribs of your body, / . . . [until] lovers no longer whisper to the presence beside
them in the dark, O corpse-to-be . . ." (BN, 49–50). Giving up all he has
learned—those we love will inevitably become corpses, that is why we love
them—Kinnell falls back on the desire to lift Maud free from the rhythms of
this dying world. But then, after a moment, the earlier imagery of the book
comes rushing back in. She clings not to be saved from loss but because of
loss, not because he represents permanence but because he will be lost some
day: "Yes, / you cling because / I, like you, only sooner / than you, will go
down / the path of vanished alphabets, / the roadlessness / to the other side of
the darkness" (BN, 50).

In a sense, Kinnell has tested himself and the earlier sections of the poem here. As if to repeat that lesson out loud, repeating his imaginative gesture at the end of the first poem, he imagines Maud at his age, walking through "the black stones / of the field, in the rain, / / and the stones saying / over their one word, *ci-gît, ci-gît, ci-gît*" (BN, 51). What he whispers this time is his hope that, surrounded by stones testifying to her losses—or as the first poem would have it, "orphaned, / emptied"—she will have relearned what she knows now as an infant: "*the wages / of dying is love*" (BN, 53). Anticipation of the "still undanced cadence of vanishing" need not lead to madness or bitterness or to the reaching out for illusory tokens of permanence—no, he whispers, it can lead to a passionate attachment to the vanishing things of this world: "Kiss / the mouth / which tells you, *here, / here is the world.* This mouth. This laughter. These temple bones" (BN, 52). He is whispering, we realize, to himself, repeating back the "healing" his song, in embracing the drunk, fly, and so on, has almost inadvertently been demonstrating all along.

The eighth poem tests the embrace out in Kinnell's own marriage. He is in bed with his wife, who is pregnant with their second child. Perhaps in response to her changed body, he describes them as "two mismatched halfnesses lying side by side in the darkness" (BN, 57). In a sense, the phrase encapsulates Kinnell's version of one possible reason Whitman's embrace must remain a limited gesture. According to Aristophanes, he muses, we were originally part of a perfect union from which we were torn away: "each of us / is a torn half / whose lost other we keep seeking across time / until we die, or give up— / or actually find her" (BN, 57–58). That theory explains both the universal sense of loss we all hold deep within and the misfitting embrace with his wife. Would it be possible to regain that original wholeness and thus avoid the need to embrace a stranger? Might we embrace fully? Kinnell is tempted to say yes. Perhaps the lost lover of the book's opening poem was his "true" other and, for a moment, he had "actually found her, / held her face a few hours / in my hands; and for reasons—cowardice, / loyalties, all which goes by the name 'necessity'— / left her" (BN, 58). Perhaps, if he had known, it would have been possible to avoid "necessity" and, as Berryman would have it, to have remained in that "sycamore . . . all at the top," entering a world not defined by loss:

> Suppose I had stayed
> with that woman of Waterloo, suppose
> we had met on a hill called Safa, in our own country,
> that we had lain out on the grass
> and looked into each other's blindness, . . .
> . . . .
> I think I might have closed my eyes, and moved
> from then on like the born blind,

> their faces
> gone into heaven already.
> (BN, 60)

With that union, he would have remained in his "own country," blind to this imperfect world and its straining and clutching after brief comforts.

But, he immediately realizes, it is precisely this world and its pleasures that are the glories of life; and it is "the wound itself," that painful sense of from what we have been torn, that causes us to sing and clutch and desire, accomplishing, "for a moment, the wholeness the drunk Greek / extrapolated from his high / or flagellated out of an *empty* heart, / / that purest, / most tragic concumbence, strangers / clasped into one, a moment, of their moment on earth" (BN, 58). To dream of regaining that original wholeness, then, is to deny the transient, tragic lights of the earth and to be blind to desire. Instead of wholeness, Kinnell admits once again, we have the riches of momentary human embraces—the memory, for example, of him and his wife, clasped as one, on Whitman's "beautiful uncut hair of graves":

> . . . the bees glittered in the blossoms
> and the bodies of our hearts
> opened
> under the knowledge
> of tree, on the grass of the knowledge
> of graves, and among the flowers of the flowers.
>
> And the brain kept blossoming
> all through the body, until the bones themselves could think,
> (BN, 59)

Such an unfolding of human potential (recall the other images of flowering) is made possible only by loss—the knowledge that drives us to vision, and consciousness, and desire. That Kinnell stresses the *knowledge* of graves" as the ground for his embrace points quite consciously toward what he has added to "Song of Myself." Where Whitman, in "joyful health," can declare "to die is different from what any one supposed, and luckier," Kinnell has forced himself to work through his own line of inner debate that might issue forth in such openness. It is, for Kinnell, the knowledge of loss that prompts our songs, the "call back across the darkness / of the valley of not-knowing / the only word tongues shape without intercession, / / *yes* . . . yes . . ." (BN, 61).

This eighth poem concludes with the prediction of "a kind of fate" toward which Kinnell and those he loves stumble, hand in hand: "some field, maybe, of flaked stone / scattered in starlight / where the flesh / swaddles its skeleton a last time / before the bones go their way without us" (BN, 61). This field of arrowheads is an imagined place where our ties with the earth are broken; it is the context for the embrace. In the ninth poem, Kinnell imagines actually walking through this field, and as he walks, he confronts one last time the temptation to flee its brokenness. He tries to release himself from the world's rhythms in two ways. First, he links himself with what seems the stones' drive away from the broken world:

> I walk out from myself,
> among the stones of the field,
> each sending up its ghost-bloom
> into the starlight, to float out
> over the trees, seeking to be one
> with the unearthly fires kindling and dying
>
> in space—
>
> (BN, 66)

But even as he speaks, he realizes that the blossoming stones are continually "falling back, knowing / the sadness of the wish / to alight / back among the glitter of bruised ground" (BN, 66). The bruised earth is all there is.

Second—reversing the direction, but under the same temptation—Kinnell imagines descending from that broken field to an inner chamber of the earth: "the unbreathable goaf / of everything I ever craved and lost." There he encounters an alchemist ("An old man, a stone / lamp at his forehead, squats / by his hell-flames, stirs into / his pot / chopped head / of crow") with the supposed power to transform the lapsed and ground-down fragments of life into something transcendent. Instead, as with the seer of Poem 4, examination reveals: "Nothing. / Always nothing. Ordinary blood / boiling away in the glare of the brow lamp" (BN, 67). And it is this discovery—gained and lost throughout the book—that the "ordinary blood" of the earth is all there is to turn to, that frees Kinnell to make his strongest account of connection.

> . . . I crawl up: I find myself alive
> in the whorled
> archway of the fingerprint of all things,
> skeleton groaning,
> blood-strings wailing the wail of all things.
> (BN, 68)

His groans are the world's; the wail of his bones and sinews is the wail of all dying things.[13] Avoiding the last false option of transcendence, he acts out his version of Whitman, deliberately "sett[ing] against his despondency all his gratefulness" (WIW, 226) and embracing his surroundings.

The final poem in the sequence serves as a summation: it reaches back and quite consciously revises a number of the book's opening images in light of Kinnell's deeper understanding of the embrace. First, returning to the "black ashes, black stones, where tramps / must have squatted down," Kinnell thinks again of the fire he built in response to his loss. Rather than sputtering out into black, dead remains, it (and the poem for which it is a figure) has proved a radiant center: "it warms / everyone who might wander into its radiance, / a tree, a lost animal, the stones, / / because in the dying world it was set burning" (BN, 71). Second, the black bear, which had appeared in the first poem as a model of instinctive acceptance of life's rhythms, appears again in the same pose. But now, the bear "understands" that Kinnell has worked his way back to its position; the poet and the bear have merged:

> . . . he understands
> a creature, a death-creature
> watches from the fringe of the trees,
> finally he understands
> I am no longer here, he himself
> from the fringe of the trees watches
> a black bear . . .
>
> (BN, 71–72)

In a sense, we see here the same embrace as earlier in the "The Bear," but an embrace worked out quite consciously now in full awareness of its grounds and limitations. Third, Kinnell's acceptance of the positive effects of emptiness are summarized: as contentedly standing near an echoing cliffside, fully conscious of the fact that the next step brings one to the point "where the voice calling from stone / no longer answers, / turns into stone, and nothing comes back" (BN, 72–73); and as the number of this last poem, "one / and zero / walk[ing] off together, / . . . one creature / walking side by side with the emptiness" (BN, 73). And finally, the book's opening image—Kinnell's cupped, empty hands—is returned to by way of a concert violinist who "puts the irreversible sorrow of his face / into the opened palm / of the wood" and produces, in a shower of rosin, "the sexual wail / of the back-alleys and blood strings we have lived." The violinist's wail, now holding an entire concert hall captive in its power, is a final refiguring of the poet's opening "howl"; that howl, made as it has been out of Kinnell's sense of a division within himself and potentially within Whitman, overcoming his fear then giving into it again, in first one voice then another, has become, in its widest sense, a concert: a "concert of one / divided among himself" (BN, 75). What is most notable about the last poem of the sequence is that there is no longer a struggle. Kinnell has passed through his confrontation with human emptiness, as he is sure Whitman must have, but in full view, and he has transformed what he sees as the unstated sense of loss in "Song of Myself" back into its obvious sense of power, splintered and brief, but directed outward toward the world.

Notes

1. Galway Kinnell, *Mortal Acts, Mortal Words* (Boston: Houghton Mifflin, 1980), p. 39. Cited in the text as MA. Other Kinnell texts referred to are: BR, *Body Rags* (Boston: Houghton Mifflin, 1968); BN, *The Book of Nightmares* (Boston: Houghton Mifflin, 1971); WDS, *Walking Down the Stairs: Selections from Interviews* (Ann Arbor: University of Michigan Press, 1978); WIW, "Whitman's Indicative Words," in *Walt Whitman: The Measure of His Song,* ed. Jim Pearlman, Ed Folsom, and Dan Campion (Minneapolis: Holy Cow! Press, 1981).

2. See my "Introduction" for a full discussion of these issues. Paul Zweig, in his recent biography *Walt Whitman: The Making of the Poet* (New York: Basic Books, 1984) makes a similar point: "Whitman would not make poetry out of the argument with himself. Instead, he would pour ecstasies of hope and anticipation into a dream of self-making, of self-transcendence, of which the fundamental discipline would be the making of poems. These poems would not be monologues of inward conflict and resolution. They would leap cleanly, with a tone of casual conviction, into a vision of expanded being" (p. 195). Lee Zimmerman, in the useful *Intricate and Simple Things: The Poetry of Galway Kinnell* (Urbana: University of Illinois Press, 1987), takes up this issue as well. Quite properly aware that for Kinnell "pain and death . . . have an insistent and tragic presence that he wants not to denigrate," Zimmerman writes: "Kinnell doesn't directly accuse Whitman of a too-quick-and-easy Tennysonian consolation or of letting his transcendentalism eclipse a proper confrontation with pain and death, but he does feel that Whitman hides his own human effort to accommodate them, to his poetic detriment" (pp. 11–12). However, Zimmerman leaves Kinnell's criticisms there, not continuing, as I do, to his statement that Whitman *did,* although outside the stated program of his poetry, work through just such a confrontation. Accordingly, Zimmerman finds Kinnell's early "The Avenue Bearing the Initial of Christ into the New World" to be "the most Whitmanesque of Kinnell's poems"—not only because of the way the poem accumulates detail, but also because it "remain[s] relatively free of struggle" (p. 49), thereby covering over where "Kinnell's poetics depart from Whitman's, [in] incorporating a truer sense of tragedy" (p. 12). Although I read this book after completing my chapter, the entire argument I make here—that struggle and a confrontation with death are exactly what Kinnell finds present and generative in Whitman—could be seen as a response to such a reading.

3. For other remarks by Kinnell on his use of Whitman, see his essay "The Poetics of the Physical World," *Iowa Review* 2, no. 3 (1971): 113–16. On the importance of this movement in Kinnell's work as a whole, see, for example, Alan Williamson, *Introspection and Contemporary Poetry* (Cambridge: Harvard University Press, 1984), pp. 87–89.

4. The most important essay to date on this poem, Cary Nelson's "Ecclesiastical Whitman" in *Our Last First Poets: Vision and History in Contemporary American Poetry* (Urbana: University of Illinois Press, 1981), pp. 63–96, examines a similar relationship between Kinnell and Whitman. Nelson makes a historical argument (pp. 63–64): that Kinnell has set himself up to compete for Whitman's "prophetic voice," to speak for his entire country, but has found "his effectiveness as a visionary speaker . . . undercut by the brute reality of American history." Thus, in contrast to Whitman, Kinnell's poem can claim only a formal resolution which, because it "cannot transform the national history it acknowledges," testifies to its own failure to embrace the world (pp. 94–96). In the following pages, I make a different argument: that the difference between the two poets is best understood in personal terms, with Kinnell competing for and modifying Whitman's more limited stance as a self-portraitist, not a prophet. In these terms, I will argue, the reality of such an experience as the Vietnam War needs only to be acknowledged, not transformed.

5. Kinnell has commented in an interview: "the poem deals with various creatures and things with whom I have an affinity. You can really write only about things you identify with, to some degree. Each creature or thing you write about brings out some aspect of yourself." Thomas Gardner, "An Interview with Galway Kinnell," *Contemporary Literature* 20

(1979): 428–29. Two useful examinations of empathy in Kinnell are Charles Molesworth, "The Poetry of Galway Kinnell" in his *The Fierce Embrace: A Study of Contemporary American Poetry* (Columbia: University of Missouri Press, [1979]), particularly pp. 104–9, and Robert Langbaum, "On Galway Kinnell's *Book of Nightmares*," *American Poetry Review* 8, no. 2 (1979): 30–31. Zimmerman (*Intricate and Simple Things*, pp. 110–27), has a strong discussion of these two poems and the question of empathy, rightly stressing the struggle involved in Kinnell's version of this act: "even as his presumption of kinship aligns him with Whitman and the others, his ingrained sense of the difficulty of this kinship distinguishes him from many of them" (p. 119).

6. In *Walking Down the Stairs*, Kinnell comments: "Children live with death almost as animals do. This natural trust in life's rhythms, infantile as it is, provides the model for the trust they may struggle to learn later on" (p. 46).

7. In *Walking Down the Stairs*, Kinnell remarks: " 'The Hen Flower' was the first poem I finished of the sequence. It expresses the dread that is the poem's starting point. It addresses the protagonist before he begins the journey of the poem, instructing him to let go, to surrender to existence" (p. 47).

8. Nelson (*Our Last First Poets*, p. 94) makes a very important point about what he rightly calls the "incredibly elaborate" system of textual repetition and variation in this poem. But what he sees as an attempt to overcome history in "the self-referential perfection of the book's formal development," I see as an acknowledgment of struggle. Each repetition is a reminder of where he has been; the mistakes and successes of the previous poems are carried forward as public testimony to the stages of the journey, demonstrating—perhaps too insistently—his distance from Whitman's "unavowed" struggle.

9. Kinnell has referred more than once to the way Dickinson's "I heard a Fly buzz—when I died" uses the fly to capture the heightened feeling one might have for the world at the moment of death. See, for example, *Walking Down the Stairs* (p. 23) and "The Poetics of the Physical World" (p. 120).

10. See also his essay "Poetry, Personality, and Death," *Field* 4 (Spring 1971): 61: "The more we conquer nature, the more nature becomes our enemy, and since we are, like it or not, creatures of nature, the more we make an enemy of the very life within us."

11. Nelson (*Our Last First Poets*, pp. 94–96) argues that this Vietnam poem subverts the book's "perfection" because Kinnell has not been able to absorb it into his "verbal matrix." As I have just tried to demonstrate, however, the poem forms a significant part of the emptiness-embrace pattern.

12. Kinnell, "The Poetics of the Physical World," p. 125.

13. See Gardner, "An Interview with Galway Kinnell," p. 428: "When I was writing that, I was, of course, thinking of some sort of sympathetic and permanent linking of my life and the life of all things on earth."

Galway Kinnell
and the Domestication of the Transcendental

LORRIE GOLDENSOHN

In 1971, *The Book of Nightmares* stood as Galway Kinnell's most ambitious attempt at a metaphysical response to death, the dense, fire-fibred poem intended as "a kind of paradigm of what the human being wants to say to the cosmos."[1] When pressed about such large intentions and the added need to address the political issues that were burning most poets in the decades of the sixties and seventies, Kinnell expanded on his notion of those urgencies pushing *The Book of Nightmares* by saying simply that the long poem represented "[t]he desire for a poem in which you can say everything, in which there is nothing that has to be left out."[2] Whatever his metaphysical curiosities, Kinnell has always sounded them from within a consistently autobiographical frame: "My poetry does stay fairly close to the experiences of my life. I don't usually write in others' voices."[3] He has named and presented himself in his work, from the early "Doppelgänger" to the late "Sheffield Ghazals," introducing us to a "Galway" and also to a "Kinnell," as he makes the poet and speaker one. A persistent and interesting tension has always been between the upper and lower registers of this voice, producing a language large-souled enough to take on the traditional Romantic peering into the borders between heaven and earth, while keeping a low-key contemporary inflection.

But by 1975, in a mid-career interview, Kinnell signaled what seemed an emphatic narrowing: "My circumstances are such that I live most of my life rather busily in the midst of the daily and ordinary . . . whatever my poetry will be, from now on it will no doubt come out of this involvement in the ordinary."[4] This was a little bald, more than a little uncompromising in its avoidance of anything that could smack of a hankering after the sublime or the titanic (for which Ralph Mills had praised, and Donald Davie condemned, him). Likewise, it suggests no more Thoreauvian isolation, or quasi–ecstatic celebration in the Whitman mode, or alchemical transformations in the vein of an earlier Kinnell. Somewhere between *The Book of Nightmares* and *Mortal*

Portions of this essay originally appeared in *The Massachusetts Review: A Quarterly of Literature, the Arts, and Public Affairs* as "Approaching Home Ground: Galway Kinnell's *Mortal Acts, Mortal Words*," 25, no. 2 (Summer 1984): 303–21. It was revised and updated by the author especially for this collection and is printed by permission of the author and *The Massachusetts Review*.

Acts, Mortal Words (1980), Kinnell's aesthetic was changing decisively enough so that the early inclusive goals—"for a poem in which you can say everything, in which there is nothing that has to be left out"—became a poetry of private and domestic event, and one that resembled less and less Whitman's cosmic selving.

Yet faithful to the penetrations of language from within new subjects, and still sensitive to metaphysical resonance, the best of Kinnell's poems remain alert to "[t]he moment / in the late night," as in "The Poem," when

> . . . objects
> on the page grow suddenly
> heavy, hugged
> by a rush of strange gravity.[5]

Language, in the 1980 volume *Mortal Acts, Mortal Words,* is still the negotiation between flesh and spirit, making up the tracks that spirit lays down in the flesh of the word. Or, looks for that curious double moment when language flashes out to the quick of things, only to show in another and reciprocal pulsation how things themselves exist as a language. Here are lines from "Blackberry Eating":

> . . . as I stand among them
> lifting the stalks to my mouth, the ripest berries
> fall almost unbidden to my tongue,
> as word sometimes do, certain peculiar words
> like *strengths* or *squinched,*
> many-lettered, one-syllabled lumps,
> which I squeeze, squinch open, and splurge well
> in the silent, startled, icy black language
> of blackberry-eating in late September.[6]

Within the objects of this blackberry language, there is an insistence on the ordinary object as the right carrier for meaning; as if more exalted objects could only blur or distort the precise fitting, the exact adjustment of language to reality. Somewhere around 1980 Kinnell's language becomes so consistently tempered and vibratoless, so committed to conversational cadence, that it seems fully protected by republican modesty against any stilts-on attack of the sublime. Yet a milk bottle, for instance, bearing a resemblance to the jar in Tennessee, works up to transcendence from just this deliberately prosy beginning:

> I imagine I can actually remember one certain
> quart of milk which has just finished clinking
> against three of its brethren
> in the milkman's great hand and stands,

> freeing itself from itself, on the rotting
> doorstep in Pawtucket circa 1932,
> to be picked up and taken inside
> by one in whom time hasn't yet completely
> woven all its tangles, and not ever set down . . .
> . . . .
> The old bottle will shatter no one knows when
> in the decay of its music, the sea eagle
> will cry itself back down into the sea
> the sea's creatures transfigure over and over.
> Look. Everything has changed.
> Ahead of us the meantime is overflowing.
> Around us its own almost-invisibility
> streams and sparkles over everything.[7]

Whatever else the language is doing, it still admits the higher celebrations. Ordinariness does not signal a rejection of significant subject, but gives notice instead of Kinnell's intention to seek significance at hand. In the diction of this poetical discourse, "ordinary" still means universal, but tilted meaningfully toward the egalitarian.

The ordinary also contains the time-bound, and from within it, Kinnell continues to advance the preoccupation that has shaped all of his poetry: the lip of the collision between eternity and human death. In *Mortal Acts, Mortal Words* Kinnell took these lines from Petrarch as his epigraph: "mortal beauty, acts, and words have put all their burden on my soul." In this fifth collection of work, he moved his poems decisively away from the larger and tighter structuring of *The Book of Nightmares,* but kept the earlier attention to all emergent fences between the dying and deathless. In "There Are Things I Tell to No One," he says,

> I say "God"; I believe,
> rather, in a music of grace
> that we hear, sometimes, playing to us
> from the other side of happiness.
> When we hear it, when it flows
> through our bodies, it lets us live
> these days lighted by their vanity
> worshipping—as the other animals do,
> who live and die in the spirit
> of the end—that backward-spreading
> brightness[8]

After writing *The Book of Nightmares,* Kinnell remarked, "A door has been closed on something. It would be foolish to go on in the same way."[9] The task he set himself in *Mortal Acts, Mortal Words,* deliberately juxtaposing word against act, was to understand that "backward-spreading brightness" and to balance the longing heavenward against the down-pulling anchor of earth's subjects, and to be determined to pay earth its measure of honor.

In 1972, in his essay "The Poetics of the Physical World," these intentions had been phrased:

> The subject of the poem is the thing which dies . . . Poetry is the wasted breath. This is why it needs the imperfect music of the human voice, this is why its words have no higher aim than to press themselves to us, to cling to the creatures and things we know and love, to be the ragged garments. It is through something radiant in our lives that we have been able to dream of paradise, that we have been able to invent the realm of eternity. But there is another kind of glory in our lives which derives precisely from our inability to enter that paradise or to experience eternity. That we last only for a time, that everyone around us lasts only for a time, that we know this, radiates a thrilling, tragic light on all our loves, all our relationships, even on those moments when the world, through its poetry, becomes almost capable of spurning time and death.[10]

As that "thrilling, tragic light" spreads over the poems that deal directly with the death of various people important to the poet—brother, mother, and first indirectly, then more directly in later years, the father—we might ask how the concessions made to poetry's mortal reach eventually affect Kinnell's style. Given the modest possibilities enumerated here, the invention but not the occupation of heaven, poetry's "wasted breath," how will the poet keep expressive faith in his bleaknesses? While clinging "to the creatures and things we know and love" will the poems of dark mortality have their edges bleached by sentimental compromise? If we take seriously Stevens's premise that death is the mother of beauty, then any poetics becomes at best a poetics of tragedy. But in the new determination to balance leaps at heaven with earthbound events, the poet risks dilution and intermittent falls into a poetry of cloying pathos or preening sentimentality, characteristics marring even strong and vital work in every collection since *Mortal Acts, Mortal Words*.

If we follow Kinnell in the things he tells to no one, God is a distant concept to be set off with quotation marks. The only knowable part of "God" is "the music of grace that we hear"—or, all that is knowable of grace is the music or poetry of life. Yet in "The Poetics of the Physical World," Kinnell sees poetry's capacity to fuse connections between life and eternity as limited: Poetry is only "almost capable" of beating back time and death, and there is no certainty where, or if, the poetic act should be divinized. In this essay, a doubt about the transfigurative powers of language eventually registers in the poetry as the lesser force of nostalgia, a conceptual scheme of reality in which language is never more than the etiolations of print. For uncomfortable stretches in Kinnell's secular humanism, uncertainty cuts edge away from the blade. In big, sloppy poems like "Flying Home," or in tight-lipped, bone-dry little ones like "Prayer," a passionless, merely "humorous" skepticism substitutes diffidently for religious conviction. The abraded vocabulary of "shining" and "singing" which Kinnell otherwise adopts to hoist poems like "Last Gods" up into the precincts of Blake's "Human Form Divine" doesn't work, betraying through halfheartedness the poetry of the human that believes in a style of holiness without gods. Suspended homelessly between invention and experience, between speaking and being, Kinnell's poet drops the prophetic mantle inherited from the old pantheons. Without a god to sear his mouth with the burning coal, the vatic poet flounders, unless he wholly and stubbornly believes that the desire for knowing and shaping experience can be generated from within his own body's truth. In the context of this dilemma, Yeats's defiantly soaring lines from "The Tower" appear unreachable:

> Death and life were not
> Till man made up the whole
> Made lock, stock and barrel
> Out of his bitter soul.[11]

Yeats's bitter soul, cresting in the high phases of early Modernism, offers an option on the uses of art no longer as accessible, perhaps, to a late–twentieth century poet. An inheritor of *l'univers concentrationnaire,* and properly wary of anything leading to a religion of art, Kinnell does not toss us bon mots in the style of Pound: "Religion: another of the numerous failures resulting from an attempt to popularize art."[12] About "God" Kinnell isn't sure; about poetry, its fitful illumination flows from what becomes "in the bedraggled poem of the modern ... the images, those lowly touchers of physical reality, which remain shining."[13] Or, in the nominalist tradition, poetic images flow and shine in the apparent power of thing over word.

Given this perspective on the bedraggled language of the modern and its dangerous exhaustions, it is instructive to compare a strong elegy for a brother, "Freedom, New Hampshire," from 1960's *What a Kingdom It Was,* with family elegies from *Mortal Acts, Mortal Words.* The early poem is quite explicit in its refusal to have its grief mitigated by belief in the comforts of the resurrection:

> When a man dies he dies trying to say without slurring
> The abruptly decaying sounds. It is true
> That only flesh dies, and spirit flowers without stop
> For men, cows, dung, for all dead things; and it is good, yes—
>
> But an incarnation is in particular flesh
> And the dust that is swirled into a shape
> And crumbles and is swirled again had but one shape
> That was this man. When he is dead the grass
> Heals what he suffered, but he remains dead,
> And the few who loved him know this until they die.[14]

Similarly, the theme of resurrection, or incarnate flesh as immortal spirit, is passed upon ironically in "The Supper After the Last," again from the early book, where Kinnell has Christ speak this doctrine:

> From the hot shine where he sits his whispering drifts:
> You struggle from flesh into wings; the change exists.
> But the wings that live gripping the contours of the dirt
> Are all at once nothing, flesh and light lifted away.
>
> You are the flesh; I am the resurrection, because I am the light.
> I cut to your measure the creeping piece of darkness
> That haunts you in the dirt. Step into light—
> I make you over. I breed the shape of your grave in the dirt.[15]

In both of these poems, the energy gained is the energy of their unbelief. Earth is read uncompromisingly as the site that confers meaning. Heavenly transfiguration is not our dominion because even as light our turf remains turf.

"The Sadness of Brothers" picks up the death of a brother again, but this time, twenty-one years later, loss is differently approached:

> He comes to me like a mouth
> speaking from under several inches of water.
> I can no longer understand what he is saying.
> He has become one
> who never belonged among us, someone
> it is useless to think about or remember.

The task of this elegy is to accept the absolute loss and suffering that the living experience. The dead brother is not lost merely to himself, or to some limited point in time, nor is imagination seen as an adequate substitute for real loss, because poetry is only an "almost capable." From within the poem, there is open acknowledgment that all moves at assuming the consciousness of others can be partially or totally blocked: and then the poem enacts that blockage. When memory picks up an isolated picture of the dead brother, and tries to animate that body with what would be its living voice—projecting the long dead into the present moment—the real nature of loss is borne. The speaker of section 4, playing at supposing his brother alive, and training his eyes on that resurrected image, says,

> I think he's going to ask
> for beer for breakfast, sooner
> or later he'll start making obnoxious
> remarks about race or sex
> and criticize our loose ways
> of raising children, while his eyes
> grow more slick, his puritan heart more pure . . .

Then he dismisses that imagining: "But no, that's fear's reading." And returns his brother to the unknowable dead. What is dead is dead, not only to itself, but more crucially, and more persuasively this time, *to us*. We long for the company of those who are dead, but fruitlessly:

> . . .—if it's true
> of love, only what
> the flesh can bear surrenders to time.[16]

Both the earlier and later elegy offer a richness of life gathered in for observation, and a steady clearsightedness. But the second elegy, unlike the first, highlights much more complex personal and familial relationships over a longer arc of time, and exposes a range of subject to be examined with increasing vitality, as well as puzzling lacunae, in all of Kinnell's subsequent poetry. The earlier elegy, freshly within the experience, shaped its retrospective pastoral icon from childhood material and interwove an account of its grief with farm imagery and animal life. Both are lovely poems; but the one less fierce, and written in middle age, draws closer to people, farther from nature, while it continues the earlier poem's stoic resignation to the rule of severance over our lives and language. The later poem also marks the coming of a more muted language of feeling, one from which the burn of a Swiftian *saeva indignatio* is fading.

In elegies for his mother, Kinnell tests other relations and perceptions, with strained results. These elegies as well as "Brother of My Heart" and "Fisherman" prefer conventional bromides, or conventional evasions and discretions. Nearing the conclusion of "The Last Hiding Places of Snow," Kinnell shifts from his earlier view of the flesh as perishable, declaring the mother "beloved dross promising heaven," and describes her ultimate transmutation from dead woman to eternal presence:

> Every so often, when I look
> at the dark sky, I know she remains
> among the old endless blue lightedness
> of stars; or finding myself out in a field
> in November, when a strange
> starry perhaps first snowfall blows
> down across the darkening air, lightly,
> I know she is there, where snow
> falls flakes down fragile softly
> falling until I can't see the world
> any longer, only its stilled shapes.[17]

This soft falling skitters uncomfortably close to bathos and matches other sections in "Fisherman" and "Two Set Out on Their Journey" where there are similar forced marches heavenward. More convinced by his religious skepticism than by his halfhearted religious faith, I would rather wait for the Kinnell who ends the poem on the human side of the grave as "in the memory / her old body slowly executes into the earth." With the marvelous turn on execute, the poem conforms to its darker finalities, and briefly, the language is once again invested.

But invested in a way that underlines the tactical problems of the work after *The Book of Nightmares,* and after Kinnell's more systematic attempts to articulate a poetics in prose. While faith in the existence of a language—of existence itself as code—is named, nevertheless, the constraints that Kinnell has voiced in prose eventually close in on poetry and shut down faith in language just as he gives himself no other ground to stand on than his junction between flesh and all forms of spirit. The hop from "lowly touchers of physical reality" to "images" is all we have left as passage over the gap between ideas and things.

As a poet turns increasingly to the personal, our closest witness to the materially authentic, the hope must be to reveal the contours of a life and the rhyme of its placement within a larger human order. But in orienting through the solid ordinariness of oneself, with wife, children, family, and friends in the nearby practice of one's seeing, the predictable difficulties surface. In putting life at the service of his work's trajectory, melting together life and poetry, there are unforeseeable consequences for all around the poet, including the critic. In this, Kinnell moves toward that union of self and poem which he has described as "disappearing right into the words."[18] But as one naturally and instinctively seeks to maintain breathing space between the published life and the lived life, the dynamic of revelation forces choices for which one is rarely ready, exaggerating the gaps between seeing and knowing, knowing and doing, and leaving the poetry the prey of these omissions. At that point, both poet and reader have the right to ask each other to what extent either is responsible to life.

As Kinnell shifted from animal totems like the bear and porcupine and headed into the domestic and tribal away from the wilderness, he moved toward a territory if not increasingly feminized, then at least within a communality influenced by the joint experience of men *and* women. In the world of the ordinary, in which family stories traditionally invoke readings of gender and generational ties, of sisters as well as brothers, of wives as well as husbands, the loneness and fierce privacy of the American male communing with nature has frayed famously in contact with the domestic, especially in the annals of American fiction. But fiction's account of the world is one that Kinnell explicitly rejected in 1974:

> There are things which novels can do and say that poetry can't. It's mostly because of the novel's capacity to create a set of people who can act upon each other. Poems can't do that easily.[19]

And for most of Kinnell's work the people or especially women acting upon him with irritant force have been discreetly absent. Daughters melt into sisters or sons, a wife stars as remote dedicatee or appears as the object of veiled reproach or disappears beneath the male's self-pitying regret, as in "When One Has Lived a Long Time Alone." Given Kinnell's approach, the lyric eye / I will become more unmanageable the more it is embedded within a "set of people" like the family which demands a *we* to complete its moral perspective. As Kinnell moves into family history, the demands of narrative strategy over lyric edge closer.

In *Mortal Acts, Mortal Words,* most of the problematic exclusions and refusals in the poems resting on his domestic life cluster around mother, wife, and daughter; without them, the emphasis on the intimate and familial not only weakens in scope but blurs in focus. In "The Last Hiding Places of Snow," Kinnell steps uneasily around the identification of woman as earth-symbol. The mother-spirit issues from "a place in the woods," at first quite a scary place; then, while "mother love" is invoked and perceived as protecting the speaker, gradually other feelings emerge:

> My mother did not want me to be born;
> afterwards, all her life, she needed me to return.
> When this more-than-love flowed toward me, it brought darkness;
> she wanted me as burial earth wants—to heap itself gently upon but
>   also to annihilate—
>
> and I knew, whenever I felt longings to go back,
> that is what wanting to die is. That is why
>
> dread lives in me,
> dread which comes when what gives life beckons toward death,
> dread which throws through me
> waves
> of utter strangeness, which wash the entire world empty.[20]

In this stance, Kinnell is not Antaeus, deriving strength from a reaffirmation of the ground of earth that is his being. While the lines depend on identifying woman as earth-mother, they also follow the traditional misogynist conflation of womb / tomb, where the chthonic female is not muse, but instead the fixedly mortal part: the dread mother who in "giving life beckons toward death." Kinnell's mother is a blurred and softened, but still recognizable form of Blake's Tirzah:

> Thou Mother of my Mortal Part
> With cruelty didst mould my Heart.
> And with false self-deceiving tears,
> Didst bind my Nostrils Eyes & Ears.
>
> Didst close my Tongue in senseless clay
> and me to Mortal Life betray.[21]

In Kinnell's poem, while he has declined both conventional Christian terms, as well as Blake's idiosyncratic enactment of the dialectical struggle of heaven and earth, his allegorized reading of gender still makes use of this significant convergence of symbols, womb / tomb, but finally neither denies nor develops its misogynist coloring. In this elegy, Kinnell's mother-dread just sits there.

Finally, the mother is absorbed into the Empyrean, and in a partial acceptance of family themes, her fearful parentage subsides into the poet's acceptance of his parenting as a way of transcending despair and discontinuity. Kinnell introduces, then backs away from the explicit gender alignment and its problems. In the poem he expresses distress:

> I was not at her bedside
> that final day, I did not grant her ancient,
> huge-knuckled hand
> its last wish, I did not let it
> gradually become empty of the son's hand—and so
> hand her, with more steadiness, into the future.[22]

But the whole argument of gender relationship in parenting, and what it negatively represents, and negatively enforces, is bypassed as the poet simply wishes to be blessed at his own deathbed by his children's presence. In "The Last Hiding Places of Snow," refusing to respond to the dread that has broken loose, Kinnell dissolves the gender issue into a spongy prose whose firmest and most vivid moment is an image, which

> . . . these hands keep, of strolling down Bethune Street in spring, a little
> creature hanging from each arm, by a hand so small it can do no more
> than press its tiny thumb pathetically into the soft beneath my thumb
> . . .[23]

Implicitly, in the context of this poem, Kinnell shows that the suicidal despair the earth-religion of the devouring mother evokes can be turned aside, its energy blessedly reconverted into a powerful and nonsmothering father love. The female womb, and earth's asphyxiating ownership, however, explicitly put in an appearance as the cause of death and failed transcendence, as they did in *The Book of Nightmares,* where the womb / tomb of earth becomes a shroud for the newborn. In two books, now, fetal life, in agreement with Wordsworth's "Intimations Ode," represents attachment to a primary great world of memory and being. Born, "memories rush out," as the newborn

> . . . sucks
> air, screams
> her first song—and turns rose,
> the slow,

> beating, featherless arms
> already clutching at the emptiness.[24]

As babies leave the kingdom of the infinite, and pass through the bone gates of the woman, they diminish, and enter mortality; still touched, if fadingly, with the greater life of the nonhuman, and trailing those clouds of glory.

In *Mortal Acts, Mortal Words,* the ground of the poem of family relationships muddies in the space between the transition from one eschatological belief to another. The belief that an individual human existence is a flower that blooms but once, hence the density of its singular sweetness, tangles with the belief suggested in *The Book of Nightmares* that life is part of a birthdeath cycle wherein we die to be born, in which a kind death returns us to our higher life in eternity, where we are mercifully free of the circling of generations of mere matter. In addition to this tension between one theology over another, one scheme of values over another, there is a strong pull towards a gender-polarized description of human nature, where the good parts are assigned to longing for celestial transcendence (male) and the wicked parts to a dully quietist chthonic restriction (female).

But in *Mortal Acts, Mortal Words,* except for the passage on dread of the female, quoted above from "The Last Hiding Places Of Snow," Kinnell does not retreat to an overtly sexist position. This brushes by for flashed seconds. Indeed, the whole plot of failing to say the potent goodbye to the mother alters in the course of his oeuvre. By the time we get to *Imperfect Thirst,* (1994) a book that culminates in the death of the sister who was his surrogate mother, in "Flies," the earlier scene has become "When I arrived almost too late at her deathbed / and she broke through her last coma and spoke," Kinnell now stresses the mother's will to acknowledge her son across the falling barrier of death.

For Kinnell and for Blake the negative symbology of woman / nature can be shelved in favor of a happier postulate: that the sexual union of male and female is the iridescent emblem of the ruling principle of love made indwelling and physically manifest, as sexual love transforms the impermanence of the flesh through time-devouring ecstasy:

> . . . the last cry in the throat
> or only dreamed into it
> by its threads too wasted to cry
> will be but an ardent note
> of gratefulness so intense
> it disappears into that music
> which carries our time on earth away
> on the great catafalque
> of spine marrowed with god's-flesh,
> thighs bruised by the blue flower,

> pelvis that makes angels shiver to know down here we mortals make
> love with our bones.[25]

This ethic of the sexual remains a doughtily fervent and frequently iterated part of Kinnell's emotional and intellectual baggage, extending all the way into the poems of *Imperfect Thirst*. If in the old scheme heaven is something we earn for ethical behavior, in Kinnell's account, heaven is something increasingly awarded for the seriously randy. Our generative parts link us to Creator and Creation in the only holiness left on earth to modern self-doubt. "Flying Home" includes this reflection:

> in the airport men's room, seeing
> middle aged men my age
> as they washed their hands after touching
> their penises—when it might have been more in accord
> with the lost order to wash first, then touch—[26]

Critics like Charles Altieri, who derides the inadequacy of Kinnell's "pathetic and portentous attempt to take God's place, with an imaginary phallus as our only weapon,"[27] or Donald Davie, who harrumphs at Kinnell's having "no special capacity for spiritual apprehensions," labelling his program an "excessive trust in the body, an ever more feverish carnality,"[28] seem to me very close to the old conservative Anglican campaign against the Enthusiast. Yet it was the pacifist Enthusiasts of the sixties and seventies who had the durable discernment to march under the banner "Make love not war," thereby recognizing as Kinnell did in the sixth section of *The Book of Nightmares,* and as Blake and Freud did before him, that military aggression, or the imperialism or "titanism" to which Davie mistakenly consigns Kinnell, has as its roots a fundamental perversion of the erotic drive. That view, which accepts the convergences between a loveless denial of the flesh, warped sexuality, and war, is one which I share, and to which too little attention has been directed in sorting out Kinnell's beliefs.

Yet the ghost of phallocentrism cannot be completely exorcised. Kinnell writes that only through mortal flesh is flesh made immortal, as human birth, fueled by holy sexual desire, cancels human death. If, in a changing poetics, language is finally too unreliable to be the conveyor of the eternal real, sex is not. And from this elevation of sexuality as death's death-blow, and until about 1985, before Kinnell's poems were jolted by the experience of divorce, it also seemed an easy transit to a usually phallocentric world, and to the elimination of woman as muse, or, in literary terms energy source.

Until the family poems of *Imperfect Thirst,* female generativity, unless attached to male desire, did not exist for Kinnell. While earlier poems drew from his animals the most resonant cry of longing for immortality, a longing for the artifice of eternity, that cry originated in a male totem: a porcupine or a bear. Philip Slater, in *The Glory of Hera*, traces the birth of Dionysus from the hiding place of Zeus' thigh as one of the classic feints of the male narcissist as he attempts to expunge his dreaded mother as inheritance and to deny his need for parental love: In this mythic replay of birth, the Greeks displaced women altogether.[29] It is interesting to see that Kinnell similarly displaces women from the birth role in "The Bear" by claiming the male totem as his source of creative energy. In "The Bear," Kinnell's speaker literally climbs into the carcass, to be reborn as poetic speech; more overtly later, but in an analogous displacement, in "The Last Hiding Places of Snow," the generative line dissolves from the problematic mothering into the speaker's fathering.

In *The Book of Nightmares*, the source of transcending mortality through mortality begins to thrust forward in Kinnell's mythology of children, where the births of his daughter Maud and son Fergus provide the framework for the sequence opening and closing the book. Speaking about *The Book of Nightmares* and after remarking that the book is "nothing but an effort to face death and live with death," Kinnell goes on to describe the special connection that infants have to transcendence:

> These little lumps of clinging flesh, and one's terrible, inexplicable closeness to them, make one feel very strongly the fragility of a person. In the company of babies, one is very close to the kingdom of death. And as children grow so quickly, as they change almost from day to day, it's hardly possible to put mortality out of mind for long.[30]

Approximately eight years after saying this, Kinnell's concern with babies as an emblem of the human link to death evolves and broadens to stress generational and familial continuity. The focus on eternal copresence is returned earthside; out Kinnell's way, however, parenting is mostly something that fathers do by themselves.

Up to *The Book of Nightmares*, Kinnell's best-known personae live comfortably within the American macho: boy, tramp, convict, logger, skier and hiker—these solitary speakers wander quite naturally and without any sense of excluded life. If in poems about parenting Kinnell later becomes the celebrant of domesticity, it is certainly not that he does so after having served a term as the poet of marriage. The adult female, abstractly celebrated as a featureless sexual partner, is only fleetingly invoked as part of Kinnell's intimate cosmos. If in *Mortal Acts, Mortal Words* we slowly work up to a family romance, it is still a romance where most of the parts are played by men.

For some poets, it would not be hard to construct an argument defending this practice. Since many worlds exist that can legitimately be characterized by the acute absence of either sex, it is unreasonable to demand equal time at all times. But Kinnell invites a poetics that will yoke physical and imaginative creativity and fuse poems and human generations within a single energy source. If mothers, wives and daughters are obliterated except for evanescent traces, Kinnell courts the return of the repressed in significant lapses in the story; important gaps, and because of the gaps, distortions. You can't take on children, parents, and the family without installing the ladies somewhere.

In *Mortal Acts, Mortal Words,* the short poem "Saint Francis and the Sow" acts to avert this distortion, as the sow is lifted into the series of animal totems including porcupine and bear. In the poem, the speaker tells the mama pig the old story of her beauty:

> . . . Saint Francis
> put his hand on the creased forehead
> of the sow, and told her in words and in touch
> blessings of earth on the sow, and the sow
> began remembering all down her thick length,
> from the earthen snout all the way
> through the fodder and slops to the spiritual curl of the tail,
> from the hard spininess spiked out from the spine
> down through the great broken heart
> to the blue milken dreaminess spurting and shuddering
> from the fourteen teats into the fourteen mouths sucking and blowing
> beneath them:
> the long, perfect loveliness of sow.[31]

Saint Francis may be casting out more than the poet consciously dreams for him, however, as this poem transforms mother-dread, or its potentially fearsome and devil-ridden sow, into a nurturant, multi-breasted "perfect loveliness."

Kinnell has eloquently pleaded for a poetics that will be personally inclusive. In "Poetry, Personality, and Death" he says,

> If we take seriously Thoreau's dictum, "Be it life or death, we crave only reality," if we are willing to face the worst in ourselves, we also have to accept the risks I have mentioned, that probing into one's own wretchedness one may just dig up more wretchedness. What justifies the risk is the hope that in the end the search may open and transfigure us.[32]

What has always been appealing in Kinnell's poetry has not been wretchedness but the sharply observant, often skeptically wary, persona who nonetheless exudes concern. The dilemma of sentimentality, however, is created when the beguiling voice lulls us into forgetting our need for language's splintery ability to reflect the relation of men and women accurately, in the minute particulars of what is to constitute, in Kinnell's 1971 phrase, "Tenderness toward Existence."[33] Clearly a tenderness that has to make its way through fears that are also conceivable by the poet, right in the midst of sexuality, in these terms:

> Just as the supreme cry
> of joy, the cry of orgasm, also has a ghastliness to it,
> as though it touched forward
> into the chaos where we break apart . . .[34]

Without a better map of that ghastliness and its kindred cohesions and disintegrations—as they are played out in the man-woman relationship and as they replay earlier family roles—Kinnell's poems have fitted too comfortably into their tenderness; without the risk-taking that an emotionally expanded subject might have provided, the poems of the middle decade roughly between 1974 and 1984 have given pleasure, but not the pleasure that readers of this copiously gifted poet might have expected. In response to "Poetry, Personality, and Death," Adrienne Rich said,

> The problem of Kinnell, I believe (and if I single him out in this essay it is not because I think his blindness is greater but his potential for vision more)—the problem for Kinnell is the problem of the masculine writer—To become truly universal, he will have to confront the closed ego of man in its most private and political mode: his confused relationship to his own femininity, and his fear and guilt towards women.[35]

These are subjects Kinnell touches gingerly at points; indeed, the closing poem of *Mortal Acts, Mortal Words* looks to be a partial engagement with Rich's program, as do other poems even more fully in later books. "Flying Home," however, instead of returning both poet and poetry to the full resonance of the *home ground*—the last two words of the book—manages rhetorical stereotype in place of the male-female engagement. The poem anticipates a stability and ease of return to that home ground that in the unaccountably divergent ways of living, as against composing, the divorce-shadowed poems of the future will render ironically inapplicable.

In *The Book of Nightmares*, both daughter and son, Maud and Fergus, become emblems of continuity; but from *Mortal Acts, Mortal Words* onward, the son becomes the emblem of the ongoing continuity of the next generation, and daughters make their appearance as late as *Imperfect Thirst* only as sisters in the previous generation. While it is true that people, even poets, have to live their lives as people rather than as symbolic portents, nevertheless, the absence of one of the earlier symbolic people belonging to this story of lives becomes noticeable. What happened to the memorable girl-child detailed in "Little Sleep's-Head Sprouting Hair in the Moonlight"?

> In a restaurant once, everyone
> quietly eating, you clambered up
> on my lap: to all
> the mouthfuls rising toward

all the mouths, at the top of your voice
you cried
your one word *caca! caca! caca!*
and each spoonful
stopped, a moment, in midair, in its withering
steam.[36]

We miss this pungent little critic of transcendence, echoing as she does the earlier feelings of her father:

The great thing about Whitman is that he knew all of our being must be loved, if we are to love any of it. I have often thought there should be a book called *Shit*, telling us that what comes out of the body is no less a part of reality, no less sacred, than what goes into it; only a little less nourishing. It's a matter of its moment in the life cycle: food eaten is on the cross, at its moment of sacrifice, while food eliminated is at its moment of ascension.[37]

In a more chastened spirit, the poem "Holy Shit," from *Imperfect Thirst*, pits this interest in post-realities against a barrage of quotations generally attributing stink and corruption to the bulk of human ends, both physical and spiritual, against which Martin Luther, Shacharit, and Whitman are ultimately allowed to triumph. In the final lines, Kinnell puts a wonderful spin on a High Romantic affirmation:

We don't know what life is, but we know
all who live on earth eat, sleep, mate, work,
shit, and die. Let us remember this is our home
and that we have become, we mad ones, its keepers.
Let us sit bent forward slightly, and be opened a moment,
as earth's holy matter passes through us.[38]

As Kinnell in his sixties accelerates his dealings with ends and endings, beginning to explore more intensely than ever before the impact of the undone and badly done in private and civic life, there is a continuing effort to make his own aesthetic draw intelligently from the American transcendental and largely patriarchal tradition what it can. In "The Last River," Kinnell dismissed Thoreau and what Thoreau himself called the "excrementitious" truths of his gravel bank in a spring thaw, and which Kinnell relabeled the failure of "Seeking Love . . . ," accusing Henry David of "failing to know I only loved / my purity." Nonetheless, Kinnell has him come back to inhabit the fisher child of *Mortal Acts, Mortal Words.* In "Fergus Falling," Kinnell outlines in fairly compact form both the strengths and dilemmas of accepting the full flowering of the *isolato,* to borrow another American writer's term for the revolutionary persona in question.

In this poem, written with a deceptively casual music, Kinnell begins,

> He climbed to the top
> of one of those million white pines
> set out across emptying pastures
> of the fifties—some program to enrich the rich
> and rebuke the forefathers
> who cleared it all one with ox and axe—
> climbed to the top, probably to get out
> of the shadow
> not of those forefathers but of this father,
> and saw for the first time,
> down in its valley, Bruce Pond, giving off
> its little steam in the afternoon.

After completing this magical climb out of the order of the generations, in full Oedipal revolt, the poem stalls the engine of ascent for a moment to look at Bruce Pond. In effective, rhythmically irregular strophes, Kinnell describes the pond. In service to a belief in the fusion of letter and literal within the real, and with the intent of tracing the same intersection between the real and the symbolic, Thoreau drew Walden Pond for us in fidelity to its deceptive ordinariness and then told us, "A lake is the landscape's most beautiful and expressive feature. It is earth's eye; looking into which the beholder measures the depth of his own nature." Kinnell follows the same intention of reflecting in language the order of language within the order of nature:

> pond where Clarence Akley came on Sunday morning to cut down the
>   cedars around the shore, I'd sometimes hear the slow spondees of
>   his work, he's gone,
> where Milton Norway came up behind me while I was fishing and stood
>   awhile before I knew he was there, he's the one who put the cedar
>   shingles on the house, some have curled or split, a few have
>   blown off, he's gone,

In banging home that refrain, "he's gone," Kinnell puts us in the book's preoccupation, mortality, but here, the mortality of a serenely repeating human order, in a persuasive syntax of continuity:

> pond where an old fisherman in a rowboat sits, drowning hooked
>   worms, when he's gone he's replaced and is never gone

And then we get to the moment of recognition preceding the fall that gives the poem its title:

> . . . when Fergus
> . . . .
> . . . saw its oldness down there

> in its old place in the valley, he became heavier suddenly
> in his bones
> the way fledglings do just before they fly,
> and the soft pine cracked . . .

Fergus falls into his own mortality, anticipating what his adult body will do later; but the pond remains for the transfixed child an exchange of gazes with "earth's eye": "Galway, Ines, I saw a pond!" The pond remains an emblem in the tradition of Emerson and Thoreau as a fusion, or crossing place of self and world, where through nature's mediation, both become known, though in the ending, emphasis shifts from the optimism of having achieved knowledge, or spirit-food, to the more phlegmatic angling and waiting for it:

> Yes—a pond
> that lets off its mist
> on clear afternoons of August, in that valley
> to which many have come, for their reasons,
> from which many have gone, a few for their reasons, most not,
> where even now an old fisherman only the pinetops can see
> sits in the dry gray wood of his rowboat, waiting for pickerel.[39]

In this poem, which takes the child protagonist into the romantic struggle to know self through nature, Kinnell only briefly attaches that task to another in which one gains self-knowledge by learning one's place in the family order of generations. In this poem, to Fergus, the shadow of father and forefathers are muted backdrop. As Kinnell evades open treatment of the family themes that have met with such partial success elsewhere, in this poem he converts avoidance into advantage: "Fergus Falling" comes into its own by freshly acknowledging an aspect of harmony that has more to do with our place in the nonhuman, physical world and much less to do with our relations to each other.

In a similar mutation of Romantic convention, two other poems, "Daybreak" and "The Grey Heron," direct the focus away from the relentless anthropomorphizing that too close an imitation of Thoreau might have engendered. In these poems, stripped of the pathetic fallacy, there is an impersonal pleasure as the work bespeaks an order of things that modestly contains, rather than prominently features, man. "The Grey Heron" notes the rhyme of heron form with "a three-foot lizard / an ill-fitting skin / and with linear mouth expressive of the even temper / of the mineral kingdom."[40] The poem then places the final line recognizing the principle of mutability in the mouth of a mutable speaker on equal terms with his bird brother. "Daybreak" is likewise interested in the flux and permeability of natural order:

> On the tidal mud, just before sunset,
> dozens of starfishes
> were creeping. It was
> as though the mud were a sky
> and enormous, imperfect stars
> moved across it as slowly
> as the actual stars cross heaven.[41]

This small, quiet poem contains the same echoing large-scale satisfactions as the famous passage about night fishing in *Walden*, where the ardent angler sinks his line down in the mysterious element only to realize that he has hooked heaven in the deep sky-water of his local pond.

In the re-ordering intensity of these last spatial paradoxes, Kinnell is in position to advance Thoreau out of the woods and if not into a family cabin, then at least into a human enclosure from which the cabin can be sighted or remembered. Stepping back more than a little from the themes of his own fatherhood, both within and after the melancholy post-divorce separations and regrets of *The Past*, Kinnell has continued to write elegies for fellow artists while reaffirming the terms of an earlier devotion to what we experience as the larger natural world.

In the transformative body of his poems attentive to the nonhuman, the tactile and aural become visible. As the metaphysical is expressed through the physical, earth and paradise, suffering and ecstasy, the momentary and the enduring, all meet. For Kinnell, within the flow of these unions a generative ground of mystery exists. In a 1972 interview, he remarked on the richness of physical verbs and adjectives in English and then goes on to say,

> If the things and creatures that live on earth don't possess mystery, then there isn't any. To touch this mystery requires, I think, love of the things and creatures that surround us, so that they are transformed within us, and so that our inner life finds expression through them. . . . In the purest poem the inner and outer meet.[42]

This spatializing fusion of inner and outer is matched by the inclusive desire to touch upper and lower, to claim heaven for earth, to beat down fences between body and mind, and to make at least these borders permeable to poetic traffic.

In a passage from *When One Has Lived a Long Time Alone*, a beach walk in "Who, on Earth" turns up a dead skate, and Kinnell muses,

> . . . In the dead
> skate the mass of whatever
> substance flesh on dying becomes
> presses down into the sand,
> trying to fall into the heaven

> inside earth almost visible
> through the half-washed windows
> of stones.[43]

The lines recall the final image of Nerval's "Vers dorées," in which a spirit gathers in stone, like a newborn eye under its eyelid. In Kinnell's poem, as in Nerval's, matter is sentient; in the symbolist tradition, the word is bound to the material, and the only heaven we need to look for occurs in the dying going on under our eyes and under our feet. As in Blake's *Marriage of Heaven and Hell* and elsewhere, there is an access of energy in the literal / symbolic revolution occurring in the reversals of up / down, heaven / hell, and immortal / mortal. Value is seen springing from the unsuspected partner in these binaries. In his own revision of the relations between heaven and earth, Kinnell has said, "The poetics of heaven agrees to the denigration of pain and death; in the poetics of the physical world these are the very elements."[44]

His late poems about love and sexuality peer with ever more intense curiosity at the sexual encounter and the intricate design of human parts, even as divorce and solitude sharpen his sense of how precarious and blessed a circumstance it is to wake up and find someone else in bed beside you. There is, however, a growing insistence on putting the human in a dues-paying relation to the world of the nonhuman, although the elision of animal into human becomes the unavoidable one that we must live. As a lyric poet faced with nuclear extinction and postindustrial commodification, Kinnell can only say with terrible dryness,

> To de-animalize human mentality, to purge it of obsolete
> evolutionary characteristics, in particular of death,
> which foreknowledge terrorizes the contents of skulls with,
> is the fundamental project of technology.[45]

At sixty-plus, one can recognize that there are worse sightlines than that of the animally human.

But as Kinnell's post-Romantic aesthetic stresses the sacralized sexual and the material body's passage over and through formative landscapes, he still clings to the female as object rather than subject of desire. A late poem like "Rapture," however, makes its hesitant stab at entering the female mind, even if the mind in question is only entertaining sexual congress with the speaker as her subject. In the "hypnopompic play" with which the speaker amuses himself, desire filters through the male mind imagining female desire:

> I can feel she has got out of bed.
> That means it is seven A.M.
> I have been lying with eyes shut,
> thinking, or possibly dreaming,
> of how she might look if, at breakfast,

> I spoke about the hidden place in her
> which, to me, is like a soprano's tremolo,
> and right then, over toast and bramble jelly,
> if such things are possible, she came.[46]

Some might see this poem as a rather limited exercise at cross-gender empathy, but there it sits, the first acknowledgment of a desire separate from male desire, even if reassuringly evoked—"hypnopompically"—by the speaker himself. *Imperfect Thirst* offers two other poems, "The Cellist" and "Parkinson's Disease," both striking portraits of female dedication and tenderness, while the concluding elegy for the poet's sister presents her at death with a blend of sweetness and rooted dignity unlike anything else in his work. All of these poems are new departures, relying as they do less on lyric and more on the ply-over-ply of character within narrative.

But Kinnell's view of parenting remains essentialist. The parent metaphor in "Last Gods" still signals whatever is mortality-defying in our lives, the belief in erotic coupling as the site of ultimate knowledge fervent as ever:

> He kneels, opens
> the dark, vertical smile
> linking heaven with the underearth
>
> . . . .
>
> The hair of their bodies
> startles up. They cry
> in the tongue of the last gods,
> who refused to go,
> chose death, and shuddered
> in joy and shattered in pieces,
> bequeathing their cries
> into the human mouth. Now in the lake
> two faces float, looking up
> at a great maternal pine whose branches
> open out in all directions
> explaining everything.[47]

These late lines accept the place of both death and sex within a terrestrial heaven. From the vantage point of a birth into language, two faces peer out from a uterine lake and celebrate a maternal pine vaguely "explaining everything." Erotic fusion here echoes the parented universe whose terms he acknowledged in a 1976 interview:

While eternity is only our word for some condition we don't understand, yet in the greatest moments of our lives, we do grasp that there's an element beyond our reach, from which we came, and into which we will dissolve, which is the mother and father of all the life of the planet, to use terms which may apply better than we think.[48]

In "Under the Maud Moon," Maud's birth became the moment when "being itself / closes down all over her," as the little exile from eternity enters mortality. But while in "Last Gods" the idea of woman repeats the familiar picture of the earth-mother, source of both life and death, elsewhere Kinnell's hold on parenting as a generative metaphor loosens. Ideas of the physical both embrace an animistic universe and acknowledge a more intermittent contact with the sources of its speech. "Divinity" says

> When the man touches through
> to the exact center of the woman,
> he lies motionless, in equilibrium,
> in absolute desire, at the threshold
> of the world to which the Creator Spirit
> knows the pass-whisper, and whispers it,
> and his loving friend becomes his divinity.[49]

But the invocation of deity by way of sexuality sounds a little tired, and the "loving friend" too closely resembles the familiar female love object up on a retrofitted pedestal. We tend to believe Kinnell when in "Oatmeal" he says gamely but glumly: "Maybe there is no sublime; only the shining of the amnion's tatters." Maybe that should be enough for anyone.

"My Mother's R & R," however, and several additional poems from *Imperfect Thirst* remembering childhood, show Kinnell opening other chapters in his relations with the female. In a reversion to family stories more extended than anything since *Mortal Acts, Mortal Words,* this poem, as well as other poems replaying childhood vacations and sibling relations and seeing both parents from new angles, allows Kinnell a less rhetorical insight into his own uneasy feelings about mother, father, and parenting. Unlike the maternal pine of "Last Gods," these poems make no claim to "explain everything." Like the stubbornly meaty shred pried from between the teeth, chewing the memory of one or the other event over again in the seventh decade of a lifetime provides a more salutary truth than mere obedience to ideology can obtain. In "My Mother's R & R" Kinnell remembers his brother and himself, climbing into their mother's bed, and the consequences:

> We climbed into bed with her.
> Perhaps she needed comforting
> and she was alone, and she let us take
> a breast each out of the loose slip.
> "Let's make believe we're babies,"
> Derry said. We put the large pink
> flowers at the end of those lax breasts
> into our mouths and sucked with enthusiasm.
> She laughed and seemed to enjoy our play.
> Perhaps intoxicated by our pleasure,

> or frustrated by the failure of the milk
> to flow, we sucked harder, probably
> our bodies writhed, our eyes flared,
> maybe she could feel our teeth.
> Abruptly she took back her breasts
> and sent us from the bed, two small
> hungry boys enflamed and driven off
> by the she-wolf. But we had got our nip,
> and in the empire we would found
> we would taste every woman and expel
> each one who came to resemble her.[50]

In the swoop at the end, gathering up both little boys in the legendary founding of Rome, the poem suddenly enlarges its space and time and releases a palpable bitterness and a sudden flare of retroactive anger at the mortified dependencies that mother love engenders in the male child.

There is a wondering tentativeness also to other similarly narrative poems, as if the finger tracing the spelling of these events had only just come upon their meaning—and there is a vivid persuasiveness to their contours because of it. *Imperfect Thirst* clearly expands Kinnell's territory. In addition to these family poems, delving deeper into the roots of personality, Kinnell has also begun to radiate awareness outward to other cast members in the sexual dramas of his lifetime. The passage in which Kinnell as a child is stung by the limits of maternal tenderness is quickly balanced by ruminative lines from "The Cellist." Kinnell harkens to

> . . . the disparity
> between all the tenderness I've received
> and the amount I've given, and the way
> I used to shrug off the imbalance
> simply as how things are, as if the male
> were constituted like those coffeemakers
> that produce less black bitter than the quantity
> of sweet clear you poured in—forgetting about
> how much I spilled through unsteady walking,
> and that lot I flung on the ground
> in suspicion, and for fear I wasn't worthy,
> and all I threw out for reasons I don't understand yet.[51]

"Running on Silk," in the live, nervy juxtapositions of this late manner, triggers a memory collapsing present and past, enveloping someone else's wife, and himself, "an unattached young man" in exuberant adultery. But the last moment of the poem splices in the husband pushed aside by that coupling:

> Will I find him, up ahead,
> standing at a closed departure gate, like that man

that night forty years ago, as if turned to wood
and put out by his murderers to sell cigars?[52]

These are newly rueful notes in the marital opera.

In the poetry published since *The Book of Nightmares,* much has happened
by way of gender awareness for the bodywork of poets like Sharon Olds (to
whom Kinnell dedicated *When One Has Lived a Long Time Alone*), Jorie Gra-
ham, and Louise Glück. Yet in Kinnell's drawing of the physical world, the
strength of his poetry occurs largely in its connection to the animal and nonhuman world and in his active celebration of the non-gender-specific praising
human tongue. Breaking past the sentimental certainties of the place "where
lovers speak" in the halo of "kingdom come," perhaps the sharper wisdom
that Kinnell has begun to offer instead is that of the isolated man in "The
Massage":

> Far down inside his chest it feels sore.
> The hands can't pass the twelve cartilaginous bars.
> The future he dreaded seems to have dissolved
> on approach, and reassembled behind as the past—
> but slightly blurred, being mostly unlived.[53]

Imperfect Thirst advances beyond these regrets; accepting the family as subject once again, in a move resembling that of many contemporary poets,
Kinnell now, however, skips the generation of his own parenting to return
to an earlier past: to childhood and youth, not blurred, but richly reassem-
bling.

In "The River That Is East," published in 1961, the poet stood on the
shore apostrophizing the river in good Wordsworthian style: "thou, River of
Tomorrow." Although filled with urban detritus, the East River was seen as
"[t]he immaculate stream, heavy, and swinging home again." In 1990, and
more markedly again in 1995, the homing future is internalized; we are the
river, with a load still mysteriously out of reach. The older voice is frequently
glum, as Kinnell's view of the sublime grows more occluded, but the
unforced sound of the late poetry is more penetrating as it plays over the
relation between flesh, world, and spirit. *Imperfect Thirst,* abandoning the
morose in favor of restless and vital appetite, is no less touched by death
than the other books, no less earnest in its search for values that reach
beyond the immediate, and yet its often pained and wondering exploration
of memory throws its subjects into a place which is more than the nineteenth-century terrain seen through a dimmer, less hopeful lens. Writing a
poetry ever more securely balanced between urban and pastoral engagement, and faithful to its transcendental roots, Kinnell, in his developing concern with the domestic, sets a new program for both himself and that tradition.

Notes

1. Galway Kinnell, *Walking Down the Stairs: Selections from Interviews* (Ann Arbor: University of Michigan Press, 1978), 24–25.

2. Kinnell, *Walking,* 26.

3. Kinnell, *Walking,* 22.

4. Kinnell, *Walking,* 85.

5. Galway Kinnell, *Body Rags* (Boston: Houghton Mifflin, 1968), 29.

6. Galway Kinnell, *Mortal Acts, Mortal Words* (Boston: Houghton Mifflin, 1980), 24.

7. Kinnell, *Mortal Acts,* 67–68.

8. Kinnell, *Mortal Acts,* 59.

9. Kinnell, *Walking,* 49.

10. Galway Kinnell, "The Poetics of the Physical World," *Iowa Review* 2, no. 3 (Summer 1971): 125.

11. *W. B. Yeats. The Poems,* ed. Richard J. Finneran (New York: MacMillan, 1983), 198.

12. Ezra Pound, Pavannes and Divigations (New York: New Directions, 1974), 231.

13. Kinnell, "Poetics," 116.

14. Galway Kinnell, *The Avenue Bearing the Initial of Christ into the New World* (Boston: Houghton Mifflin, 1974), 99.

15. Kinnell, *Avenue C,* 102.

16. Kinnell, *Mortal Acts,* 33–36.

17. Kinnell, *Mortal Acts,* 45.

18. Kinnell, *Walking,* 68.

19. Kinnell, *Walking,* 60.

20. Kinnell, *Mortal Acts,* 42–43.

21. William Blake, *The Poetry and Prose of William Blake,* ed. David B. Erdman (New York: Doubleday, 1965), 30.

22. Kinnell, *Mortal Acts,* 43.

23. Kinnell, *Mortal Acts,* 43.

24. Galway Kinnell, *The Book of Nightmares* (Boston: Houghton Mifflin, 1971), 6–7.

25. Kinnell, *Mortal Acts,* 60–61.

26. Kinnell, *Mortal Acts,* 70.

27. Charles Altieri, "The Dominant Poetic Mode of the Late Seventies," in *On the Poetry of Galway Kinnell: The Wages of Dying,* ed. Howard Nelson (Ann Arbor: University of Michigan Press, 1990), 139.

28. Donald Davie, "Slogging for the Absolute," in *On the Poetry of Galway Kinnell: The Wages of Dying,* ed. Howard Nelson (Ann Arbor: University of Michigan Press, 1990), 143, 149.

29. Philip Slater, *The Glory of Hera: Greek Mythology and the Greek Family* (Boston: Beacon Press, 1971).

30. Kinnell, *Walking,* 44.

31. Kinnell, *Mortal Acts,* 9.

32. Galway Kinnell, "Poetry, Personality, and Death," *Field* 4 (Spring 1971): 67.

33. Kinnell, *Nightmares,* 29.

34. Kinnell, *Mortal Acts,* 60.

35. Adrienne Rich, "Poetry, Personality and Wholeness: A Response to Galway Kinnell," *Field* 7 (Fall 1972): 17.

36. Kinnell, *Nightmares,* 50.

37. Kinnell, "Poetry, Personality and Death," 70.

38. Galway Kinnell, *Imperfect Thirst* (New York: Houghton Mifflin, 1994), 67.

39. Kinnell, *Mortal Acts,* 3–4.

40. Kinnell, *Mortal Acts,* 20.

41. Kinnell, *Mortal Acts,* 19.
42. Kinnell, *Walking,* 52.
43. Galway Kinnell, *When One Has Lived a Long Time Alone* (New York: Knopf, 1990), 34.
44. Kinnell, "Poetics," 119.
45. Galway Kinnell, *The Past* (Boston: Houghton Mifflin, 1985), 48.
46. Kinnell, *Imperfect Thirst,* 50.
47. Kinnell, *When One Has Lived,* 48.
48. Kinnell, *Walking,* 97–98.
49. Kinnell, *When One Has Lived,* 46.
50. Kinnell, *Imperfect Thirst,* 9.
51. Kinnell, *Imperfect Thirst,* 19.
52. Kinnell, *Imperfect Thirst,* 22.
53. Kinnell, *When One Has Lived,* 17.

Index

♦

The Editor

◆

Dr. James Nagel, J. O. Eidson Distinguished Professor of American Literature at the University of Georgia, founded the scholarly journal *Studies in American Fiction* and edited it for 20 years. He is the general editor of the Critical Essays on American Literature series published by G. K. Hall / Macmillan, a program that now contains over 130 volumes. He was one of th founders of the American Literature Association and serves as its executive coordinator. He is also a past president of the Ernest Hemingway Society. Among his 17 books are *Stephen Crane and Literary Impressionism,* Critical Essays on *The Sun Also Rises, Ernest Hemingway: The Writer in Context, Ernest Hemingway: The Oak Park Legacy,* and *Hemingway in Love and War,* which was selected by the New York Times as one of the outstanding books of 1989 and which has been made into a major motion picture. Dr. Nagel has published over 50 articles in scholarly journals, and has lectured on American literature in 15 countries.